STEVE BIKO - I WRITE WHAT I LIKE

STEVE BIKO -

A selection of his writings
edited with a personal memoir by
Aelred Stubbs C.R.

I WRITE WHAT I LIKE

1817

Published in San Francisco by
HARPER & ROW, PUBLISHERS
New York, Hagerstown, San Francisco, London

Grateful acknowledgement is made for permission to reprint the following:
"White Racism and Black Consciousness" from *Student Perspectives on
South Africa Capetown* copyright © 1972 by David Philip Publisher (Pty) Ltd.;
"Black Consciousness and the Quest for a True Humanity" from *Black Theology:
The South African Voice* copyright © 1973 by C. Hurst & Co.; "Our Strategy
for Liberation" from the January 16, 1978 issue of *Christianity and Crisis*;
"On Death" from the January 7, 1976 issue of *The New Republic*.

FIRST U.S. EDITION

LIBRARY OF CONGRESS NUMBER: 78-19499

INTERNATIONAL STANDARD BOOK NUMBER: 0-06-250052-X

79 80 81 82 83 10 9 8 7 6 5 4 3 2 1

Contents

Acknowledgements: The Editor and Publishers wish to thank the following for their valuable help in the compilation of this book: the Lawyers' Committee for Civil Rights Under Law in Washington D.C., for providing us with various articles written by Steve Biko which the Committee had in its possession; Gale Gerhart; C. Hurst and Co. for permission to reproduce 'Black Consciousness and the Quest for a True Humanity'; David Philip Publisher (Pty) Ltd for permission to reproduce the chapter entitled 'White Supremacy and Black Consciousness'; The New Republic Inc for the chapter 'On Death'; Christianity and Crisis and Episcopal Churchmen for South Africa for permission to reproduce 'Our Strategy for Liberation'; The International University Exchange Fund; Hugh Lewin.

Preface

The time for a comprehensive biography of Steve Biko is not yet. But it is hoped that the production of a book containing a selection of his writings, together with a personal memoir, may be timely, that it may serve to inform those who all over the world know the name Biko only in the dreadful context of his death, a little more fully what manner of man he was. For this reason nothing is said in depth about his death, crucial as this is in a final assessment of the man.

I am acutely aware that the definitive writing on Steve can only come from one who writes from within his own tradition, historic, linguistic and political. Unfortunately at the moment those who are so qualified are either in detention, banned, on Robben Island or in exile. I can claim to have known him from the mid-1960s, and with a deepening intimacy, as the memoir indicates, from 1973 until his death. I am a priest of the Anglican Community of the Resurrection. Our headquarters is at Mirfield in Yorkshire. We have worked in South Africa since 1903. I was sent out in 1959 to join the staff of St Peter's Theological College, Rosettenville, Johannesburg, of which I became Principal in 1960. Forced by government legislation to close at Rosettenville, in 1963 we took St Peter's to form the Anglican constituent college in the new ecumenical Federal Theological Seminary at Alice, next to Fort Hare. I was expelled from the Republic in July 1977.

The compilation of this book would have been impossible but for a generous grant from World University Service, an organisation devoted (amongst other excellent aims) to the service of Steve's cause. Even then, because of my inability to enter South Africa, the material could not have been collected but for the initiative, diligence and skill of Mr David Mesenbring. He has also read through the manuscript of the memoir, and made valuable criticisms. To them I express my grateful thanks, as also to a Sister who typed the manuscript of the memoir, and to the Librarian and staff of the National University of Lesotho. Much of the material

here gathered together was supplied from sources who do not wish
for public acknowledgement, but I am nevertheless grateful for their
co-operation. Thanks are due to the editors and publishers of the
articles contained in chapters 11, 14, 18 and 19 and for permission to
reproduce them.

The royalties from this book will go to the Biko family, to be
devoted by them to a project of which they know Steve would have
approved.

AELRED STUBBS, C.R
Masite, Lesotho, 1978

1
Introduction

Stephen Bantu Biko was born in Kingwilliamstown, Cape Province, on 18 December 1946, the third child and second son of Mr and Mrs Mzimgayi Biko. His father died when Stephen was four. He received primary and secondary education locally before proceeding to Lovedale Institution, Alice. He did not stay long at that Bantu Education Department-run school however, and his formative higher schooling was received at the Roman Catholic Mariannhill, in Natal. Matriculating at the end of 1965 he entered the medical school of the (white) University of Natal, Non-European section, Durban, at the beginning of 1966. Active at first in NUSAS (National Union of South African Students), he broke with them in 1968 to form SASO (South African Students' Organisation), of which he was elected first President in July 1969, and in July 1970 he was appointed Publicity Secretary.

In December 1970 he married Miss Nontsikelelo (Ntsiki) Mashalaba from Umtata. From 1971 his heart was increasingly in political activity, and in the middle of 1972 his course at Wentworth was terminated. Immediately he began to work for BCP (Black Community Programmes) in Durban, but at the beginning of March 1973, together with seven other SASO leaders, was banned. Restricted to his home town of Kingwilliamstown, he founded the Eastern Cape Branch of BCP and worked as Branch Executive until an extra clause was inserted in his banning order at the end of 1975 prohibiting him from working for BCP.

In 1975 he was instrumental in founding the Zimele Trust Fund. He was detained for 101 days under section 6 of the Terrorism Act from August to December 1976, and was then released without being charged. He was many times charged under security legislation, but never convicted. In January 1977 he was appointed Honorary President of BPC (Black People's Convention) for five years – an organisation he had helped to found in 1972.

On 18 August 1977, he was again detained under section 6 of the

Terrorism Act. He was taken to Port Elizabeth, where he was kept naked and manacled, as was revealed at the inquest after his death. He died in detention on 12 September. The cause of death was established as brain damage. His death and the inquest have been so extensively reported that it is unnecessary to add further details here. He leaves a widow and two small boys aged seven and three.

The writings which follow belong or refer to the period 1969–72, when Steve was active in the Black Consciousness Movement, of which he is now regarded as the "father". After his banning in March 1973 he could no longer travel, speak in public, or write for publication. It seems logical, therefore, to place these before the memoir, which deals mainly with the period after he was banned. The evidence at the BPC-SASO Trial in Pretoria was given in the first week of May 1976, but refers to events which took place during the earlier period. Thus the book follows a chronological sequence as far as can be ascertained.

2
South African Students' Organisation—its Role, its Significance and its Future

In the early 1960s there had been abortive attempts to found non-white student organisations. In 1961 and 1962 the African Students' Association (ASA) and the African Students' Union of South Africa (ASUSA) were established. The Durban Students' Union and the Cape Peninsular Students' Union, which later merged to form the Progressive National Students' Organisation, were fanatically opposed to NUSAS initially. ASA and ASUSA were divided by ideological loyalties connected with (ANC) African National Congress and Pan Africanist Congress (PAC). None of these organisations survived. NUSAS was by no means a spent force on the black campuses, but the fact that its own power base was on white campuses (Wits – the University of Witwatersrand – Rhodes, University of Cape Town, Natal) meant that it was virtually impossible for black students to attain leadership positions. Least of all could NUSAS speak for non-white campuses, though it often assumed that role.

The formation of the University Christian Movement (UCM) in 1967 gave blacks a greater chance of coming together. Its initial political respectability in the eyes of the black university college authorities gave it a chance to function on those campuses in a way impossible for NUSAS. At the UCM Conference at Stutterheim in July 1968 about 40 blacks from all the main black centres of higher education in the Republic formed themselves into a caucus and agreed on the need for a nationally representative black student organisation. The UNB group (University of Natal Black), which of course included Steve, was asked to continue investigations. As a result a representative conference was held at Mariannhill, Natal, in December 1968, when SASO was formed, to be officially inaugurated at Turfloop in July 1969, when Steve was elected President.

4

*This is Steve's Presidential address to the 1st National Formation
School of SASO, held at University of Natal – Black Section,
Wentworth, Durban, 1–4 December 1969.*

SASO – ITS ROLE, ITS SIGNIFICANCE AND ITS FUTURE

Very few of the South African students' organisations have elicited
as mixed a response on their establishment as SASO seems to have
done. It would seem that only the middle-of-the-roaders have
accepted SASO. Cries of "shame" were heard from the white students who have struggled for years to maintain interracial contact.
From some of the black militants' point of view SASO was far from
the answer, it was still too amorphous to be of any real help. No one
was sure of the real direction of SASO. Everybody expressed fears
that SASO was a conformist organisation. A few of the white students expressed fears that this was a sign to turn towards militancy.
In the middle of it all was the SASO executive. Those people were
called upon to make countless explanations on what this all was
about.

I am surprised that this had to be so. Not only was the move taken
by the non-white students defensible but it was a long overdue step. It
seems sometimes that it is a crime for the non-white students to think
for themselves. The idea of everything being done for the blacks is an
old one and all liberals take pride in it; but once the black students
want to do things for themselves suddenly they are regarded as becoming "militant".

Probably it would be of use at this stage to paraphrase the aims of
SASO as an organisation. These are:

1. To crystallise the needs and aspirations of the non-white students
   and to seek to make known their grievances.
2. Where possible to put into effect programmes designed to meet
   the needs of the non-white students and to act on a collective basis
   in an effort to solve some of the problems which beset the centres
   individually.
3. To heighten the degree of contact not only amongst the non-white
   students but also amongst these and the rest of the South African
   student population, to make the non-white students accepted on
   their own terms as an integral part of the South African student
   community.
4. To establish a solid identity amongst the non-white students and

to ensure that these students are always treated with the dignity and respect they deserve.

5. To protect the interests of the member centres and to act as a pressure group on all institutions and organisations for the benefit of the non-white students.
6. To boost up the morale of the non-white students, to heighten their own confidence in themselves and to contribute largely to the direction of thought taken by the various institutions on social, political and other current topics.

The above aims give in a nutshell the role of SASO as an organisation. The fact that the whole ideology centres around non-white students as a group might make a few people to believe that the organisation is racially inclined. Yet what SASO has done is simply to take stock of the present scene in the country and to realise that not unless the non-white students decide to lift themselves from the doldrums will they ever hope to get out of them. What we want is not black visibility but real black participation. In other words it does not help us to see several quiet black faces in a multiracial student gathering which ultimately concentrates on what the white students believe are the needs for the black students. Because of our sheer bargaining power as an organisation we can manage in fact to bring about a more meaningful contact between the various colour groups in the student world.

The idea that SASO is a form of "Black NUSAS" has been thrown around. Let it be known that SASO is *not* a national union and has never claimed to be one. Neither is SASO opposed to NUSAS as a national union. SASO accepts the principle that in any one country at any time a national union must be open to all students in that country, and in our country NUSAS is the national union and SASO accepts her fully as such and offers no competition in that direction. What SASO objects to is the dichotomy between principle and practice so apparent among members of that organisation. While very few would like to criticise NUSAS policy and principles as they appear on paper one tends to get worried at all hypocrisy practised by the members of that organisation. This serves to make the non-white members feel unaccepted and insulted in many instances. One may also add that the mere numbers fail to reflect a true picture of the South African scene. There shall always be a white majority in the organisation. This in itself does not matter except that where there is conflict of interests between the two colour groups the non-white always get off the poorer. These are some of the problems SASO looks into. We would not like to see the black centres being forced out of NUSAS by a swing to the right. Hence it becomes our concern to exert our influence on NUSAS where possible for the benefit of the non-white centres who are members of that organisation.

Another popular question is why SASO does not affiliate to NUSAS. SASO has a specific role to play and it has been set up as the custodian of non-white interests. It can best serve this purpose by maintaining only functional relationships with other student organisations but not structural ones. It is true that one of the reasons why SASO was formed was that organisations like NUSAS were anathema at the University Colleges.* However our decision not to affiliate to NUSAS arises out of the consideration of our role as an organisation in that we do not want to develop any structural relationships that may later interfere with our effectiveness.

SASO has met with a number of difficulties shortly after its inception.

1. There is the chronic problem of not having enough financial resources. It does seem that this is where most non-white organisations fail. However we hope to clear out of this difficulty soon and we shall in the process need lots of help from the stronger centres.

2. Traditional sectionalisation still makes correspondence a very sluggish business with some centres. Most of the university colleges have a long history of isolation. Some of them have grabbed the chance to break free from their cocoons. A few still cling tenaciously to them. We have for instance been unable to get through to Bellville. We have difficulty in getting to a few other centres. But I am happy to say that most centres realise the exciting possibilities of this meaningful form of communication. We hope in time that we shall all be able to join in the happy community of those who share their problems.

3. The bogey of authority also seems a real problem. Understandably lots of students are afraid that any involvement with anybody beyond their own university might attract unwarranted attention not only from local but also from national authority.

* The "University Colleges" were the ethnic institutions established by the Nationalist government, e.g. at Ngoye for the Zulus, Turfloop for the Tswanas and Sotho, the takeover of the formerly non-ethnic Fort Hare (where many leaders of the independent African countries were educated) for the Xhosas, Bellville for the Coloureds, and Duran Westville for the Indians. Editor's note.

However one hopes that there will be more examples of those courageous few who built up the SRC at places like Turfloop to the point where it had a lot of bargaining power with the Rector.

4. Non-acceptance by NUSAS sparked off lots of unwelcome problems. To many centres accepting SASO became an automatic step towards withdrawing from NUSAS. Very few centres seemed to be able to grasp the differences in focal points between the two organisations.

5. There has been considerable lack of support from the various SRCs for those involved in the organisation. A lot of people even from the affiliated centres seem to regard themselves as observers.

However besides these problems the Executive has continued applying itself diligently towards setting a really solid foundation for the future. There is reason to believe that SASO will grow from strength to strength as more and more centres join.

The future of SASO highly depends on a number of things. Personally I believe that there will be a swing to the right on the white campuses. This will result in the death of NUSAS or a change in that organisation that will virtually exclude all non-whites. All sensible people will strive to delay the advent of that moment. I believe that SASO too should. But if the day when it shall come is inevitable, when it does come SASO will shoulder the full responsibility of being the only student organisation catering for the needs of the non-white students. And in all probability SASO will be the only student organisation still concerned about contact between various colour groups.

Lastly I wish to call upon all student leaders at the non-white institutions to put their weight solidly behind SASO and to guarantee the continued existence of the organisation not only in name but also in effectiveness. This is a challenge to test the independence of the non-white student leaders not only organisationally but also ideologically. The fact that we have differences of approach should not cloud the issue. We have a responsibility not only to ourselves but also to the society from which we spring. No one else will ever take the challenge up until we, of our own accord, accept the inevitable fact that ultimately the leadership of the non-white peoples in this country rests with us.

3
Letter to Students' Representative Council Presidents

This chapter consists of a letter sent by Steve, as President of SASO, in February 1970 to the SRC (Students' Representative Council) Presidents of English and Afrikaans medium universities, to national student and other (including overseas) organisations. It gives the historical background and an authoritative rationale for the founding of SASO. The tone is conciliatory towards NUSAS, which is still recognised as "the true National Union of students in South Africa today". Steve was aware of the strength of opposition to a segregated body, particularly outside South Africa which is where it was hoped that some of the money for the support of SASO would come from. It was necessary to present the positive purpose in the formation of SASO which would make it clear that the "withdrawal" was only in order to re-group and be more effective in striving towards the common ultimate aim of both NUSAS and SASO – a non-racial, egalitarian society.

The historical background section displays Steve's strong sense of history and particularly of the continuity of African resistance to the various forms of white oppression. In reading this document readers should remember that from his first arrival at Medical School Steve had taken a leading part in NUSAS activities, and had been an outstandingly successful NUSAS local Chairman. It could never be said of him that he turned to founding a rival organisation because of his failure to "make the grade" in NUSAS. Also it is remarkable, but entirely typical, that the implicit attack on NUSAS which the founding of SASO involved never led to a breach of the good personal relationships he continued to enjoy with the white NUSAS leaders.

This document is not only an excellent account of the reasons for the founding of SASO, and a stout defence of its non-racialist intentions. It is also a good example of that combination of tough, even aggressive, language with a basically friendly underlying spirit which was so marked a feature always of Steve's statesmanlike approach to other organisations and persons.

*As an interesting follow-up to this chapter, Chapter 4 is a report by
Steve on his presidential tour of most of the black campuses, which was
published in the June 1970 issue of the SASO Newsletter, i.e. four
months after the letter to the SRC Presidents. Steve spent a great part
of his presidential year touring the campuses and building up support
for the young movement.*

To: SRC Presidents (English and Afrikaans Modium Universities)
National Student Organisations
Other Organisations
Overseas Organisations

Dear Sir,
      Re: *South African Students' Organisation*
Allow us at this late stage to introduce the South African Students'
Organisation to you. This is a one-year-old organisation which was
established at the inaugural conference at the University of the
North in July 1969.

This circular is meant to give your organisation a true and first-
hand account of the factors that led to the establishment of the
organisation. We also intend giving you a clear picture of where we
stand today in relation to the other student organisations in the
country.

HISTORICAL BACKGROUND
The implementation in 1960 of the Fort Hare Transfer Act of 1959
which brought Fort Hare under direct government control dealt a
blow to student contact between that University and the rest of the
student population. The dissolution of the SRC at Fort Hare in
August that year by the students themselves was a sequel to the
stringent measures applied at this then only black University to
suppress the freedom of the students to meet and discuss with
whomsoever they wanted to.

Even more contained were the sister "Universities" that were established that same year i.e. University College of the Western
Cape (for Coloureds) University College of Zululand (for Zulus)

University College of the North (for Sothos), University College of Durban (for Indians).

The concept of an independent SRC was never known at these places. The Rector had virtually limitless powers of veto over anything the students decided to do. This power of veto was especially applied to all moves by students to associate with NUSAS. Hence the long period of isolation started.

The establishment of the University Christian Movement in 1967 opened new avenues for contact. UCM had a special appeal to students at the University Colleges. The fact that within a year and a half of its existence the UCM had already a black majority in its sessions is indicative of this. Hence with the continued getting together of students from the University Colleges dialogue began again amongst black students.

One of the most talked-about topics was the position of the black students in the "open" organisations like NUSAS and UCM. Concern was expressed that these were white-dominated and paid very little attention to problems peculiar to the black community. In fact some people began to question the very competence of pluralistic groups to examine without bias problems affecting one group especially if the unaffected group is from the oppressor camp. It was felt that a time had come when blacks had to formulate their own thinking, unpolluted by ideas emanating from a group with lots at stake in the *status quo*.

There was nothing new in this kind of thinking. In bodies like African Students' Association and African Students' Union of South Africa, founded between 1960 and 1961 in the older black campuses, essentially the same underlying thinking was embodied. However these organisations died off for various reasons. The Durban Students' Union also came and went. The problem remained unsolved.

Some people amongst the black communities felt that the best approach would be a black take-over of the "open" student organisations engineered from within. However this idea never got any real support since to start with black students at the University Colleges were not even allowed to participate freely in these organisations.

In the NUSAS Conference of 1967 the blacks were made to stay at a church building somewhere in the Grahamstown location, each day being brought to Conference site by cars etc. On the other hand their white "brothers" were staying in residence around the conference site. This is perhaps the turning point in the history of black support for NUSAS. So appalling were the conditions that it showed the blacks just how valued they were in the organisation.

The 1968 NUSAS Congress was uneventful. The overriding impression was that the blacks were there in name only. The swing to the right in the organisation did not meet with the usual counter from the blacks. It was clear that none of the blacks felt a part of the organisation. Hence the Executive that was elected was all white.

Shortly thereafter, still in July, black students at a UCM conference demanded time to meet alone as a group. Ostensibly they were to discuss what to do in the face of the "72 hour" clause which forbade them to remain in a white area for more than 72 hours at a stretch. However once together they discussed for the first time, formally, the idea of forming a black organisation.

They had to choose between a structured and non-structured alliance and they decided on the former for the sake of continuity. The problem was that none of them were student leaders and therefore they could not take binding decisions.

In December 1968 a conference of SRCs from the black campuses decided overwhelmingly in favour of a black organisation and in July 1969 at the inaugural conference of SASO the organisation was formally founded.

It might probably be untrue to give the impression that everything was smooth. However most of the debate arose because of the tendency not to want to do what appears to conform with government policy – i.e. to segregate against another group. To quote from the SASO communique released in July 1969:

1. At a time when events are moving so fast in the country, it is not totally advisable to show any form of division amongst students' ranks – especially now that students appear to be a power to be reckoned with in this country.
2. Any move that tends to divide the student population into separate laagers on the basis of colour is in a way a tacit submission to having been defeated and apparently seems an agreement with apartheid.
3. In a racially sensitive country like ours, provision for racially exclusive bodies tends to build up resentment and to widen the gap that exists between the races, and the student community should resist all attempts to fall into this temptation.

4. Any formation of a purely non-white body shall be subject to a lot of scrutiny and so the chances of the organisations lasting are very little.

This shows, in a nutshell, just how strong the doubts were amongst some black student leaders. However the argument to go ahead was much stronger. While, as a matter of principle, we would reject separation in a normal society, we have to take cognizance of the fact that ours is far from a normal society. It is difficult not to look at white society as a group of people bent on perpetuating the *status quo*. The situation is not made easier by the non-acceptance that black students have met with in all the so called open organisations both religious and secular. All suffer from the same fault basically of accepting as a fact that there shall be white leadership and even worse, that they shall occupy themselves predominantly with problems affecting white society first.

Another important point was that in the interest of preserving a farcical non-racial front, almost 80% of the black students were regarded as expendable. These are the students who for instance were not allowed to participate freely in organisations like NUSAS because they were at government-controlled University Colleges. To quote once more from the SASO communiqué:

> In choosing to meet on a limited scale rather than not meeting at all, the non-white students shall be choosing the lesser evil, and striving to offset some of the evils that have accrued from the same evil system that made it impossible for them to meet freely with other students.

STRUCTURE

In terms of structure SASO operates *like* a National Union although she does not claim to be one. The basic type of affiliation is "centre affiliation". The SRCs are the power bases. They affiliate on behalf of their students. Where there is no SRC we accept a majority student body decision as an automatic affiliation by that centre. Individual membership is also catered for.

The governing body of SASO is the General Students' Council which meets once a year. It consists of the delegates from the various centres and branches and also the Executive. This is the official policy-making body of SASO.

The Executive governs in between GSC sessions, working according to mandates given to it by the GSC. The President is the sole interpreter of policy in between sessions.

POLICY
SASO has thus far taken policy only on a few topics, these mainly being student organisation, our broad basis of operation etc.

(a) *NUSAS*
1. SASO recognises NUSAS as the true National Union of students in South Africa today. This is based on the paper policy of the organisation. We offer no competition to NUSAS for black membership.
2. SASO criticises the dichotomy between principle and practice found in the organisation. We reject their basis of integration as being based on standards predominantly set by white society. It is more of what the white man expects the black man to do than the other way round. We feel we do not have to prove ourselves to anybody.
3. The fact that there are 27,000 white students and 3,000 black students in the organisation is not complementary to black opinion being fairly listened to.
4. The commitment of white students to the principles of the organisation is limited to very few individuals and hence NUSAS' credentials as a sincere and committed aspirant for change are wanting.

(b) *ASB*
This is the Afrikaanse Studentebond, a culturally inclined organisation operating predominantly at the Afrikaans medium Universities. It lays stress on Calvinism and Afrikanerdom as criteria for membership.
1. We uphold the right of any group to want to perpetuate their culture via this sort of organisation.
2. Where this promotion of a group culture implies cultivation of racist tendencies then the "right" becomes a negative right like the right to kill.
3. We tend to dismiss ASB as an incorrigible group with whom no worthwhile contact can be maintained.

(c) *UCM*

The University Christian Movement is a religious group concerning itself with ecumenical topics and modernisation of the archaic Christian religious practice. It also concerns itself with a practical application of Christian principles in an immoral society like the South African one.

1. We believe to a great extent that UCM has overcome the problems of adjustment to a two-tier society like ours. However we still feel that the fact that the blacks are in the majority in the organisation has not been sufficiently evidenced in the direction of thought and in the leadership of the organisation.
2. We nevertheless feel that UCM's progress is commendable especially in the direction of provoking meaningful thinking amongst clergymen, and its members.

(d) *The Press*

SASO rejects the press and believes in having as little to do with it as possible. The press is largely directed at white society or the so-called electorate whose values are laced with racial prejudice against black people.

Equally SASO rejects the black press which up to now has been largely controlled and some of it financed by government institutions. We believe that alongside Radio Bantu, most of the black press is being used as instruments of propaganda to get people to swallow most of the unbalanced and inflated stories about "what the government is doing for the Bantus" or ". . . for the Indians" or ". . . for the Coloureds".

AIMS

The aims of SASO are concerned primarily with black students and also with contact amongst students in general. Put in a paraphrased form these are:

1. To crystallise the needs and aspirations of the non-white students and to seek to make known their grievances.
2. Where possible to put into effect programmes designed to meet the needs of the non-white students and to act on a collective basis in an effort to solve some of the problems which beset the centres individually.
3. To heighten the degree of contact not only amongst the non-white

but also amongst these and the rest of the South African student population to make the non-white students accepted on their own terms as an integral part of the South African community.

4. To establish a solid identity amongst the non-white students and to ensure that these students are always treated with the dignity and respect they deserve.

5. To protect the interest of the member centres and to act as a pressure group on all institutions and organisations for the benefit of the non-white students.

6. To boost up the morale of the non-white student to heighten their own confidence in themselves and to contribute largely to the direction of thought taken by the various institutions on social, political and other current topics.

While these aims might appear to be couched in racialistic language, they are in fact a sign that the black student community has at last lost faith with their white counterparts and is now withdrawing from the open society.

The blacks are tired of standing at the touchlines to witness a game that they should be playing. They want to do things for themselves and all by themselves.

CONCLUSION

Too much caution has had to be taken at the beginning and the progress has been slow. We have reached a stage now where our existence has become an accomplished fact and our way of seeing things has been adopted by a substantial number on the black campuses.

Our limited dialogue with NUSAS, which has been along lines of constructive criticism, has been interpreted deliberately by some groups, including officials of ASB as a rejection of nonracialism as a political goal. Yet while critics to the right of NUSAS might rejoice, one thing they have to keep in mind is that with all its shortcomings NUSAS is still worth talking to. It is on the other hand, we believe, a painful waste of time to engage in any dialogue with racially-bigoted organisations like the ASB. Hence some people at the last SASO conference felt that this organisation "should be left alone to their small world of isolation whose boundaries are the four wheels of an ossewa".*

SASO adopts the principle that blacks should work themselves

---

* A waggon. Editor's note.

into a powerful group so as to go forth and stake their rightful claim in the open society rather than to exercise that power in some obscure part of the Kalahari. Hence this belies the belief that our withdrawal is an end in itself.

STEVE BIKO
PRESIDENT

4
Black Campuses and Current Feelings

The article that follows below is a brief summary of observations I made during the tour of most of the black campuses. It is based on discussions at student body meetings, SRC meetings and with small groups of individuals outside local leadership circles.

Slowly at first and quite fast of late, the black student community is casting aside the old approach towards solving its problems. A definite spirit of independence and an awareness of ourselves as a group with potential strength is beginning to manifest itself in many ways. On many an occasion I found the various campuses not only ready to support but also eager to join in directing the thinking of SASO. It was generally agreed that at this stage of our history, the most logical step is to follow the directive given by SASO i.e. that of concentrating on ourselves as a group and amalgamating our forces.

One striking feature is the steep decline in the intensity of the "morality" argument. Some time ago quite a lot of people used to be violently opposed to "segregation" even when practised by blacks against whites. Of late people of this persuasion are beginning to see the logic of rejecting the so called bilateral approach. The idea that blacks and whites can participate as equal partners in an open organisation is being questioned even by the most ardent black supporters of non-racialism. These people realise now that a lot of time and strength is wasted in maintaining artificial and token nonracialism at student level – artificial not in the sense that it is natural to segregate but rather because even those involved in it have certain prejudices that they cannot get rid of and are therefore basically dishonest to themselves, to their black counterparts and to the community of black people who are called upon to have faith in such people.

Another noticeable feature is that most of the students, while very sure of what they did not like in it, and who were quite harsh in their criticism of the old approach, yet lacked a depth of insight into what can be done. One found wherever he went the question being asked repeatedly "where do we go from here?" This again is a tragic result of the old approach, where the blacks were made to fit into a pattern largely and often wholly, determined by white students. Hence our originality and imagination have been dulled to the point where it takes a supreme effort to act logically even in order to follow one's beliefs and convictions.

A third and also important observation was the eagerness of the students to wish to relate whatever is done to their situation in the community. There is growing awareness of the role the black students may be called upon to play in the emancipation of their community. The students realise that the isolation of the black intelligentsia from the rest of the black society is a disadvantage to black people as a whole.

When everything is said and done one must express pleasant surprise at the quality of leadership on the various campuses. The history of most of the black campuses is marred with restrictions and intimidations. One would have thought that by now everybody has been cowed down to the point of dogged acceptance of all that comes from authority. Yet at many places I was surprised by the sheer bargaining power that the SRCs have built with their respective authorities.

Strong delegations are being sent from most of the black campuses to the SASO conference where a concerted effort will be made to get answers to some of the questions. The conference promises to be both interesting and enlightening especially in view of the diversity that one finds in approach. But some things are common to all – to bear witness to the unity of the black students, to give proper direction and depth to the movement and to make themselves worthy of the claim that they are the leaders of tomorrow.

STEVE BIKO

5
Black Souls in White Skins?

At the 1st General Students Council of SASO in July 1970 Steve was succeeded as President by Barney Pityana. Steve was elected Chairman of SASO Publications. The following month the monthly SASO Newsletter began to appear carrying articles by himself called "I write what I like" and signed Frank Talk. At the BPC/SASO Trial the Judge at one point interjected: "Isn't (accused) number 9 [Strini Moodley] Frank Talk?" to which Steve replied, "No, no, he was never Frank Talk, I was Frank Talk" (see p. 108). This article and the one that follows, from the August and September 1970 issues of the Newsletter respectively, give an authentic exposition of the philosophy of Black Consciousness.

I WRITE WHAT I LIKE

The following is the first of a series of articles under the above topic, that will appear regularly in our Newsletter.

BLACK SOULS IN WHITE SKINS?

Basically the South African white community is a homogeneous community. It is a community of people who sit to enjoy a privileged position that they do not deserve, are aware of this, and therefore spend their time trying to justify why they are doing so. Where differences in political opinion exist, they are in the process of trying to justify their position of privilege and their usurpation of power.

With their theory of "separate freedoms for the various nations in the multinational state of South Africa" the Nationalists have gone a long way towards giving most of white South Africa some sort of moral explanation for what is happening. Everyone is quite content to point out that these people – meaning the blacks – will be free when they are ready to run their own affairs in their own areas. What more could they possibly hope for?

But these are not the people we are concerned with. We are concerned with that curious bunch of nonconformists who explain their participation in negative terms: that bunch of do-gooders that goes under all sorts of names – liberals, leftists etc. These are the people who argue that they are not responsible for white racism and the country's "inhumanity to the black man". These are the people who claim that they too feel the oppression just as acutely as the blacks and therefore should be jointly involved in the black man's struggle for a place under the sun. In short, these are the people who say that they have black souls wrapped up in white skins.

The role of the white liberal in the black man's history in South Africa is a curious one. Very few black organisations were not under white direction. True to their image, the white liberals always knew what was good for the blacks and told them so. The wonder of it all is that the black people have believed in them for so long. It was only at the end of the 50s that the blacks started demanding to be their own guardians.

Nowhere is the arrogance of the liberal ideology demonstrated so well as in their insistence that the problems of the country can only be solved by a bilateral approach involving both black and white. This has, by and large, come to be taken in all seriousness as the *modus operandi* in South Africa by all those who claim they would like a change in the *status quo*. Hence the multiracial political organisations and parties and the "nonracial" student organisations, all of which insist on integration not only as an end goal but also as a means.

The integration they talk about is first of all artificial in that it is a response to conscious manoeuvre rather than to the dictates of the inner soul. In other words the people forming the integrated complex have been extracted from various segregated societies with their in-built complexes of superiority and inferiority and these continue to manifest themselves even in the "nonracial" set-up of the integrated complex. As a result the integration so achieved is a one-way course, with the whites doing all the talking and the blacks the listening. Let me hasten to say that I am not claiming that segregation is necessarily the natural order; however, given the facts of the situation where a group experiences privilege at the expense of others, then it becomes obvious that a hastily arranged integration cannot be the solution to the problem. It is rather like expecting the slave to work together with the slave-master's son to remove all the conditions leading to the former's enslavement.

Secondly, this type of integration as a means is almost always unproductive. The participants waste lots of time in an internal sort of mudslinging designed to prove that A is more of a liberal than B. In other words the lack of common ground for solid identification is all the time manifested in internal strifes inside the group.

It will not sound anachronistic to anybody genuinely interested in real integration to learn that blacks are asserting themselves in a society where they are being treated as perpetual under-16s. One does not need to plan for or actively encourage real integration. Once the various groups within a given community have asserted themselves to the point that mutual respect has to be shown then you have the ingredients for a true and meaningful integration. At the heart of true integration is the provision for each man, each group to rise and attain the envisioned self. Each group must be able to attain its style of existence without encroaching on or being thwarted by another. Out of this mutual respect for each other and complete freedom of self-determination there will obviously arise a genuine fusion of the life-styles of the various groups. This is true integration.

From this it becomes clear that as long as blacks are suffering from inferiority complex – a result of 300 years of deliberate oppression, denigration and derision – they will be useless as co-architects of a normal society where man is nothing else but man for his own sake. Hence what is necessary as a prelude to anything else that may come is a very strong grass-roots build-up of black consciousness such that blacks can learn to assert themselves and stake their rightful claim.

Thus in adopting the line of a nonracial approach, the liberals are playing their old game. They are claiming a "monopoly on intelligence and moral judgement" and setting the pattern and pace for the realisation of the black man's aspirations. They want to remain in good books with both the black and white worlds. They want to shy away from all forms of "extremisms", condemning "white supremacy" as being just as bad as "Black Power!". They vacillate between the two worlds, verbalising all the complaints of the blacks beautifully while skilfully extracting what suits them from the exclusive pool of white privileges. But ask them for a moment to give a concrete meaningful programme that they intend adopting, then you will see on whose side they really are. Their protests are directed at and appeal to white conscience, everything they do is directed at finally convincing the white electorate that the black man is also a man and that at some future date he should be given a place at the white man's table.

The myth of integration as propounded under the banner of liberal ideology must be cracked and killed because it makes people believe that something is being done when in actual fact the artificial integrated circles are a soporific on the blacks and provide a vague satisfaction for the guilty-stricken whites. It works on a false premise that because it is difficult to bring people from different races together in this country, therefore achievement of this is in itself a step forward towards the total liberation of the blacks. Nothing could be more irrelevant and therefore misleading. Those who believe in it are living in a fool's paradise.

First the black-white circles are almost always a creation of white liberals. As a testimony to their claim of complete identification with the blacks, they call a few "intelligent and articulate" blacks to "come around for tea at home", where all present ask each other the same old hackneyed question "how can we bring about change in South Africa?" The more such tea-parties one calls the more of a liberal he is and the freer he shall feel from the guilt that harnesses and binds his conscience. Hence he moves around his white circles – whites-only hotels, beaches, restaurants and cinemas – with a lighter load, feeling that he is not like the rest of the others. Yet at the back of his mind is a constant reminder that he is quite comfortable as things stand and therefore should not bother about change. Although he does not vote for the Nats (now that they are in the majority anyway), he feels quite secure under the protection offered by the Nats and subconsciously shuns the idea of a change. This is what demarcates the liberal from the black world. The liberals view the oppression of blacks as a problem that has to be solved, an eye sore spoiling an otherwise beautiful view. From time to time the liberals make themselves forget about the problem or take their eyes off the eyesore. On the other hand, in oppression the blacks are experiencing a situation from which they are unable to escape at any given moment. Theirs is a struggle to get out of the situation and not merely to solve a peripheral problem as in the case of the liberals. This is why blacks speak with a greater sense of urgency than whites.

A game at which the liberals have become masters is that of deliberate evasiveness. The question often comes up "what can I do?". If you ask him to do something like stopping to use segregated facilities or dropping out of varsity to work at menial jobs like all blacks or defying and denouncing all provisions that make him privileged, you always get the answer – "but that's unrealistic!". While this may be true, it only serves to illustrate the fact that no matter what a white man does, the colour of his skin – his passport to privilege – will always put him miles ahead of the black man. Thus in the ultimate analysis no white person can escape being part of the oppressor camp.

"There exists among men, because they are men, a solidarity through which each shares responsibility for every injustice and every wrong committed in the world, and especially for crimes that are committed in his presence or of which he cannot be ignorant".

This description of "metaphysical guilt" explains adequately that white racism "is only possible because whites are indifferent to suffering and patient with cruelty" meted out to the black man. Instead of involving themselves in an all-out attempt to stamp out racism from their white society, liberals waste lots of time trying to prove to as many blacks as they can find that they are liberal. This arises out of the false belief that we are faced with a black problem. There is nothing the matter with blacks. The problem is WHITE RACISM and it rests squarely on the laps of the white society. The sooner the liberals realise this the better for us blacks. Their presence amongst us is irksome and of nuisance value. It removes the focus of attention from essentials and shifts it to ill-defined philosophical concepts that are both irrelevant to the black man and merely a red herring across the track. White liberals must leave blacks to take care of their own business while they concern themselves with the real evil in our society – white racism.

Secondly, the black-white mixed circles are static circles with neither direction nor programme. The same questions are asked and the same naiveté exhibited in answering them. The real concern of the group is to keep the group going rather than being useful. In this sort of set-up one sees a perfect example of what oppression has done to the blacks. They have been made to feel inferior for so long that for them it is comforting to drink tea, wine or beer with whites who seem to treat them as equals. This serves to boost up their own ego to the extent of making them feel slightly superior to those blacks who do not get similar treatment from whites. These are the sort of blacks who are a danger to the community.

Instead of directing themselves at their black brothers and looking at their common problems from a common platform they choose to sing out their lamentations to an apparently sympathetic audience that has become proficient in saying the chorus of "shame!". These dull-witted, self-centred blacks are in the ultimate analysis as guilty of the arrest of progress as their white friends for it is from such groups that the theory of gradualism emanates and this is what keeps the blacks confused and always hoping that one day God will step down from heaven to solve their problems. It is people from such groups who keep on scanning the papers daily to detect any sign of the change they patiently await without working for. When Helen Suzman's* majority is increased by a couple of thousands, this is regarded as a major milestone in the "inevitable change". Nobody looks at the other side of the coin – the large-scale removals of Africans from the urban areas or the impending zoning of places like Grey Street in Durban and a myriad of other manifestations of change for the worse.

Does this mean that I am against integration? If by integration you understand a breakthrough into white society by blacks, an assimilation and acceptance of blacks into an already established set of norms and code of behaviour set up by and maintained by whites, then YES I am against it. I am against the superior-inferior white-black stratification that makes the white a perpetual teacher and the black a perpetual pupil (and a poor one at that). I am against the intellectual arrogance of white people that makes them believe that white leadership is a *sine qua non* in this country and that whites are the divinely appointed pace-setters in progress. I am against the fact that a settler minority should impose an entire system of values on an indigenous people.

If on the other hand by integration you mean there shall be free participation by all members of a society, catering for the full expression of the self in a freely changing society as determined by the will of the people, then I am with you. For one cannot escape the fact that the culture shared by the majority group in any given society must ultimately determine the broad direction taken by the joint culture of that society. This need not cramp the style of those who feel differently but on the whole, a country in Africa, in which the majority of the people are African must inevitably exhibit African values and be truly African in style.

What of the claim that the blacks are becoming racists? This is a favourite pastime of frustrated liberals who feel their trusteeship

* At that time, and for many years, the only Progressive Party MP. Editor's note.

ground being washed off from under their feet. These self-appointed trustees of black interests boast of years of experience in their fight for the 'rights of the blacks'. They have been doing things for blacks, on behalf of blacks, and because of blacks. When the blacks announce that the time has come for them to do things for themselves and all by themselves all white liberals shout blue murder!

"Hey, you can't do that. You're being a racist. You're falling into their trap."

Apparently it's alright with the liberals as long as you remain caught by *their* trap.

Those who know, define racism as discrimination by a group against another for the purposes of subjugation or maintaining subjugation. In other words one cannot be a racist unless he has the power to subjugate. What blacks are doing is merely to respond to a situation in which they find themselves the objects of white racism. We are in the position in which we are because of our skin. We are collectively segregated against – what can be more logical than for us to respond as a group? When workers come together under the auspices of a trade union to strive for the betterment of their conditions, nobody expresses surprise in the Western world. It is the done thing. Nobody accuses them of separatist tendencies. Teachers fight their battles, garbagemen do the same, nobody acts as a trustee for another. Somehow, however, when blacks want to do their thing the liberal establishment seems to detect an anomaly. This is in fact a counter-anomaly. The anomaly was there in the first instance when the liberals were presumptuous enough to think that it behoved them to fight the battle *for* the blacks.

The liberal must understand that the days of the Noble Savage are gone; that the blacks do not need a go-between in this struggle for their own emancipation. No true liberal should feel any resentment at the growth of black consciousness. Rather, all true liberals should realise that the place for their fight for justice is within their white society. The liberals must realise that they themselves are oppressed if they are true liberals and therefore they must fight for their own freedom and not that of the nebulous "they" with whom they can hardly claim identification. The liberal must apply himself with absolute dedication to the idea of educating his white brothers that the history of the country may have to be rewritten at some stage and that we may live in "a country where colour will not serve to put a man in a box". The blacks have heard enough of this. In other words, the liberal must serve as a lubricating material so that as we change the gears in trying to find a better direction for South Africa, there should be no grinding noises of metal against metal but a free and easy flowing movement which will be characteristic of a well-looked-after vehicle.

FRANK TALK

6
We Blacks

In the last issue, I took a look at a section of the white community. Today I propose to concern myself with the black world – the validity of the new approach.

WE BLACKS

Born shortly before 1948*, I have lived all my conscious life in the framework of institutionalised separate development. My friendships, my love, my education, my thinking and every other facet of my life have been carved and shaped within the context of separate development. In stages during my life I have managed to outgrow some of the things the system taught me. Hopefully what I propose to do now is to take a look at those who participate in opposition to the system – not from a detached point of view but from the point of view of a black man, conscious of the urgent need for an understanding of what is involved in the new approach – "black consciousness".

One needs to understand the basics before setting up a remedy. A number of the organisations now currently "fighting against apartheid" are working on an oversimplified premise. They have taken a brief look at what is, and have diagnosed the problem incorrectly. They have almost completely forgotten about the side effects and have not even considered the root cause. Hence whatever is improvised as a remedy will hardly cure the condition.

Apartheid – both petty and grand – is obviously evil. Nothing can justify the arrogant assumption that a clique of foreigners has the right to decide on the lives of a majority. Hence even carried out faithfully and fairly the policy of apartheid would merit condemnation and vigorous opposition from the indigenous peoples as well as those who see the problem in its correct perspective. The fact that apartheid has been tied up with white supremacy, capitalist exploitation, and deliberate oppression makes the problem much more

* The year in which the Nationalist Party came to power. Editor's note.

complex. Material want is bad enough, but coupled with spiritual poverty it kills. And this latter effect is probably the one that creates mountains of obstacles in the normal course of emancipation of the black people.

One should not waste time here dealing with manifestations of material want of the black people. A vast literature has been written on this problem. Possibly a little should be said about spiritual poverty. What makes the black man fail to tick? Is he convinced of his own accord of his inabilities? Does he lack in his genetic make-up that rare quality that makes a man willing to die for the realisation of his aspirations? Or is he simply a defeated person? The answer to this is not a clearcut one. It is, however, nearer to the last suggestion than anything else. The logic behind white domination is to prepare the black man for the subservient role in this country. Not so long ago this used to be freely said in parliament even about the educational system of the black people. It is still said even today, although in a much more sophisticated language. To a large extent the evil-doers have succeeded in producing at the output end of their machine a kind of black man who is man only in form. This is the extent to which the process of dehumanisation has advanced.

Black people under the Smuts government were oppressed but they were still men. They failed to change the system for many reasons which we shall not consider here. But the type of black man we have today has lost his manhood. Reduced to an obliging shell, he looks with awe at the white power structure and accepts what he regards as the "inevitable position". Deep inside his anger mounts at the accumulating insult, but he vents it in the wrong direction – on his fellow man in the township, on the property of black people. No longer does he trust leadership, for the 1963 mass arrests were blameable on bungling by the leadership, nor is there any to trust. In the privacy of his toilet his face twists in silent condemnation of white society but brightens up in sheepish obedience as he comes out hurrying in response to his master's impatient call. In the home-bound bus or train he joins the chorus that roundly condemns the white man but is first to praise the government in the presence of the police or his employers. His heart yearns for the comfort of white society and makes him blame himself for not having been "educated" enough to warrant such luxury. Celebrated achievements by whites in the field of science – which he understands only hazily – serve to make him rather convinced of the futility of resistance and to throw away any hopes that change may ever come. All in all the black man has become a shell, a shadow of man, completely defeated, drowning in his own misery, a slave, an ox bearing the yoke of oppression with sheepish timidity.

This *is* the first truth, bitter as it may seem, that we have to acknowledge before we can start on any programme designed to change the status quo. It becomes more necessary to see the truth as it is if you realise that the only vehicle for change are these people who have lost their personality. The first step therefore is to make the black man come to himself; to pump back life into his empty shell; to infuse him with pride and dignity, to remind him of his complicity in the crime of allowing himself to be misused and therefore letting evil reign supreme in the country of his birth. This is what we mean by an inward-looking process. This is the definition of "Black Consciousness".

One writer makes the point that in an effort to destroy completely the structures that had been built up in the African Society and to impose their imperialism with an unnerving totality the colonialists were not satisfied merely with holding a people in their grip and emptying the Native's brain of all form and content, they turned to the past of the oppressed people and distorted, disfigured and destroyed it. No longer was reference made to African culture, it became barbarism. Africa was the "dark continent". Religious practices and customs were referred to as superstition. The history of African Society was reduced to tribal battles and internecine wars. There was no conscious migration by the people from one place of abode to another. No, it was always flight from one tyrant who wanted to defeat the tribe not for any positive reason but merely to wipe them out of the face of this earth.

No wonder the African child learns to hate his heritage in his days at school. So negative is the image presented to him that he tends to find solace only in close identification with the white society.

No doubt, therefore, part of the approach envisaged in bringing about "black consciousness" has to be directed to the past, to seek to rewrite the history of the black man and to produce in it the heroes who form the core of the African background. To the extent that a vast literature about Gandhi in South Africa is accumulating it can be said that the Indian community already has started in this direction. But only scant reference is made to African heroes. A people without a positive history is like a vehicle without an engine. Their emotions cannot be easily controlled and channelled in a recognisable direction. They always live in the shadow of a more successful society. Hence in a country like ours they are forced to celebrate holidays like Paul Kruger's day. Heroes' day, Republic day etc., – all of which are occasions during which the humiliation of defeat is at once revived.

Then too one can extract from our indigenous cultures a lot of positive virtues which should teach the Westerner a lesson or two. The oneness of community for instance is at the heart of our culture. The easiness with which Africans communicate with each other is not forced by authority but is inherent in the make-up of African people. Thus whereas the white family can stay in an area without knowing its neighbours, Africans develop a sense of belonging to the community within a short time of coming together. Many a hospital official has been confounded by the practice of Indians who bring gifts and presents to patients whose names they can hardly recall. Again this is a manifestation of the interrelationship between man and man in the black world as opposed to the highly impersonal world in which Whitey lives. These are characteristics we must not allow ourselves to lose. Their value can only be appreciated by those of us who have not as yet been made slaves to technology and the machine. One can quote a myriad of other examples. Here again "black consciousness" seeks to show the black people the value of their own standards and outlook. It urges black people to judge themselves according to these standards and not to be fooled by white society who have white-washed themselves and made white standards the yardstick by which even black people judge each other.

It is probably necessary at this stage to warn all and sundry about the limits of endurance of the human mind. This is particularly necessary in the case of the African people. Ground for a revolution is always fertile in the presence of absolute destitution. At some stage one can foresee a situation where black people will feel they have nothing to live for and will shout unto their God "Thy will be done." Indeed His will shall be done but it shall not appeal equally to all mortals for indeed we have different versions of His will. If the white God has been doing the talking all along, at some stage the black God will have to raise His voice and make Himself heard over and above noises from His counterpart. What happens at that stage depends largely on what happens in the intervening period. "Black consciousness" therefore seeks to give positivity in the outlook of the black people to their problems. It works on the knowledge that "white hatred" is negative, though understandable, and leads to precipitate and shot-gun methods which may be disastrous for black and white alike. It seeks to channel the pent-up forces of the angry black masses to meaningful and directional opposition basing its entire struggle on realities of the situation. It wants to ensure a singularity of purpose in the minds of the black people and to make possible total involvement of the masses in a struggle essentially theirs.

What of the white man's religion – Christianity? It seems the people involved in imparting Christianity to the black people steadfastly refuse to get rid of the rotten foundation which many of the missionaries created when they came. To this date black people find no message for them in the Bible simply because our ministers are still too busy with moral trivialities. They blow these up as the most important things that Jesus had to say to people. They constantly urge the people to find fault in themselves and by so doing detract from the essence of the struggle in which the people are involved. Deprived of spiritual content, the black people read the bible with a gullibility that is shocking. While they sing in a chorus of "mea culpa" they are joined by white groups who sing a different version – "tua culpa". The anachronism of a well-meaning God who allows people to suffer continually under an obviously immoral system is not lost to young blacks who continue to drop out of Church by the hundreds. Too many people are involved in religion for the blacks to ignore. Obviously the only path open for us now is to redefine the message in the bible and to make it relevant to the struggling masses. The bible must not be seen to preach that all authority is divinely instituted. It must rather preach that it is a sin to allow oneself to be oppressed. The bible must continually be shown to have something to say to the black man to keep him going in his long journey towards realisation of the self. This is the message implicit in "black theology". Black theology seeks to do away with spiritual poverty of the black people. It seeks to demonstrate the absurdity of the assumption by whites that "ancestor worship" was necessarily a superstition and that Christianity is a scientific religion. While basing itself on the Christian message, black theology seeks to show that Christianity is an adaptable religion that fits in with the cultural situation of the people to whom it is imparted. Black theology seeks to depict Jesus as a fighting God who saw the exchange of Roman money – the oppressor's coinage – in His father's temple as so sacrilegious that it merited a violent reaction from Him – the Son of Man.

Thus in all fields "Black Consciousness" seeks to talk to the black man in a language that is his own. It is only by recognising the basic set-up in the black world that one will come to realise the urgent need for a re-awakening of the sleeping masses. Black consciousness seeks to do this. Needless to say it shall have to be the black people themselves who shall take care of this programme for indeed Sekou Toure was right when he said:

To take part in the African revolution, it is not enough to write a revolutionary song; you must fashion the revolution with the people. And if you fashion it with the people, the songs will come by themselves and of themselves.

In order to achieve real action you must yourself be a living part of Africa and of her thought; you must be an element of that popular energy which is entirely called forth for the freeing, the progress and the happiness of Africa. There is no place outside that fight for the artist or for the intellectual who is not himself concerned with, and completely at one with the people in the great battle of Africa and of suffering humanity.

FRANK TALK

7
Fragmentation of the Black Resistance

This article, from the SASO Newsletter of June 1971, deals with the problem faced by black leaders, whether African, Coloured or Indian, of working "within the system" ("the system" being the whole white racist apartheid structure built up by the Nationalists since 1948). Over and over again the pattern of resistance to the apartheid-created structures has been the same. First, open and defiant rejection: second, sullen acquiescence and reluctant collaboration; lastly, capitulation and corruption. The system operates with a cruel relentlessness, and also with seductive bribery: hence the "success" of Chief Matanzima's ruling party in the Transkei, alluded to by Steve in one of the closing paragraphs of this article.

Of particular interest here is the reference in the last paragraph but two to the amount of "community work that neeeds to be done in promoting a spirit of self-reliance". This article was written a year before Steve decided to devote himself full-time to this kind of work by joining Black Community Programmes.

It would be instructive to compare the consistent integrity of all Steve's writings and attitudes on this key issue of "working within the system" with the utterances over a comparable period of time of any other black politician.

I WRITE WHAT I LIKE

FRAGMENTATION OF THE BLACK RESISTANCE

Just who can be regarded as representative of black opinion in South Africa? This question often crosses my mind in many conversations with people throughout the country and on reading various newspaper reports on what blacks have to say on topical matters. Once more the issue was highlighted during the debate on whether or not to celebrate the 10th Anniversary of the "Republic" of South Africa. On the one hand Mr Pat Poovalingam in Durban was urging the Indian people to celebrate whilst, on the other, people like Mr Mewa Ramgobin and the Labour Party argued the case against celebration. In Zululand Chief Gatsha Buthelezi stated that the Zulu people would celebrate whilst elsewhere pamphlets were distributed from various black sources reminding the people that they would be celebrating the countless sins of the Nationalist Government. The interesting thing of course was the conspicuous silence of the urban African people except for the hushed objections of Soweto's UBC* Not at any stage did anybody state a representative opinion.

Anyone staying in South Africa will not be completely surprised by this. Political opinion is probably very clear-cut on issues of this nature amongst the African people especially. However, since the banning and harassment of black political parties – a dangerous vacuum has been created. The African National Congress and later the Pan-African Congress were banned in 1960; the Indian Congress was routed out of existence and ever since there has been no co-ordinated opinion emanating from the black ranks. Perhaps the Kliptown Charter – objectionable as the circumstances surrounding it might have been – was the last attempt ever made to instil some amount of positiveness in stating categorically what blacks felt on political questions in the land of their forefathers.

After the banning of the black political parties in South Africa, people's hearts were gripped by some kind of foreboding fear for anything political. Not only were politics a closed book, but at every corner one was greeted by a slave-like apathy that often bordered on timidity. To anyone living in the black world, the hidden anger and turmoil could always be seen shining through the faces and actions of these voiceless masses but it was never verbalised. Even the active phase, thuggery and vandalism – was directed to one's kind – a clear manifestation of frustration. To make it worse, no real hope was offered by the output from the recently created black universities. Sons and fathers alike were concerned about cutting themselves a niche in a situation from which they saw no hope of escaping.

After this brief spell of silence during which political activity was

* Urban Bantu Council. Editor's note.

mainly taken up by liberals, blacks started dabbling with the dangerous theory – that of working within the system. This attitude was exploited to the full by the Nationalist party. Thus the respectability of Matanzima's Transkei was greatly boosted by Ndamse's decision to join hands with him. Clearly Ndamse, being a one-time banned man, convinced many people by his decision that there was something to be gained out of these apartheid institutions. Soon thereafter the Coloured Labour Party, operating on an anti-apartheid ticket was formed to oppose the pro-apartheid Federal Party within the all-Coloured Coloured Representative Council. People's logic became strangely twisted. Said a member of the Transkei's opposition Democratic Party: "We know that the Transkeian parliament is a stooge body. We ask you to elect us to that stooge body!"

But it seems that nothing influenced people more to "accept" the "working within the system" theory than the decision by Chief Gatsha Buthelezi to join in and lead the Zulu Territorial Authority. Chief Gatsha Buthelezi had for a long time been regarded as the bastion of resistance to the institution of a territorial authority in Zululand. Then one morning a newspaper intimated that he might just agree to take it up and within weeks Chief Gatsha Buthelezi was indeed the Chief Executive Officer of the Zululand Territorial Authority.

Following the capitulation of Chief Gatsha Buthelezi, a burst of activity manifested itself in these apartheid institutions. On the one hand the Labour Party was making full use of the sanctified platform – the CRC – to air their grievances against the government, on the other Chief Gatsha was fast becoming an embarrassment to the government with the kind of things he was saying.

I believe it is just here that the confusion over who are the leaders of the black world began to arise. Because of the increased verbalisation of black man's complaints, the people – especially the white world – began to take these various voices as speaking on behalf of and as leaders of the black world. This kind of picture was particularly built up by the English press, who followed in detail everything people like Chief Gatsha Buthelezi did and said. Of course in the absence of any organized opinion it began to sound even to some black people themselves as if this were the case. The fact that Matanzima also joined in the bandwagon of militant demands has made everyone sit back and clap. People argue that the Nationalists have been caught in their own game. The black lion is beginning to raise its voice. This is a gross over-simplification.

What in fact is happening is that the black world is beginning to be completely fragmented and that people are beginning to talk sectional politics. I would rather like to believe that this was foreseen long ago by the Nationalist Party and that it is in fact a part of the programme. After the kind of noises made by Buthelezi, the Labour Party and of late Matanzima, who can argue that black opinion is being stifled in South Africa? Moreover any visitor is made to see that these people are fighting for more concessions in their own area (13% of the land). They accept that the rest of South Africa is for whites. Also none of them sees himself as fighting the battle for all black people. Xhosas want their Transkei, the Zulus their Zululand etc. Coloured people harbour secret hopes of being classified as "brown Afrikaners" and therefore meriting admittance into the white laager while Indian people might be given a vote to swell the buffer zone between whites and Africans. Of course these promises will never be fulfilled – at least not in a hurry – and in the meantime the enemy bestrides South Africa like a colossus laughing aloud at the fragmented attempts by the powerless masses making appeals to his deaf ears.

"The Transkei is the Achilles' heel of the Nationalists" claim intellectual politicians who are always quick to see a loophole even in a two-foot-thick iron wall. This is false logic. The Transkei, the CRC, Zululand and all these other apartheid institutions are modern-type laagers behind which the whites in this country are going to hide themselves for a long time to come. Slowly the ground is being swept off from under our feet and soon we as blacks will believe completely that our political rights are in fact in our "own" areas. Thereafter we shall find that we have no leg to stand on in making demands for any rights in "mainland White South Africa" which incidentally will comprise more than three-quarters of the land of our forefathers.

This is the major danger that I see facing the black community at the present moment – to be so conditioned by the system as to make even our most well-considered resistance to fit within the system both in terms of the means and of the goals. Witness the new swing amongst leaders of the Indian community in Durban. (I must admit I say this with pain in my heart). Ever since word was let loose that the Indian Council will at some near future be elected, a number of intelligent people are thinking of reviving the Indian Congress and letting

it form some kind of opposition within the system. This is dangerous retrogressive thinking which should be given no breathing space.
These apartheid institutions are swallowing too many good people
who would be useful in a meaningful programme of emancipation of
the black people.

Who are the leaders of the black world then if they are not to be
found in the apartheid institution? Clearly, black people know that
their leaders are those people who are now either in Robben Island or
in banishment or in exile – voluntary or otherwise. People like Mandela, Sobukwe, Kathrada, M.D. Naidoo and many others will
always have a place of honour in our minds as the true leaders of the
people. They may have been branded communists, saboteurs, or
similar names – in fact they may have been convicted of similar offences in law courts but this does not subtract from the real essence of
their worth. These were people who acted with a dedication unpar-
alleled in modern times. Their concern with our plight as black people
made them gain the natural support of the mass of black people. We
may disagree with some things they did but know that they spoke the
language of the people.

Does this necessarily mean that I see absolutely no advantage in
the present set-up? Unless the political astuteness of the black people
involved in these various apartheid institutions is further sharpened,
I am afraid we are fast approaching an impasse. The new generation
may be right in accusing us of collaboration in our own destruction.
In Germany the petty officials who decided on which Jews were to be
taken away were also Jews. Ultimately Hitler's gangs also came for
them. As soon as the dissident factors outside the apartheid institutions are completely silenced, they will come for those who make
noise inside the system. Once that happens the boundaries of our
world will forever be the circumference of the 13% "black spots".

Perhaps one should be a little positive at this stage. I completely
discourage the movement of people from the left to join the institutions of apartheid. In laying out a strategy we often have to take
cognizance of the enemy's strength and as far as I can assess all of us
who want to fight within the system are completely underestimating
the influence the system has on us. What seems to me to be logical at
this stage is for the left to continually pressurise the various apartheid institutions to move in the direction of testing the limits of possibility within the system, to prove the whole game a sham and to
break off the system. I will take the example of the Labour Party be-

cause it sounds as the most well-organised dissident group in the system.

The Coloured Labour Party stood for elections on an anti-apartheid ticket and won most of the elected seats. Further, the Labour Party wasted no time in spelling out its anti-apartheid stance and revived political activity to a great extent within the Coloured community. In fact the growing consciousness of the possibility of political action amongst the Coloured people is due to the Labour Party. Pretty soon the Labour Party will find that it is singing the same tune and whatever they say will cease to be of news value. In the meantime Tom Swartz will start making demands for the Coloured people and will probably gain a few concessions. The Coloured people will then realise that in fact a positive stand like that of Tom Swartz's is more welcome than a negative attitude like that of the Labour Party who keep on saying the same things. Then the Labour Party will start falling into disfavour.

This is not just theoretical. It has happened in the past with Matanzima and Guzana in the Transkei. Guzana's party – once the pride of dissident Transkeians who wanted to demonstrate their rejection of the system – has now been relegated to the background, operating even on the right of Matanzima's party whose militant demands are being seen as a more meaningful opposition to the system than a rehashed debate on the protection of white interests in the Transkei.

Therefore I see the real value of the Labour Party being in galvanising its forces now, organising them and pulling out of the Coloured Representative Council together with the support of all the Coloured people. The longer they stay in the CRC, the more they risk being irrelevant. "Pull out and do what"? this is the next question. There is a lot of community work that needs to be done in promoting a spirit of self-reliance and black consciousness among all black people in South Africa.

This is what the Labour Party should resort to doing. By now they have sufficiently demonstrated that the CRC is rejected by the Coloured People. Further operation within the system may only lead to political castration and a creation of an "I-am-a-Coloured" attitude which will prove a set back to the black man's programme of emancipation and will create major obstacles in the establishment of a non-racial society once our problems are settled. This to me sounds the only way of turning a disadvantage into an advantage. It is true of not only the Labour Party but also of all black people of conscience who are now operating within the system.

Thus in an effort to maintain our solidarity and relevance to the situation we must resist all attempts at the fragmentation of our resistance. Black people must recognise the various institutions of apartheid for what they are – gags intended to get black people fighting separately for certain "freedoms" and "gains" which were prescribed for them long ago. We must refuse to accept it as inevitable that the only political action the blacks may take is through these institutions.

Granted that it may be more attractive and even safer to join the system, we must still recognise that in doing so we are well on the way towards selling our souls.

FRANK TALK

8
Some African Cultural Concepts

This is a paper given by Steve at a conference called by IDAMASA (Interdenominational Association of African Ministers of Religion) and ASSECA (Association for the Educational and Cultural Development of the African people) at the Ecumenical Lay Training Centre, Edendale, Natal in 1971. The conference drew together a number of black organisations who might be interested in a closer association. Several papers were given including one by Chief Gatsha Buthelezi. This conference proved to be a staging post on the way to the formation of the Black People's Convention in Johannesburg in December of that year.

SOME AFRICAN CULTURAL CONCEPTS

One of the most difficult things to do these days is to talk with authority on anything to do with African culture. Somehow Africans are not expected to have any deep understanding of their own culture or even of themselves. Other people have become authorities on all aspects of the African life or to be more accurate on BANTU life. Thus we have the thickest of volumes on some of the strangest subjects – even "the feeding habits of the Urban Africans", a publication by a fairly "liberal" group, Institute of Race Relations.

In my opinion it is not necessary to talk with Africans about African culture. However, in the light of the above statements one realises that there is so much confusion sown, not only amongst casual non-African readers, but even amongst Africans themselves, that perhaps a sincere attempt should be made at emphasising the authentic cultural aspects of the African people by Africans themselves.

Since that unfortunate date – 1652 – we have been experiencing a process of acculturation. It is perhaps presumptuous to call it "acculturation" because this term implies a fusion of different cultures. In our case this fusion has been extremely one-sided. The two major cultures that met and "fused" were the African Culture and the Anglo-Boer Culture. Whereas the African culture was unsophisticated and simple, the Anglo-Boer culture had all the trappings of a colonialist culture and therefore was heavily equipped for conquest. Where they could, they conquered by persuasion, using a highly exclusive religion that denounced all other Gods and demanded a strict code of behaviour with respect to clothing, education ritual and custom. Where it was impossible to convert, fire-arms were readily available and used to advantage. Hence the Anglo-Boer culture was the more powerful culture in almost all facets. This is where the African began to lose a grip on himself and his surroundings.

Thus in taking a look at cultural aspects of the African people one inevitably finds himself having to compare. This is primarily because of the contempt that the "superior" culture shows towards the indigenous culture. To justify its exploitative basis the Anglo-Boer culture has at all times been directed at bestowing an inferior status to all cultural aspects of the indigenous people.

I am against the belief that African culture is time-bound, the notion that with the conquest of the African all his culture was obliterated. I am also against the belief that when one talks of African culture one is necessarily talking of the pre-Van Riebeeck culture. Obviously the African culture has had to sustain severe blows and may have been battered nearly out of shape by the bellingerent cultures it collided with, yet in essence even today one can easily find the fundamental aspects of the pure African culture in the present day African. Hence in taking a look at African culture I am going to refer as well to what I have termed the modern African culture.

One of the most fundamental aspects of our culture is the importance we attach to Man. Ours has always been a Man-centred society. Westerners have in many occasions been surprised at the capacity we have for talking to each other – not for the sake of arriving at a particular conclusion but merely to enjoy the communication for its own sake. Intimacy is a term not exclusive for particular friends but applying to a whole group of people who find themselves together either through work or through residential requirements.

In fact in the traditional African culture, there is no such thing as two friends. Conversation groups were more or less naturally determined by age and division of labour. Thus one would find all boys whose job was to look after cattle periodically meeting at popular spots to engage in conversation about their cattle, girlfriends, parents, heroes etc. All commonly shared their secrets, joys and woes. No one felt unnecessarily an intruder into someone else's business. The curiosity manifested was welcome. It came out of a desire to share. This pattern one would find in all age groups. House visiting was always a feature of the elderly folk's way of life. No reason was needed as a basis for visits. It was all part of our deep concern for each other.

These are things never done in the Westerner's culture. A visitor to someone's house, with the exception of friends, is always met with the question "what can I do for you?". This attitude to see people not as themselves but as agents for some particular function either to one's disadvantage or advantage is foreign to us. We are not a suspicious race. We believe in the inherent goodness of man. We enjoy man for himself. We regard our living together not as an unfortunate mishap warranting endless competition among us but as a deliberate act of God to make us a community of brothers and sisters jointly involved in the quest for a composite answer to the varied problems of life. Hence in all we do we always place Man first and hence all our action is usually joint community oriented action rather than the individualism which is the hallmark of the capitalist approach. We always refrain from using people as stepping stones. Instead we are prepared to have a much slower progress in an effort to make sure that all of us are marching to the same tune.

Nothing dramatises the eagerness of the African to communicate with each other more than their love for song and rhythm. Music in the African culture features in all emotional states. When we go to work, we share the burdens and pleasures of the work we are doing through music. This particular facet strangely enough has filtered through to the present day. Tourists always watch with amazement the synchrony of music and action as African working at a road side use their picks and shovels with well-timed precision to the accompaniment of a background song. Battle songs were a feature of the long march to war in the olden days. Girls and boys never played any games without using music and rhythm as its basis. In other words with Africans, music and rhythm were not luxuries but part and parcel of our way of communication. Any suffering we experienced was made much more real by song and rhythm. There is no doubt that the so called "Negro spirituals" sung by Black slaves in the States as they toiled under oppression were indicative of their

African heritage.

The major thing to note about our songs is that they never were songs for individuals. All African songs are group songs. Though many have words, this is not the most important thing about them. Tunes were adapted to suit the occasion and had the wonderful effect of making everybody read the same things from the common experience. In war the songs reassured those who were scared, highlighted the determination of the regiment to win a particular encounter and made much more urgent to the need to settle the score; in suffering, as in the case of the Black slaves, they derived sustenance out of a feeling of togetherness, at work the binding rhythm makes everybody brush off the burden and hence Africans can continue for hours on end because of this added energy.

Attitudes of Africans to property again show just how unindividualistic the African is. As everybody here knows, African society had the village community as its basis. Africans always believed in having many villages with a controllable number of people in each rather than the reverse. This obviously was a requirement to suit the needs of a community-based and man-centred society. Hence most things were jointly owned by the group, for instance there was no such thing as individual land ownership. The land belonged to the people and was merely under the control of the local chief on behalf of the people. When cattle went to graze it was on an open veld and not on anybody's specific farm.

Farming and agriculture, though on individual family basis, had many characteristics of joint efforts. Each person could by a simple request and holding of a special ceremony, invite neighbours to come and work on his plots. This service was returned in kind and no remuneration was ever given.

Poverty was a foreign concept. This could only be really brought about to the entire community by an adverse climate during a particular season. It never was considered repugnant to ask one's neighbours for help if one was struggling. In almost all instances there was help between individuals, tribe and tribe, chief and chief etc. even in spite of war.

Another important aspect of the African culture is our mental attitude to problems presented by life in general. Whereas the Westerner is geared to use a problem-solving approach following very trenchant analyses, our approach is that of situation-experiencing. I will quote from Dr Kaunda to illustrate this point :

> The Westerner has an aggressive mentality. When he sees a problem he will not rest until he has formulated some solution to it. He cannot live with contradictory ideas in his mind; he must settle for one or the other or else evolve a third idea in his mind which harmonises or reconciles the other two. And he is vigorously scientific in rejecting solutions for which there is no basis in logic. He draws a sharp line between the natural and the supernatural, the rational and non-rational, and more often than not, he dismisses the supernatural and non-rational as superstition. . . .

> Africans being a pre-scientific people do not recognise any conceptual cleavage between the natural and supernatural. They experience a situation rather than face a problem. By this I mean they allow both the rational and non-rational elements to make an impact upon them, and any action they may take could be described more as a response of the total personality to the situation than the result of some mental exercise.

This I find a most apt analysis of the essential difference in the approach to life of these two groups. We as a community are prepared to accept that nature will have its enigmas which are beyond our powers to solve. Many people have interpreted this attitude as lack of initiative and drive yet in spite of my belief in the strong need for scientific experimentation I cannot help feeling that more time also should be spent in teaching man and man to live together and that perhaps the African personality with its attitude of laying less stress on power and more stress on man is well on the way to solving our confrontation problems.

All people are agreed that Africans are a deeply religious race. In the various forms of worship that one found throughout the Southern part of our Continent there was at least a common basis. We all accepted without any doubt the existence of a God. We had our own community of saints. We believed – and this was consistent with out views of life – that all people who died had a special place next to God. We felt that a communication with God, could only be through these people. We never knew anything about hell – we do not believe that God can create people only to punish them eternally after a short period on earth.

Another aspect of religious practices was the occasion of worship. Again we did not believe that religion could be featured as a separate part of our existence on earth. It was manifest in our daily lives. We thanked God through our ancestors before we drank beer, married, worked etc. We would obviously find it artificial to create special occasions for worship. Neither did we see it logical to have a particular building in which all worship would be conducted. We believed that God was always in communication with us and therefore merited attention everywhere and anywhere.

It was the missionaries who confused our people with their new religion. By some strange logic, they argued that theirs was a scientific religion and ours was mere superstition in spite of the biological discrepancies so obvious in the basis of their religion. They further went on to preach a theology of the existence of hell, scaring our fathers and mothers with stories about burning in eternal flames and gnashing of teeth and grinding of bone. This cold cruel religion was strange to us but our fore-fathers were sufficiently scared of the unknown impending anger to believe that it was worth a try. Down went our cultural values!

Yet it is difficult to kill the African heritage. There remains, in spite of the superficial cultural similarities between the detribalised and the Westerner, a number of cultural characteristics that mark out the detribalised as an African. I am not here making a case for separation on the basis of cultural differences. I am sufficiently proud to believe that under a normal situation, Africans can comfortably stay with people of other cultures and be able to contribute to the joint cultures of the communities they have joined. However, what I want to illustrate here is that even in a pluralistic society like ours, there are still some cultural traits that we can boast of which have been able to withstand the process of deliberate bastardisation. These are aspects of the modern African culture – a culture that has used concepts from the white world to expand on inherent cultural characteristics.

Thus we see that in the area of music, the African still expresses himself with conviction. The craze about jazz arises out of a conversion by the African artists of mere notes to meaningful music, expressive of real feelings. The Monkey Jive, Soul etc. are all aspects of a modern type African culture that expresses the same original feelings. Solos like those of Pat Boone and Elvis Presley could never really find expression within the African culture because it is not in us to listen passively to pure musical notes. Yet when soul struck with its all-engulfing rhythm it immediately caught on and set hundreds of millions of black bodies in gyration throughout the world. These were people reading in soul the real meaning – the defiant message "say it loud! I'm black and I'm proud". This is fast becoming our modern culture. A culture of defiance, self-assertion and group pride and solidarity. This is a culture that emanates from a situation of common experience of oppression. Just as it now finds expression in our music and our dress, it will spread to other aspects. This is the new and modern black culture to which we have given a major contribution. This is the modern black culture that is responsible for the restoration of our faith in ourselves and therefore offers a hope in the direction we are taking from here.

Thus in its entirety the African Culture spells us out as people particularly close to nature. As Kaunda puts it, our people may be unlettered and their physical horizons may be limited yet "they inhabit a larger world than the sophisticated Westerner who has magnified his physical senses through inverted gadgets at the price all too often of cutting out the dimension of the spiritual." This close proximity to Nature enables the emotional component in us to be so much richer in that it makes it possible for us, without any apparent difficulty to feel for people and to easily identify with them in any emotional situation arising out of suffering.

The advent of the Western Culture has changed our outlook almost drastically. No more could we run our own affairs. We were required to fit in as people tolerated with great restraint in a western type society. We were tolerated simply because our cheap labour is needed. Hence we are judged in terms of standards we are not responsible for. Whenever colonisation sets in with its dominant culture it devours the native culture and leaves behind a bastardised culture that can only thrive at the rate and pace allowed it by the dominant culture. This is what has happened to the African culture. It is called a sub-culture purely because the African people in the urban complexes are mimicking the white man rather unashamedly.

In rejecting Western values, therefore, we are rejecting those things that are not only foreign to us but that seek to destroy the most cherished of our beliefs – that the corner-stone of society is man himself – not just his welfare, not his material wellbeing but just man himself with all his ramifications. We reject the power-based society of the Westerner that seems to be ever concerned with perfecting their technological know-how while losing out on their spiritual dimension. We believe that in the long run the special contribution to the world by Africa will be in this field of human relationship. The great powers of the world may have done wonders in giving the world an industrial and military look, but the great gift still has to come from Africa – giving the world a more human face.

9
The Definition of Black Consciousness

This is a paper produced for a SASO leadership training course, probably in December 1971, and is included here as an example of Steve talking to members of his own organisation, and therefore speaking from the heart of his and their experience.

THE DEFINITION OF BLACK CONSCIOUSNESS

We have in our policy manifesto defined blacks as those who are by law or tradition politically, economically and socially discriminated against as a group in the South African society and identifying themselves as a unit in the struggle towards the realisation of their aspirations. This definition illustrates to us a number of things:
1. Being black is not a matter of pigmentation – being black is a reflection of a mental attitude.
2. Merely by describing yourself as black you have started on a road towards emancipation, you have committed yourself to fight against all forces that seek to use your blackness as a stamp that marks you out as a subservient being.

From the above observations therefore, we can see that the term black is not necessarily all-inclusive; i.e. the fact we are all *not white* does not necessarily mean that we are all *black*. Non-whites do exist and will continue to exist and will continue to exist for quite a long time. If one's aspiration is whiteness but his pigmentation makes attainment of this impossible, then that person is a non-white. Any man who calls a white man "Baas", any man who serves in the police force or Security Branch is *ipso facto* a non-white. Black people – real black people – are those who can manage to hold their heads high in defiance rather than willingly surrender their souls to the white man.

Briefly defined therefore, Black Consciousness is in essence the realisation by the black man of the need to rally together with his brothers around the cause of their operation – the blackness of their skin – and to operate as a group in order to rid themselves of the shackles that bind them to perpetual servitude. It seeks to demonstrate the lie that black is an aberration from the "normal" which is white. It is a manifestation of a new realisation that by seeking to run away from themselves and to emulate the white man, blacks are insulting the intelligence of whoever created them black. Black Consciousness therefore, takes cognizance of the deliberateness of God's plan in creating black people black. It seeks to infuse the black community with a new-found pride in themselves, their efforts, their value systems, their culture, their religion and their outlook to life.

The interrelationship between the consciousness of the self and the emancipatory programme is of paramount importance. Blacks no longer seek to reform the system because so doing implies acceptance of the major points around which the system revolves.

Blacks are out to completely transform the system and to make of it what they wish. Such a major undertaking can only be realised in an atmosphere where people are convinced of the truth inherent in their stand. Liberation therefore, is of paramount importance in the concept of Black Consciousness, for we cannot be conscious of ourselves and yet remain in bondage. We want to attain the envisioned self which is a free self.

The surge towards Black Consciousness is a phenomenon that has manifested itself through out the so-called Third World. There is no doubt that discrimination against the black man the world over fetches its origin from the exploitative attitude of the white man. Colonisation of white countries by whites has throughout history resulted in nothing more sinister than mere cultural or geographical fusion at worst, or language bastardisation at best. It is true that the history of weaker nations is shaped by bigger nations, but nowhere in the world today do we see whites exploiting whites on a scale even remotely similar to what is happening in South Africa. Hence, one is forced to conclude that it is not coincidence that black people are exploited. It was a deliberate plan which has culminated in even so called black independent countries not attaining any real independence.

With this background in mind we are forced, therefore, to believe that it is a case of *haves* against *have-nots* where whites have been deliberately made *haves* and blacks *have-nots*. There is for instance no worker in the classical sense among whites in South Africa, for even the most down-trodden white worker still has a lot to lose if the system is changed. He is protected by several laws against competition at work from the majority. He has a vote and he uses it to return the Nationalist Government to power because he sees them as the only people who, through job reservation laws, are bent on looking after his interests against competition with the "Natives".

It should therefore be accepted that an analysis of our situation in terms of one's colour at once takes care of the greatest single determinent for political action – i.e. colour – while also validly describing the blacks as the only real workers in South Africa. It immediately kills all suggestions that there could ever be effective rapport between the real workers, i.e. blacks, and the privileged white workers since we have shown that the latter are the greatest supporters of the system. True enough, the system has allowed so dangerous an anti-black attitude to build up amongst whites that it is taken as almost a sin to be black and hence the poor whites, who are economically nearest to the blacks, demonstrate the distance between themselves and the blacks by an exaggerated reactionary attitude towards blacks. Hence the greatest anti-black feeling is to be found amongst the very poor whites whom the Class Theory calls upon to be with black workers in the struggle for emancipation. This is the kind of twisted logic that the Black Consciousness approach seeks to eradicate.

In terms of the Black Consciousness approach we recognise the existence of one major force in South Africa. This is White Racism. It is the one force against which all of us are pitted. It works with unnerving totality, featuring both on the offensive and in our defence. Its greatest ally to date has been the refusal by us to club together as blacks because we are told to do so would be racialist. So, while we progressively lose ourselves in a world of colourlessness and amorphous common humanity, whites are deriving pleasure and security in entrenching white racism and further exploiting the minds and bodies of the unsuspecting black masses. Their agents are ever present amongst us, telling us that it is immoral to withdraw into a cocoon, that dialogue is the answer to our problem and that it is unfortunate that there is white racism in some quarters but you must understand that things are changing. These in fact are the greatest racists for they refuse to credit us with any intelligence to know what we want. Their intentions are obvious; they want to be barometers by which the rest of the white society can measure feelings in the black world. This then is WHAT MAKES US believe that white power presents its self as a totality not only provoking us but also controlling our response to the provocation. This is an important point to note because it is often missed by those who believe that there are a few good whites. Sure there are a few good whites just as much as there are a few bad blacks.

However what we are concerned here with is group attitudes and group politics. The exception does not make a lie of the rule – it merely substantiates it.

The overall analysis therefore, based on the Hegelian theory of dialectic materialism, is as follows. That since the thesis is a white racism there can only be one valid antithesis i.e. a solid black unity to counterbalance the scale. If South Africa is to be a land where black and white live together in harmony without fear of group exploitation, it is only when these two opposites have interplayed and produced a viable synthesis of ideas and a *modus vivendi*. We can never wage any struggle without offering a strong counterpoint to the white races that permeate our society so effectively.

One must immediately dispel the thought that Black Consciousness is merely a methodology or a means towards an end. What Black Consciousness seeks to do is to produce at the output end of the process real black people who do not regard themselves as appendages to white society. This truth cannot be reversed. We do not need to apologise for this because it is true that the white systems have produced through the world a number of people who are not aware that they too are people. Our adherence to values that we set for ourselves can also not be reversed because it will always be a lie to accept white values as necessarily the best. The fact that a synthesis may be attained only relates to adherence to power politics. Some one somewhere along the line will be forced to accept the truth and here we believe that ours is the truth.

The future of South Africa in the case where blacks adopt Black Consciousness is the subject for concern especially among initiates. What do we do when we have attained our Consciousness? Do we propose to kick whites out? I believe personally that the answers to these questions ought to be found in the SASO Policy Manifesto and in our analysis of the situation in South Africa. We have defined what we mean by true integration and the very fact that such a definition exists does illustrate what our standpoint is. In any case we are much more concerned about what is happening now, than what will happen in the future. The future will always be shaped by the sequence of present-day events.

The importance of black solidarity to the various segments of the black community must not be understated. There have been in the past a lot of suggestions that there can be no viable unity amongst blacks because they hold each other in contempt. Coloureds despise Africans because they, (the former) by their proximity to the Africans, may lose the chances of assimilation into the white world. Africans despise the Coloureds and Indians for a variety of reasons. Indians not only despise Africans but in many instances also exploit the Africans in job and shop situations. All these stereotype attitudes have led to mountainous inter-group suspicions amongst the blacks.

What we should at all times look at is the fact that:

1. We are all oppressed by the same system.
2. That we are oppressed to varying degrees is a deliberate design to stratify us not only socially but also in terms of aspirations.
3. Therefore it is to be expected that in terms of the enemy's plan there must be this suspicion and that if we are committed to the problem of emancipation to the same degree it is part of our duty to bring to the attention of the black people the deliberateness of the enemy's subjugation scheme.
4. That we should go on with our programme, attracting to it only committed people and not just those eager to see an equitable distribution of groups amongst our ranks. This is a game common amongst liberals. The one criterion that must govern all our action is commitment.

Further implications of Black Consciousness are to do with correcting false images of ourselves in terms of Culture, Education, Religion, Economics. The importance of this also must not be understated. There is always an interplay between the history of a people i.e. the past, and their faith in themselves and hopes for their future. We are aware of the terrible role played by our education and religion in creating amongst us a false understanding of ourselves. We must therefore work out schemes not only to correct this, but further to be our own authorities rather than wait to be interpreted by others. Whites can only see us from the outside and as such can never extract and analyse the ethos in the black community. In summary therefore one need only refer this house to the SASO Policy Manifesto which carries most of the salient points in the definition of Black Consciousness. I wish to stress again the need for us to know very clearly what we mean by certain terms and what our understanding is when we talk of Black Consciousness.

10

The Church as seen by a Young Layman

This paper was given at a Conference of Black Ministers of Religion organised by Black Community Programmes and held at the Ecumenical Lay Training Centre, Edendale, Natal in May 1972. Ministers of religion have an importance in black society which a secularised Westerner will find hard to understand. At the same time the pressures on them to conform to the status quo *are formidable. Ben Khoapa, executive director of BCP, and Steve realised the importance of trying to "conscientise" this key section of the black community. A small measure of the change in the traditionally conservative attitudes of black ministers of religion is the fact that five of the old students of St Peter's (Anglican) Theological College have been or are currently banned or detained. This would have been unimaginable ten years ago.*

THE CHURCH AS SEEN BY A YOUNG LAYMAN

I am aware that today I am addressing myself to a group of people with whom I differ in two respects:

Firstly, I am a layman talking to a group of religious ministers.
Secondly, I am a young man talking to fairly elderly people.

These are perhaps the two aspects that brought me here. An attempt to close the generation gap is always fundamental in the re-examination of any hitherto orthodox situation which seems to be fast becoming obsolete in the minds of young people. Also important, is the need to make common the concept of religion, especially Christianity, understanding of which is fast becoming the monopoly of so-called theologians. For this reason I am going to deal with the topic in a lay fashion.

To my mind religion can be defined as an attempt by man to relate to a supreme being or force to which he ascribes all creation. Our particular model at this moment is Christianity. It is not quite clear just how important it is for the various religions that exist in this world to be uniform. One thing is certain though, that all religions have got similar characteristics:

1. They form man's moral conscience; in other words, embodied within each religion is a set of moral stipulations that govern the spiritual well-being of a particular people within a given context.
2. They all attempt to explain the origin and destiny of man. All are agreed that man in the human form is a transient being in the world; all agree about man's origin as being from some force, the precise nature of which is defined differently. Where religions tend to differ is in the enunciation of the destiny of men.
3. All religions claim or almost claim a monopoly on truth about the nature of the supreme being and about the way to identify with his original intention about men.

Each religion is highly ritualistic. Through years of practice, the religion develops a certain pattern and procedure that in later years becomes inseparable from the central message of that religion.

If one takes religion as nothing else but what it is – i.e. a social institution attempting to explain what cannot be scientifically known about the origin and destiny of man, then from the beginning we can see the necessity of religion. All societies and indeed all individuals, ancient or modern, young or old, identify themselves with a particular religion and when none is existent, they develop one. In most cases religion is intricately intertwined with the rest of cultural traits of society. In a sense this makes the religion part and parcel of the behavioural pattern of that society and makes the people bound by the limits of that religion through a strong identification with it. Where people are subjected to a religion that is removed from their cultural make-up, then elements of disgruntlement begin to be noted and sometimes open defiance is soon displayed. Hence one can make the claim that most religions are specific and where they fail to observe the requirements of specificity then they must be sufficiently adaptable to convey relevant messages to different people in different situations. For indeed, each religion has a message for the people amongst whom it is operative.

These are perhaps some of the things that never were uppermost in the minds of the people who brought Christianity into South Africa. Whereas Christianity had gone through rigorous cultural adaptation from ancient Judea through Rome, through London, through Brussels and Lisbon, somehow when it landed in the Cape, it was made to look fairly rigid. Christianity was made the central point of a culture which brought with it new styles of clothing, new customs, new forms of etiquette, new medical approaches, and perhaps new armaments. The people amongst whom Christianity was spread had to cast away their indigenous clothing, their customs, their beliefs which were all described as being pagan and barbaric.

Usage of the spear became a hall-mark of savagery. All too soon the people were divided into two camps – the converted (*amagqobhoka*) and the pagans (*amaqaba*). The difference in clothing between these two groups made what otherwise could have been merely a religious difference actually become at times internecine warfare. Stripped of the core of their being and estranged from each other because of their differences the African people became a playground for colonialists. It has always been the pattern throughout history that whosoever brings the new order knows it best and is therefore the perpetual teacher of those to whom the new order is being brought. If the white missionaries were "right" about their God in the eyes of the people, then the African people could only accept whatever these new know-all tutors had to say about life. The acceptance of the colonialist-tainted version of Christianity marked the turning point in the resistance of African people.

The Church and its operation in modern-day South Africa has therefore to be looked at in terms of the way it was introduced in this country. Even at this late stage, one notes the appalling irrelevance of the interpretation given to the Scriptures. In a country teeming with injustice and fanatically committed to the practice of oppression, intolerance and blatant cruelty because of racial bigotry; in a country where all black people are made to feel the unwanted step-children of a God whose presence they cannot feel; in a country where father and son, mother and daughter alike develop daily into neurotics through sheer inability to relate the present to the future because of a completely engulfing sense of destitution, the Church further adds to their insecurity by its inward-directed definition of the concept of sin and its encouragement of the "mea culpa" attitude.

Stern-faced ministers stand on pulpits every Sunday to heap loads of blame on black people in townships for their thieving, house-breaking, stabbing, murdering, adultery etc. No-one ever attempts to relate all these vices to poverty, unemployment, overcrowding, lack of schooling and migratory labour. No one wants to completely condone abhorrent behaviour, but it frequently is necessary for us to analyse situations a little bit deeper than the surface suggests.

Because the white missionary described black people as thieves, lazy, sex-hungry etc., and because he equated all that was valuable with whiteness, our Churches through our ministers see all these vices I have mentioned above not as manifestations of the cruelty and injustice which we are subjected to by the white man but inevitable proof that after all the white man was right when he described us as savages. Thus if Christianity in its *introduction* was corrupted by the inclusion of aspects which made it the ideal religion for the *colonisation* of people, nowadays in its *interpretation* it is the ideal religion for the maintenance of the *subjugation* of the same people.

It must also be noted that the Church in South Africa as everywhere else has been spoilt by bureaucracy. No more is it just only an expression of the sum total of people's religious feelings, it has become in fact highly institutionalised not as one unit but as several powerful units, differing perhaps not so much on scriptural interpretation as in institutional aims. It has become inconceivable to think of South Africa without a Roman Catholic church or a Methodist Church or an Anglican Church etc. in spite of the fact that the average Methodist from the street hardly knows how he differs from an Anglican or Congregationalist. This bureaucracy and institutionalisation tends to make the Church removed from important priorities and to concentrate on secondary and tertiary functions like structures and finance etc. And because of this, the Church has become very irrelevant and in fact an "ivory tower" as some people refer to it.

Going hand in hand with the bureaucratisation and institutionalisation of the Church is a special brand of a problem which also makes the Church extremely irrelevant – the concentration of that bureaucracy and institutionalisation in the hands of white people. It is a known fact that, barring the Afrikaans Churches, most of the Churches have 70, 80 or 90% of their membership within the black world. It is also a known fact that most of the Churches have 70, 80, or 90% of controlling power in white hands. It is still a known fact that white people simply don't know black people, and in most cases do not have the interests of black people at heart.

Therefore it can be reasonably concluded that either the black people's Churches are governed by a small non-sympathetic foreign minority or that too many black people are patronising foreign Churches. Which of these two it is is not quite clear, but let us assume that it is the former, since the majority of the people in this country are black people.

In that case therefore, black people who are Christians are not only conniving at the hitherto irrelevant nature of Christianity as spelt out by the Churches, but they also allow a non-sympathetic minority which is not interested in making Christianity relevant to people remain in control of the workings of the Churches. This is an untenable situation which if allowed to continue much longer will deplete from the already thinning crowds that go to Church on Sunday.

Then too, the tendency by Christians to make interpretation of religion a specialist job, results in general apathy in a world which is fast departing from identification with mysticism. Young people nowadays would like to feel that they can interpret Christianity and extract from it messages relevant to them and their situation without being stopped by orthodox limitations. This is why the Catholic Church with its dozens of dogmas either has to adjust fast to a changing world or risk the chance of losing the young constituency. In various aspects, this applies to all Churches in the Christian world.

Before looking at suggested changes within the Church, let me then summarise what I regard as my major criticisms of it:
1. It makes Christianity too much of a "turn the other cheek" religion whilst addressing itself to a destitute people.
2. It is stunted with bureaucracy and institutionalisation.
3. It manifests in its structures a tacit acceptance of the system i.e. "white equals value".
4. It is limited by too much specialisation.

The most important area to which we should perhaps direct ourselves is gaining the control that is rightfully ours within these Churches. In order to do this, we must agree that in fact we have a common purpose, a common goal, a common problem. Equally we should agree that through living in a privileged society, and through being socialised in a corrupt system, our white Christian counterparts though brothers in Christ have not proved themselves brothers in South Africa. We must agree also that tacitly or overtly, deliberately or unawares, white Christians within the Churches are preventing the

Church from assuming its natural character in the South African context, and therefore preventing it from being relevant to the black man's situation.

It has been said by many a black church man, that whites are in power within the Churches, because the Churches are modelled on Western lines which white people know best. In order to be able therefore to change the Churches, we have first to gain ascendance over them in that white model, then thereafter turn that model into one we cherish, we love, we understand, and one that is relevant to us. I can only point out here that it cannot be conceivable that all the white people in controlling positions within the Church are elected by other white people. Obviously some get into their positions because they caucus vote-wielding blacks to put them in those positions. It is high time that black people learn the highly tried method of *caucusing* to put other black people in control of Churches in which black people have something at stake. Such elected blacks will obviously have to function according to a mandate clearly outlined by the same black caucus that put them in power.

The second area in which we must focus our attention is a thorough understanding of what many people have hitherto scorned, namely Black Theology. There is a truth in the statement that many people can say one thing differently because they look at it from different angles. Christianity can never hope to remain abstract and removed from the people's environmental problems. In order to be applicable to people, it must have meaning for them in their given situation. If they are an oppressed people, it must have something to say about their oppression.

Black Theology therefore is a situational interpretation of Christianity. It seeks to relate the present-day black man to God within the given context of the black man's suffering and his attempts to get out of it. It shifts the emphasis of man's moral obligations from avoiding wronging false authorities by not losing his Reference Book, not stealing food when hungry and not cheating police when he is caught, to being committed to eradicating all cause for suffering as represented in the death of children from starvation, outbreaks of epidemics in poor areas, or the existence of thuggery and vandalism in townships. In other words it shifts the emphasis from petty sins to major sins in a society, thereby ceasing to teach the people to "suffer peacefully".

These are topics that black ministers of religion must begin to talk about seriously if they are to save Christianity from falling foul with black people particularly young black people. The time has come for our own theologians to take up the cudgels of the fight by restoring a meaning and direction in the black man's understanding of God. No nation can win a battle without faith, and if our faith in our God is spoilt by our having to see Him through the eyes of the same people we are fighting against then there obviously begins to be something wrong in that relationship.

Finally, I would like to remind the black ministry, and indeed all black people that God is not in the habit of coming down from heaven to solve people's problems on earth.

11

White Racism and Black Consciousness

The Abe Bailey Institute for Inter-racial Studies sponsored a student conference which was held at Cape Town in January 1971. The idea was to bring together student leaders from all the main national student organisations, from the Afrikaanse Studentebond on the right through NUSAS to SASO on the left. Steve and Barney were invited to deliver papers which were subsequently published in Student Perspectives on South Africa *edited by Hendrik W. van der Merwe and David Welsh (published by David Philip, Cape Town, 1972). The following is Steve's paper.*

WHITE RACISM AND BLACK CONSCIOUSNESS

THE TOTALITY OF WHITE POWER IN SOUTH AFRICA

"No race possesses the monopoly of beauty, intelligence, force, and there is room for all of us at the rendezvous of victory." I do not think Aimé Césaire was thinking about South Africa when he said these words. The whites in this country have placed themselves on a path of no return. So blatantly exploitative in terms of the mind and body is the practice of white racism that one wonders if the interests of blacks and whites in this country have not become so mutually exclusive as to exclude the possibility of there being "room for all of us at the rendezvous of victory".

The white man's quest for power has led him to destroy with utter ruthlessness whatever has stood in his way. In an effort to divide the black world in terms of aspirations, the powers that be have evolved a philosophy that stratifies the black world and gives preferential treatment to certain groups. Further, they have built up several tribal cocoons, thereby hoping to increase inter-tribal ill-feeling and to divert the energies of the black people towards attaining false prescribed "freedoms". Moreover, it was hoped, the black people could be effectively contained in these various cocoons of repression, euphemistically referred to as 'homelands'. At some stage, however, the powers that be had to start defining the sphere of activity of these apartheid institutions. Most blacks suspected initially the barrenness of the promise and have now realised that they have been taken for a big ride. Just as the Native Representative Council became a political flop that embarrassed its creators, I predict that a time will come when these stooge bodies will prove very costly not only in terms of money but also in terms of the credibility of the story the Nationalists are trying to sell. In the meantime the blacks are beginning to realise the need to rally around the cause of their suffering – their black skin – and to ignore the false promises that come from the white world.

Then again the progressively sterner legislation that has lately filled the South African statute books has had a great effect in convincing the people of the evil inherent in the system of apartheid. No amount of propaganda on Radio Bantu or promises of freedom being granted to some desert homeland will ever convince the blacks that the government means well, so long as they experience manifestations of the lack of respect for the dignity of man and for his property as shown during the mass removals of Africans from the urban areas. The unnecessary harassment of Africans by police, both in towns and inside townships, and the ruthless application of that scourge of the people, the pass laws, are constant reminders that the white man is on top and that the blacks are only tolerated – with the greatest restraints. Needless to say, anyone finding himself at the receiving end of such deliberate (though uncalled for) cruelty must ultimately ask himself the question: what do I have to lose? This is what the blacks are beginning to ask themselves.

To add to this, the opposition ranks have been thrown into chaos and confusion. All opposition parties have to satisfy the basic demands of politics. They want power and at the same time they want to be *fair*. It never occurs to them that the surest way of being unfair is to withhold power from the native population. Hence one ultimately comes to the conclusion that there is no real difference between the United Party and the Nationalist Party. If there is, a strong possibility exists that the United Party is on the right of the

Nationalists. One needs only to look at their famous slogan, "White supremacy over the whole of South Africa", to realise the extent to which the quest for power can cloud even such supposedly immortal characteristics as the "English sense of fair play". Africans long ago dismissed the United Party as a great political fraud. The Coloured people have since followed suit. If the United Party is gaining any votes at all it is precisely because it is becoming more explicit in its racist policy. I would venture to say that the most overdue political step in South African White politics is a merger between the United and Nationalist Parties.

The flirtation between the Progressive Party and blacks was brought to a rude stop by legislation. Some blacks argue that at that moment the Progressives lost their only chance of attaining some semblance of respectability by not choosing to disband rather than lose their black constituents. Yet I cannot help feeling that the Progressives emerged more purified from the ordeal. The Progressives have never been a black man's real hope. They have always been a white party at heart, fighting for a more lasting way of preserving white values in this southern tip of Africa. It will not be long before the blacks relate their poverty to their blackness in concrete terms. Because of the tradition forced onto the country, the poor people shall always be black people. It is not surprising, therefore, that the blacks should wish to rid themselves of a system that locks up the wealth of the country in the hands of a few. No doubt Rick Turner was thinking of this when he declared that "any black government is likely to be socialist", in his article on "The Relevance of Contemporary Radical Thought".

We now come to the group that has longest enjoyed confidence from the black world – the liberal establishment, including radical and leftist groups. The biggest mistake the black world ever made was to assume that whoever opposed apartheid was an ally. For a long time the black world has been looking only at the governing party and not so much at the whole power structure as the object of their rage. In a sense the very political vocabulary that the blacks have used has been inherited from the liberals. Therefore it is not surprising that alliances were formed so easily with the liberals.

Who are the liberals in South Africa? It is that curious bunch of non-conformists who explain their participation in negative terms; that bunch of do-gooders that goes under all sorts of names – liberals, leftists, etc. These are the people who argue that they are not responsible for white racism and the country's "inhumanity to the black man"; these are the people who claim that they too feel the oppression just as acutely as the blacks and therefore should be jointly involved in the black man's struggle for a place under the sun; in short, these are the people who say that they have black souls wrapped up in white skins.

The liberals set about their business with the utmost efficiency. They made it a political dogma that all groups opposing the *status quo* must *necessarily* be non-racial in structure. They maintained that if you stood for a principle of non-racialism you could not in any way adopt what they described as racialist policies. They even defined to the black people what the latter should fight for.

With this sort of influence behind them, most black leaders tended to rely too much on the advice of liberals. For a long time, in fact, it became the occupation of the leadership to "calm the masses down", while they engaged in fruitless negotiation with the *status quo*. Their whole political action, in fact, was a programmed course in the art of gentle persuasion through protests and limited boycotts and they hoped the rest could be safely left to the troubled conscience of the fair-minded English folk.

Of course this situation could not last. A new breed of black leaders was beginning to take a dim view of the involvement of liberals in a struggle that they regarded as essentially theirs, when the political movements of the blacks were either banned or harassed into non-existence. This left the stage open once more for the liberals to continue with their work of "fighting for the rights of the blacks".

It never occurred to the liberals that the integration they insisted upon as an effective way of opposing apartheid was impossible to achieve in South Africa. It had to be artificial because it was being foisted on two parties whose entire upbringing had been to support the lie that one race was superior and others inferior. One has to overhaul the whole system in South Africa before hoping to get black and white walking hand in hand to oppose a *common* enemy. As it is, both black and white walk into a hastily organised integrated circle carrying with them the seeds of destruction of that circle – their inferiority and superiority complexes.

The myth of integration as propounded under the banner of the liberal ideology must be cracked and killed because it makes people believe that something is being done when in reality the artificially integrated circles are a soporific to the blacks while salving the consciences of the guilt-sticken white. It works from the false premise that, because it is difficult to bring people from different races together in this country, achievement of this is in itself a step towards the total liberation of the blacks. Nothing could be more misleading.

How many white people fighting for their version of a change in South Africa are really motivated by genuine concern and not by guilt? Obviously it is a cruel assumption to believe that all whites are not sincere, yet methods adopted by some groups often do suggest a lack of real commitment. The essence of politics is to direct oneself to the group which wields power. Most white dissident groups are aware of the power wielded by the white power structure. They are quick to quote statistics on how big the defence budget is. They know exactly how effectively the police and the army can control protesting black hordes – peaceful or otherwise. They know to what degree the black world is infiltrated by the security police. Hence they are completely convinced of the impotence of the black people. Why then do they persist in talking to the blacks? Since they are aware that the problem in this country is white racism, why do they not address themselves to the white world? Why do they insist on talking to blacks?

In an effort to answer these questions one has to come to the painful conclusion that the liberal is in fact appeasing his own conscience, or at best is eager to demonstrate his identification with the black people only so far as it does not sever all his ties with his relatives on the other side of the colour line. Being white, he possesses the natural passport to the exclusive pool of white privileges from which he does not hesitate to extract whatever suits him. Yet, since he identifies with the blacks, he moves around his white circles – white-only beaches, restaurants, and cinemas – with a lighter load, feeling that he is not like the rest. Yet at the back of his mind is a constant reminder that he is quite comfortable as things stand and therefore should not bother about change. Although he does not vote for the Nationalists (now that they are in the majority anyway), he feels secure under the protection offered by the Nationalists and subconsciously shuns the idea of change.

The limitations that have accompanied the involvement of liberals in the black man's struggle have been mostly responsible for the arrest of progress. Because of their inferiority complex, blacks have tended to listen seriously to what the liberals had to say. With their characteristic arrogance of assuming a 'monopoly on intelligence

66

and moral judgement', these self-appointed trustees of black interests have gone on to set the pattern and pace for the realisation of the black man's aspirations.

I am not sneering at the liberals and their involvement. Neither am I suggesting that they are the most to blame for the black man's plight. Rather I am illustrating the fundamental fact that total identification with an oppressed group in a system that forces one group to enjoy privilege and to live on the sweat of another, is impossible. White society collectively owes the blacks so huge a debt that no one member should automatically expect to escape from the blanket condemnation that needs must come from the black world. It is not as if whites are allowed to enjoy privilege only when they declare their solidarity with the ruling party. They are born into privilege and are nourished by and nurtured in the system of ruthless exploitation of black energy. For the 20-year-old white liberal to expect to be accepted with open arms is surely to overestimate the powers of forgiveness of the black people. No matter how genuine a liberal's motivations may be, he has to accept that, though he did not choose to be born into privilege, the blacks cannot but be suspicious of his motives.

The liberal must fight on his own and for himself. If they are true liberals they must realise that they themselves are oppressed, and that they must fight for their own freedom and not that of the nebulous 'they' with whom they can hardly claim identification.

What I have tried to show is that in South Africa political power has always rested with white society. Not only have the whites been guilty of being on the offensive but, by some skilful manoeuvres, they have managed to control the responses of the blacks to the provocation. Not only have they kicked the black but they have also told him how to react to the kick. For a long time the black has been listening with patience to the advice he has been receiving on how best to respond to the kick. With painful slowness he is now beginning to show signs that it is his right and duty to respond to the kick *in the way he sees fit.*

BLACK CONSCIOUSNESS

"We Coloured men, in this specific moment of historical evolution, have consciously grasped in its full breath, the notion of our peculiar uniqueness, the notion of just who we are and what, and that we are ready, on every plane and in every department, to assume the responsibilities which proceed from this coming into consciousness. The peculiarity of our place in the world is not to be confused with anyone else's. The peculiarity of our problems which aren't to be reduced to subordinate forms of any other problem. The peculiarity of our history, laced with terrible misfortunes which belong to no other history. The peculiarity of our culture, which we intend to live and to make live in an ever realler manner.' (Aimé Césaire, 1956, in his letter of resignation from the French Communist Party.)

At about the same time that Césaire said this, there was emerging in South Africa a group of angry young black men who were beginning to "grasp the notion of (their) peculiar uniqueness" and who were eager to define who they were and what. These were the elements who were disgruntled with the direction imposed on the African National Congress by the "old guard" within its leadership. These young men were questioning a number of things, among which was the "go slow" attitude adopted by the leadership, and the ease with which the leadership accepted coalitions with organisations other than those run by blacks. The 'People's Charter' adopted in Kliptown in 1955 was evidence of this. In a sense one can say that these were the first real signs that the blacks in South Africa were beginning to realise the need to go it alone and to evolve a philosophy based on, and directed by, blacks. In other words, Black Consciousness was slowly manifesting itself.

It may be said that, on the broader political front, blacks in South Africa have not shown any overt signs of new thinking since the banning of their political parties; not were the signs of disgruntlement with the white world given a real chance to crystallise into a positive approach. Black students, on the other hand, began to rethink their position in black-white coalitions. The emergence of SASO and its tough policy of non-involvement with the white world set people's minds thinking along new lines. This was a challenge to the age-old tradition in South Africa that opposition to apartheid was enough to qualify whites for acceptance by the black world. Despite protest and charges of racialism from liberal-minded white students, the black students stood firm in their rejection of the principle of unholy alliances between blacks and whites. A spokesman of the new right-of-middle group, NAFSAS, was treated to a dose of the new thinking when a black student told him that 'we shall lead ourselves, be it to the sea, to the mountain or to the desert; we shall have nothing to do with white students'.

The importance of the SASO stand is not really to be found in SASO *per se* – for SASO has the natural limitations of being a student organisation with an ever-changing membership. Rather it is to be found in the fact that this new approach opened a huge crack in the traditional approach and made the blacks sit up and think again. It heralded a new era in which blacks are beginning to take care of their own business and to see with greater clarity the immensity of their responsibility.

The call for Black Consciousness is the most positive call to come from any group in the black world for a long time. It is more than just a reactionary rejection of whites by blacks. The quintessence of it is the realisation by the blacks that, in order to feature well in this game of power politics, they have to use the concept of group power and to build a strong foundation for this. Being an historically, politically, socially and economically disinherited and dispossessed group, they have the strongest foundation from which to operate. The philosophy of Black Consciousness, therefore, expresses group pride and the determination by the blacks to rise and attain the envisaged self. At the heart of this kind of thinking is the realisation by the blacks that the most potent weapon in the hands of the oppressor is the mind of the oppressed. Once the latter has been so effectively manipulated and controlled by the oppressor as to make the oppressed believe that he is a liability to the white man, then there will be nothing the oppressed can do that will really scare the powerful masters. Hence thinking along lines of Black Consciousness makes the black man see himself as a being, entire in himself, and not as an extension of a broom or additional leverage to some machine. At the end of it all, he cannot tolerate attempts by anybody to dwarf the significance of his manhood. Once this happens, we shall know that the real man in the black person is beginning to shine through.

I have spoken of Black Consciousness as if it is something that can be readily detected. Granted this may be an over-statement at this stage, yet it is true that, gradually, the various black groups are becoming more and more conscious of the self. They are beginning to rid their minds of imprisoning notions which are the legacy of the control of their attitude by whites. Slowly, they have cast aside the 'morality argument' which prevented them from going it alone and are now learning that a lot of good can be derived from specific exclusion of whites from black institutions.

Of course it is not surprising to us that whites are not very much aware of these developing forces since such consciousness is essentially an inward-looking process. It has become common practice in this country for people to consult their papers to see what is said by black leaders – by which they understand the leaders of the various apartheid institutions. While these bodies are often exploited by individuals in them for candid talking, they certainly cannot be taken seriously as yardsticks by which to measure black feeling on any topic.

The growth of awareness among South African blacks has often been ascribed to influence from the American 'Negro' movement. Yet it seems to me that this is a sequel to the attainment of independence by so many African states within so short a time. In fact I remember that at the time I was at high school, Dr Hastings Kamuzu Banda was still a militant and used to be a hero of a friend of mine. His often quoted statement was, 'This is a black man's country; any white man who does not like it must pack up and go'. Clearly at this stage the myth of the invincibility of the white man had been exposed. When fellow Africans were talking like that how could we still be harbouring ideas of continued servitude? We knew he had no right to be there; we wanted to remove him from our table, strip the table of all trappings put on it by him, decorate it in true African style, settle down and then ask him to join us on our own terms if he liked. This is what Banda was saying. The fact that American terminology has often been used to express our thoughts is merely because all new ideas seem to get extensive publicity in the United States.

National consciousness and its spread in South Africa has to work against a number of factors. First there are the traditional complexes, then the emptiness of the native's past and lastly the question of black-white dependency. The traditional inferior-superior black-white complexes are deliberate creations of the colonialist. Through the work of missionaries and the style of education adopted, the blacks were made to feel that the white man was some kind of god whose word could not be doubted. As Fanon puts it: "Colonialism is not satisfied merely with holding a people in its grip and emptying the Native's brain of all form and content; by a kind of perveted logic, it turns to the past of the oppressed people and distorts, disfigures, and destroys it." At the end of it all, the blacks have nothing to lean on, nothing to cheer them up at the present moment and very much to be afraid of in the future.

The attitude of some rural African folk who are against education is often misunderstood, not least by the African intellectual. Yet the reasons put forward by these people carry with them the realisation of their inherent dignity and worth. They see education as the quickest way of destroying the substance of the African culture. They complain bitterly of the disruption in the life pattern, non-observation of customs, and constant derision from the non-conformists whenever any of them go through school. Lack of respect for the elders is, in the African tradition, an unforgivable and cardinal sin. Yet how can one prevent the loss of respect of child for father when the child is actively taught by his know-all white tutors to disregard his family's teachings? How can an African avoid losing respect for his tradition when in school his whole cultural background is summed up in one word: barbarism?

To add to the white-oriented education received, the whole history of the black people is presented as a long lamentation of repeated defeats. Strangely enough, everybody has come to accept that the history of South Africa starts in 1652. No doubt this is to support the often-told lie that blacks arrived in this country at about the same time as the whites. Thus, a lot of attention has to be paid to our history if we as blacks want to aid each other in our coming into consciousness. We have to rewrite our history and describe in it the heroes that formed the core of resistance to the white invaders. More has to be revealed and stress has to be laid on the successful nation-building attempts by people like Chaka, Moshoeshoe and Hintsa.*

Our culture must be defined in concrete terms. We must relate the past to the present and demonstrate an historical evolution of the modern African. We must reject the attempts by the powers that be to project an arrested image of our culture. This is not the sum total of our culture. They have deliberately arrested our culture at the tribal stage to perpetuate the myth that African people were near-cannibals, had no real ambitions in life, and were preoccupied with sex and drink. In fact the wide-spread vice often found in the African townships is a result of the interference of the White man in the natural evolution of the true native culture. 'Wherever colonisation is a fact, the indigenous culture begins to rot and among the ruins something begins to be born which is condemned to exist on the margin allowed it by the European culture.' It is through the evolution of our genuine culture that our identity can be fully rediscovered.

We must seek to restore to the black people a sense of the great

* Famous tribal chieftains of respectively, the Zulus, Basotho and Tswana.

stress we used to lay on the value of human relationships; to highlight the fact that in the pre-Van Riebeeck days we had a high regard for people, their property and for life in general; to reduce the hold of technology over man and to reduce the materialistic element that is slowly creeping into the African character.

"Is there any way that my people can have the blessings of technology without being eaten away by materialism and losing the spiritual dimension from their lives?" asks President Kaunda and then, talking of the typical tribal African community, he says:

> Those.people who are dependent upon and live in closest relationship with Nature are most conscious of the operation of these forces: the pulse of their lives beats in harmony with the pulse of the Universe; they may be simple and unlettered people and their horizons may be strictly limited, yet I believe that they inhabit a larger world than the sophisticated Westerner who has magnified his physical senses through invented gadgets at the price, all too often, of cutting out the dimension of the spiritual.

It goes without saying that the black people of South Africa, in order to make the necessary strides in the new direction they are thinking of, have to take a long look at how they can use their economic power to their advantage. As the situation stands today, money from the black world tends to take a unidirectional flow to the white society. Blacks buy from white supermarkets, white greengrocers, white bottle stores, white chemists, and, to crown it all, those who can, bank at white-owned banks. Needless to say, they travel to work in government-owned trains or white-owned buses. If then we wish to make use of the little we have to improve our lot, it can only lead to greater awareness of the power we wield as a group. The 'Buy Black' campaign that is being waged by some people in the Johannesburg area must not be scoffed at.

It is often claimed that the advocates of Black Consciousness are hemming themselves in into a closed world, choosing to weep on each other's shoulders and thereby cutting out useful dialogue with the rest of the world. Yet I feel that the black people of the world, in choosing to reject the legacy of colonialism and white domination and to build around themselves their own values, standards and outlook to life, have at last established a solid base for meaningful co-operation amongst themselves in the larger battle of the Third World against the rich nations. As Fanon puts it; "The consciousness of the self is not the closing of a door to communication. . . . National consciousness, which is not nationalism, is the only thing that will give us an international dimension." This is an encouraging sign, for there is no doubt that the black-white power struggle in South Africa is but a microcosm of the global confrontation between the Third World and the rich white nations of the world which is manifesting itself in an ever more real manner as the years go by.

Thus, in this age and day, one cannot but welcome the evolution of a positive outlook in the black world. The wounds that have been inflicted on the black world and the accumulated insults of oppression over the years were bound to provoke reaction from the black people. Now we can listen to the Barnett Potters concluding with apparent glee and with a sense of sadistic triumph that the fault with the black man is to be found in his genes, and we can watch the rest of the white society echoing 'amen', and still not be moved to the reacting type of anger. We have in us the will to live through these trying times; over the years we have attained moral superiority over the white man; we shall watch as time destroys his paper castles and know that all these little pranks were but frantic attempts of frightened little people to convince each other that they can control the minds and bodies of indigenous people of Africa indefinitely.

12

Fear-an Important Determinant in South African Politics

In his judgement at the BPC/SASO trial, Mr Justice Boshoff made the following statement. ". . . Biko, under the pseudonym of 'Frank Talk', wrote an article under the heading of 'Fear – An Important Determinant in South African Politics', which in effect condemned white society . . . The claim by whites of a monopoly on comfort and security had always been so exclusive that blacks saw whites as the major obstacle in their progress towards peace, prosperity and a sane society."

This comment was made at the very end of 1976, while Steve wrote the piece in question in 1971. At that time the theory of Black Consciousness was still very much being filled out through discussion and writing. In this piece Steve was making the point that ever since the white man arrived as a settler in Southern Africa he had created and then preserved for himself a special position of privilege. This position was created and preserved by the use of violence and fear, but the use of these methods was in itself a result of the white's fear of the black population.

I WRITE WHAT I LIKE

FEAR – AN IMPORTANT DETERMINANT IN
SOUTH AFRICAN POLITICS

It would seem that the greatest waste of time in South Africa is to try and find logic in why the white government does certain things. If anything else, the constant inroads into the freedom of the black people illustrates a complete contempt for this section of the community.

My premise has always been that black people should not at any one stage be surprised at some of the atrocities committed by the government. This to me follows logically after their initial assumption that they, being a settler minority, can have the right to be supreme masters. If they could be cruel enough to cow the natives down with brutal force and install themselves as perpetual rulers in a foreign land, then anything else they do to the same black people becomes logical in terms of the initial cruelty. To expect justice from them at any stage is to be naive. They almost have a duty to themselves and to their "electorate" to show that they still have the upper hand over the black people. There is only one way of showing that upper hand – by ruthlessly breaking down the back of resistance amongst the blacks, however petty that resistance is.

One must look at the huge security force that South Africa has in order to realise this. These men must always report something to their masters in order to justify their employment. It is not enough to report that "I have been to Pondoland and the natives are behaving well and are peaceful and content." This is not satisfactory, for the perpetrators of evil are aware of the cruelty of their system and hence do not expect the natives to be satisfied. So the security boys are sent back to Pondoland to find out who the spokesman is who claims that the people are satisfied and to beat him until he admits that he is not satisfied. At that point he is either banned or brought forward to be tried under one of the many Acts. The absolutely infantile evidence upon which the State builds up its cases in some of the trials does suggest to me that they are quite capable of arresting a group of boys playing hide and seek and charging them with high treason.

This is the background against which one must see the many political trials that are held in this country. To them it looks as if something would be dangerously wrong if no major political trial was held for a period of one year. It looks as if someone will be accused by his superior for not doing his work. The strangest thing is that people are hauled in for almost nothing to be tried under the most vicious of Acts – like the Terrorism Act.

It is also against this background that one must view the recent banning and house arrest imposed on Mr Mewa Ramgobin. No amount of persuasion by anyone can convince me that Ramgobin had something sinister up his sleeve. To all those who know him,

Mewa was the last man to be considered a serious threat to anyone – let alone a powerful State with an army of perhaps 10,000 security men and informers. But then, as we said, logic is a strange word to these people.

Aimé Césaire once said: "When I turn on my radio, when I hear that Negroes have been lynched in America, I say that we have been lied to: Hitler is not dead: when I turn on my radio and hear that in Africa, forced labour has been inaugurated and legislated, I say that we have certainly been lied to: Hitler is not dead".

Perhaps one need add only the following in order to make the picture complete:

"When I turn on my radio, when I hear that someone in the Pondoland forest was beaten and tortured, I say that we have been lied to: Hitler is not dead, when I turn on my radio, when I hear that someone in jail slipped off a piece of soap, fell and died I say that we have been lied to: Hitler is not dead, he is likely to be found in Pretoria".

To look for instances of cruelty directed at those who fall into disfavour with the security police is perhaps to look too far. One need not try to establish the truth of the claim that black people in South Africa have to struggle for survival. It presents itself in ever so many facets of our lives. Township life alone makes it a miracle for anyone to live up to adulthood. There we see a situation of absolute want in which black will kill black to be able to survive. This is the basis of the vandalism, murder, rape and plunder that goes on while the real sources of the evil – white society – are suntanning on exclusive beaches or relaxing in their bourgeois homes.

While those amongst blacks who do bother to open their mouths in feeble protest against what is going on are periodically intimidated with security visits and occasional banning orders and house arrests, the rest of the black community lives in absolute fear of the police. No average black man can ever at any moment be absolutely sure that he is not breaking a law. There are so many laws governing the lives and behaviour of black people that sometimes one feels that the police only need to page at random through their statute book to be able to get a law under which to charge a victim.

The philosophy behind police action in this country seems to be "harass them! harass them!". And one needs to add that they interpret the word in a very extravagant sense. Thus even young traffic policemen, people generally known for their grace, occasionally find it proper to slap adult black people. It sometimes looks obvious here that the great plan is to keep the black people thoroughly intimidated and to perpetuate the "super-race" image of the white man, if not intellectually, at least in terms of force. White people, working through their vanguard – the South African Police – have come to realise the truth of that golden maxim – if you cannot make a man respect you, then make him fear you.

Clearly black people cannot respect white people, at least not in this country. There is such an obvious aura of immorality and naked cruelty in all that is done in the name of white people that no black man, no matter how intimidated, can ever be made to respect white society. However, in spite of their obvious contempt for the values cherished by whites and the price at which white comfort and security is purchased, blacks seem to me to have been successfully cowed down by the type of brutality that emanates from this section of the community.

It is this fear that erodes the soul of black people in South Africa – a fear obviously built up deliberately by the system through a myriad of civil agents, be they post office attendants, police, CID officials, army men in uniform, security police or even the occasional trigger-happy white farmer or store owner. It is a fear so basic in the considered actions of black people as to make it impossible for them to behave like people – let alone free people. From the attitude of a servant to his employer, to that of a black man being served by a white attendant at a shop, one sees this fear clearly showing through. How can people be prepared to put up a resistance against their overall oppression if in their individual situations, they cannot insist on the observance of their manhood? This is a question that often occurs to overseas visitors who are perceptive enough to realise that all is not well in the land of sunshine and milk.

Yet this is a dangerous type of fear, for it only goes skin deep. It hides underneath it an immeasurable rage that often threatens to erupt. Beneath it, likes naked hatred for a group that deserves absolutely no respect. Unlike in the rest of the French or Spanish former colonies where chances of assimilation made it not impossible for blacks to aspire towards being white, in South Africa whiteness has always been associated with police brutality and intimidation, early morning pass raids, general harassment in and out of townships and hence no black really aspires to being white. The claim by whites of monopoly on comfort and security has always been so exclusive that blacks see whites as the major obstacle in their progress towards peace, prosperity and a sane society. Through its association with all these negative aspects, whiteness has thus been soiled beyond recognition. At best therefore blacks see whiteness as a concept that warrants being despised, hated, destroyed and replaced by an aspiration with more human content in it. At worst blacks envy white society for the comfort it has usurped and at the centre of this envy is the wish – nay, the secret determination – in the innermost minds of most blacks who think like this, to kick whites off those comfortable garden chairs that one sees as he rides in a bus, out of town, and to claim them for themselves. Day by day, one gets more convinced that Aimé Césaire could not have been right when he said "no race possesses the monopoly on truth, intelligence, force and there is room for all of us at the rendezvous of victory."

It may, perhaps, surprise some people that I should talk of whites in a collective sense when in fact it is a particular section i.e. the government – that carries out this unwarranted vendetta against blacks.

There are those whites who will completely disclaim responsibility for the country's inhumanity to the black man. These are the people who are governed by logic for 4½ years but by fear at election time. The Nationalist party has perhaps many more English votes than one imagines. All whites collectively recognise in it a strong bastion against the highly played-up *swart gevaar*.* One must not underestimate the deeply imbedded fear of the black man so prevalent in white society. Whites know only too well what exactly they have been doing to blacks and logically find reason for the black man to be angry. Their state of insecurity however does not outweigh their greed for power and wealth, hence they brace themselves to react against this rage rather than to dispel it with openmindedness and fair play. This interaction between fear and reaction then sets on a vicious cycle that multiplies both the fear and the reaction. This is what makes meaningful coalitions between the black and white totally impossible. Also this is what makes whites act as a group and hence become culpable as a group.

In any case, even if there was a real fundamental difference in thinking amongst whites *vis-à-vis* blacks, the very fact that those disgruntled whites remain to enjoy the fruits of the system would alone

* "Black peril". Editor's note.

be enough to condemn them at Nuremburg. Listen to Karl Jaspers writing on the concept of metaphysical guilt:

There exists amongst men, because they are men, a solidarity through which each shares responsibility for every injustice and every wrong committed in the world and especially for crimes that are committed in his presence or of which he cannot be ignorant. If I do not do whatever I can to prevent them, I am an accomplice in them. If I have risked my life in order to prevent the murder of other men, if I have stood silent, I feel guilty in a sense that cannot in any adequate fashion be understood jurisdically or politically or morally . . . That I am still alive after such things have been done weighs on me as a guilt that cannot be expiated.

Somewhere in the heart of human relations, an absolute command imposes itself: in case of criminal attack or of living conditions that threaten physical being, accept life for all together or not at all.

Thus if whites in general do not like what is happening to the black people, they have the power in them to stop it here and now. We, on the other hand, have every reason to bundle them together and blame them jointly.

One can of course say that blacks too are to blame for allowing the situation to exist. Or to drive the point even further, one may point out that there are black policemen and black special branch agents. To take the last point first, I must state categorically that there is no such thing as a black policeman. Any black man who props the system up actively has lost the right to being considered part of the black world: he has sold his soul for 30 pieces of silver and finds that he is in fact not acceptable to the white society he sought to join. These are colourless white lackeys who live in a marginal world of unhappiness. They are extensions of the enemy into our ranks. On the other hand, the rest of the black world is kept in check purely because of powerlessness.

Powerlessness breeds a race of beggars who smile at the enemy and swear at him in the sanctity of their toilets; who shout "Baas" willingly during the day and call the white man a dog in their buses as they go home. Once again the concept of fear is at the heart of this two-faced behaviour on the part of the conquered blacks.

This concept of fear has now taken a different dimension. One frequently hears people say of someone who has just been arrested or banned – "there is no smoke without fire" or if the guy was out-spoken – "he asked for it, I am not surprised". In a sense this is almost deifying the security police; they cannot be wrong; if they could break the Rivonia plot, what makes them afraid of an individual to the point of banning him unless there is something – which we do not know? This kind of logic, found to varying degrees in the Afrikaner, the English and the black communities, is dangerous for it completely misses the point and reinforces irrational action on the part of the security police.

The fact of the matter is that the government and its security forces are also ruled by fear, in spite of their immense power. Like anyone living in mortal fear, they occasionally resort to irrational actions in the hope that a show of strength rather than proper intelligence might scare the resistors satisfactorily. This is the basis of security operations in South Africa most of the time. If they know that there are some three missionaries who are dangerous to their interest but whose identity is unknown, they would rather deport about 80 missionaries and hope that the three are among them than use some brains and find out who the three are. This was also the basis of the arrest of about 5,000 during the so-called "Poqo" raids of 1963.* And of course the laws from which security police derive their power are so vague and sweeping as to allow for all this. Hence one concludes that the South African security system is force-oriented rather than intelligence-oriented. One may of course add that this type of mentality, in this country, stretches all the way from State security to the style of rugby whites adopt. It has become their way of life.

One will therefore not be surprised if it proves very difficult to accept that "there is room for all of us at the rendezvous of victory". The tripartate system of fear – that of white fearing the blacks, blacks fearing whites and the government fearing blacks and wishing to allay the fear amongst whites – makes it difficult to establish rapport amongst the two segments of the community. The fact of living apart adds a different dimension and perhaps a more serious one – it makes the aspirations of the two groups diametrically opposed. The white strategy so far has been to systematically break down the resistance of the blacks to the point where the latter would accept crumbs from the white table. This we have shown we reject unequivocally; and now the stage is therefore set for a very interesting turn of events.

FRANK TALK

* See memoir, section one.

13
Let's talk about Bantustans

The concept of "bantustans", or independent/autonomous African "homelands", is the cornerstone of the Nationalist Government's "native" policy. The theory is that South Africa consists of many ethnic groups, and that peaceful co-existence can only be attained by enabling each group to develop in its own way in its own area. Introduced practically in the early 1960s, it attempted to put the clock back, to "re-patriate" to their alleged "homelands" an already extensively de-urbanised people. But it is only now with the granting of so-called "independence" to two of the "stans", Transkei and Bophuthatswana, that the cynical cruelty of the policy is fully revealed. The Minister of Plural relations (euphemism for Bantu Administration), Connie Mulder, recently stated that there were no black citizens of South Africa: *and it is still the Nationalists' intention forcibly to "repatriate" to these "homelands" all blacks who still live in that 87% of South Africa which is deemed to belong to the whites. Even if an inconceivably massive aid programme was poured in to these impoverished, unconsolidated areas they could never support the weight of population forced to reside there.*

But the ultimate wickedness lies in the attempt to strip of their South African citizenship men like Steve, who have worked for the unification of one of the potentially greatest countries in the world. For the real thinking behind the policy is the old Roman imperialist idea of "Divide and Rule"; and it is the Black Consciousness Movement's resolute and militant opposition to the Afrikaners' "baasskap" (boss-ship) policy which has led to its persecution and attempted crushing by the Nationalist Government. Thus the wholesale detentions of BPC leaders in the second half of 1976 were in order to forestall the massive protests which that organisation was planning against the inauguration of Transkei as an "independent country."

This chapter needs to be read in conjunction with chapter 16.

I WRITE WHAT I LIKE

LET'S TALK ABOUT BANTUSTANS

It is now almost ten years since the bantustan idea was practically introduced by the Nationalist Government as a lasting measure towards the solution of the "native problem". Of course the idea of territorial segregation in South Africa is an old one. It was in 1913 that Sauer, a supposed liberal Cabinet Minister in the then Government, first suggested the apportionment of parts of the country to accommodate aspirations of the native population. In the many years that followed, the percentage allotted to natives varied until it was established in 1936 to the present 13%.

What the Nationalists did under the "able" guidance of their theoretician, Verwoerd, was to convert the naked policy of wanton discrimination and segregation to the euphemistic "separate development" policy which "guaranteed" the eventual growth into complete sovereignty of eight bantustans or homelands which would be autonomous states to cater for the various "nations" that make up the South African native population.

At first the whole idea of separate development was rejected by the entire population, including elements of the Afrikaner camp. It was rejected by the liberals, Progressives, United Party, and naturally by the blacks. It was seen by the blacks naturally as a big fraud calculated to dampen the enthusiasm with which they picked the cudgels in the broader political fight for their rights in the country of their birth. People who took part in it were roundly condemned by everybody as sell-outs and Uncle Toms and nobody took them seriously. They were clearly seen as people who deliberately allowed themselves into an unholy collusion with the enemy.

In the white ranks, too, the idea was heavily criticised and seen as extremely immoral. However as the *verligte** elements of the Afrikaner section began to show interest in the ideology, a number of people began to pay attention to the idea. This was boosted up mostly by the attack launched by *verligtes* on what they called "petty apartheid". Typical of opposition politics in this country, these *verligtes* were given a lot of support by the English press simply because of their small difference with the Nationalist staunch line. In the process, a lot of people began to see merit in the *verligte* view of separate

* 'Liberal' as opposed to *verkrampte* – 'conservative.' Editor's note.

development primarily because a number of newspapers had changed their policies in an attempt to appease the *verligte* movement.

With this background in mind it therefore became necessary for us black people to restate in very strong terms the case against the bantustan idea. There are two views regarding bantustans. The first one is that of total acceptance with the hope that any demands made by the blacks through peaceful negotiation will lead to granting of further concessions by the white power structure placement. The second is that as a strategy the bantustan philosophy can be exploited towards attainment of our overall goals. Both views are dangerously short-sighted. The first one needs but little attention since it is an obvious sell-out and can only be accepted by people who have already sold their souls to the white man. The second one leads to a lot of confusion part of which is in fact a subconscious acceptance of the bantustan idea *per se* by the masses who cannot appreciate the nuances of the debate surrounding the so-called strategy.

Why are we against the bantustan idea? Black people reject this approach for so many reasons, none of which are as fundamental as the fact that it is a solution given to us by the same people who have created the problem. In a land rightfully ours we find people coming to tell us where to stay and what powers we shall have without even consulting us. The whole idea is made to appear as if for us, while working against our very existence; a look at some aspects of the policy shows this very clearly.

Geographically, i.e. in terms of land distribution, bantustans present a gigantic fraud that can find no moral support from any quarters. We find that 20% of the population are in control of 87% of the land while 80% "control" only 13%. To make this situation even more ridiculous, not one of the so-called "Bantustan nations" have an intact piece of land. All of them are scattered little bits of the most unyielding soil. In each area the more productive bits are white-controlled islands on which white farms or other types of industry are situated.

Economically, the blacks have been given a raw deal. Generally speaking the areas where bantustans are located are the least developed in the country, often very unsuitable either for agricultural or pastoral work. Not one of the bantustans have access to the sea* and in all situations mineral rights are strictly reserved for the South Afri-

* i.e. to a major port. Editor's note.

can government. In other words bantustans only have rights extending to 6 feet below surface of the land.*

Added to these observations is the fact that the operative budgets allowed the bantustans for development projects are kept so low. Control of industry and its growth in all the bantustans is locked up in the hands of the Bantu investment co-operative which though meant to be non-profitmaking, is reputed for its exploitation of the aspirant African traders and industrialists in all the bantustans. The so called Border industries now beginning to mushroom at the edges of the bantustans are orientated to exploit the labour force from within the bantustans. Most of them are subsidised by the government and their products are tax free. In spite of such advantages, they go on to pay all-time low wages which are about one-third of what they would normally pay in urban areas. In addition it should be noted that these industries at border areas are often outside the geographical confines in which most Industrial Council agreements operate; and since the black workers have no trade unions to push their case they are virtually left at the mercy of employers who are under no obligation to pay them according to rates operative elsewhere in the country.

Politically, the bantustans are the greatest single fraud ever invented by white politicians (with the possible exception of the new United Party federal policy). The same people who are guilty of the subjugation and oppression of the black man want us to believe that they can now design for blacks means of escape from that situation. The point is that this is not the intention of the policy. The actual intentions of the bantustan practices are the following:

To create a false sense of hope amongst the black people so that any further attempt by blacks to collectively enunciate their aspirations should be dampened.

To offer a new but false direction in the struggle of the Black people. By making it difficult to get even the 13% of the land the powers that be are separating our "struggles" into eight different struggles for eight false freedoms that were prescribed long ago. This has also the overall effect of making us forget about the 87% of land that is in white hands.

To cheat the outside world into believing that there is some val-

* This matter has been and continues to be subject to negotiations between the South African and Bantustan governments and may change accordingly. Editor's note.

idity in the multinational theory so that South Africa can now go back into international sport, trade, politics, etc. with a soothed conscience.

To boost up as much as possible the intertribal competition and hostility that is bound to come up so that the collective strength and resistance of the black people can be fragmented.

The question then that immediately arises is whether the bantustan leaders do not see the barreness and fraudulence implicit in this scheme. We have some men in these bantustans who would make extremely fine leaders if they had not decided to throw in their lot with the oppressors. A few of them argue that they are not selling out but are carrying on with the fight from within. There is no way of ascertaining the truth of these assumptions. Perhaps it is not necessary that this should be ascertained at all especially because no matter how one views it, the ultimate truth is that participation in the bantustan set-up is dangerously misleading to the black population. We shall concentrate here on the merits and demerits of using the system to fight the system, and forget about these bantustan leaders who believe sincerely in the policy of apartheid. After all, as one writer once said, there is no way of stopping fools from dedicating themselves to useless causes.

There are in South Africa at the moment a number of people whose participation in bantustan politics has led the black people in part and political observers throughout the world to begin to take a second look at bantustans with the belief that something can be achieved through a systematic exploitation of the bantustan approach. The argument runs that all other forms of protest, disagreement and opposition are closed to black people and that we can call the bluff of the government by accepting what they give and using it to get what we want. What most people miss is the fact that what we want is well known to the enemy and that the bantustan theory was designed precisely to prevent us from getting what we want. The authors of the system know it best and they give us any concessions we may demand according to a plan prearranged by them. When they createa these dummy platforms, these phoney telephones, they knew that some opportunists might want to use them to advance the black cause and hence they made all the arrangements to be able to control such "ambitious natives".

Matanzima and Buthelezi can shout their lungs out trying to speak to Pretoria through the phoney telephone. No one is listening in Pretoria because the telephone is a toy. The real lines between Pretoria and Zululand, between Pretoria and the Transkei are very busy day and night with Torlage and Abrahams* telling their system every step Matanzima and Buthelezi† are likely to take three months hence and how best the system should respond to such stances.

What is most painful is that Matanzima and Buthelezi are perhaps more than anybody else acutely aware of the limitations surrounding them. It may also be true that they are extremely dedicated to the upliftment of black people and perhaps to their liberation. Many times they have manifested a fighting spirit characterising true courage and determination. But if you want to fight your enemy you do not accept from him the unloaded of his two guns and then challenge him to a duel.

Bantustan leaders are subconsciously siding and abetting in the total subjugation of the black people of this country. By making the kind of militant noise they are now making they have managed to confuse the blacks sufficiently to believe that something great is about to happen. As a result blacks are sitting on the touchlines cheering loudly while Matanzima and Mangope are performing. The picture is also confused by the exaggeration given by the white press to the possibilities open to these leaders. The white press knows fully well of course that it is to their advantage to misdirect the attention of the blacks. The white press knows only too well the limitations of bantustan theory; that it is a far cry from what the blacks want but goes on to build up the image of Matanzima and Buthelezi in order to harness them to the path they have already chosen and to make the non-analytic masses believe that a great victory is just about to be achieved. Also, by widely publicising the pronouncements of the bantustan leaders and attaching extremely liberal connotations to these pronouncements, the white press has confused the outside world to think that in South Africa not only is there freedom of speech but that the Bantustan leaders are actively plotting for the ousting of the white government without the government taking any action.

Thus for white South Africa, it is extremely important to have a man like Buthelezi speaking and sounding the way he is doing. It

---

* The "Commissioners" at the time for KwaZulu and Transkei respectively. Editor's note.

† Kaiser Matanzima, leader of Transkei, Gatsha Buthelezi of Zululand, Lucas Mangope of Bophuthatswana. Editor's note.

solves so many conscience problems that South Africa has been having for so long. It has been said that the combination of Buthelezi and the white press make up the finest ambassadors that South Africa has ever had.

For me as a black person it is extremely painful to see a man who could easily have been my leader being so misused by the cruel and exploitative white world. It becomes so apparent that whatever one does in the context of the bantustans is likely to be exploited for self-aggrandisement by the white world. When you agree with the government you are an exemplary native, who sees value in being led by whites. When you use bantustan platforms to attack what you do not like you epitomise the kind of militant black leader who in South Africa is freely allowed to speak and oppose the system. You exonerate the country from the blame that it is a police state. South African information bureaux throughout the world carry long coverages of activities and pronouncements by bantustan leaders to highlight the degree of open-mindedness and fair play to be found in this country.

No, black people must learn to refuse to be pawns in a white man's game. This type of politics calls upon us to provide our own initiative and to act at our own pace and not that created for us by the system. No bantustan leader can tell me that he is acting at his own initiative when he enters the realms of bantustan politics. At this stage of our history we cannot have our struggle being tribalised through the creation of Zulu, Xhosa and Tswana politicians by the system.

These tribal cocoons called "homelands" are nothing else but sophisticated concentration camps where black people are allowed to "suffer peacefully". Black people must constantly pressurise the bantustan leaders to pull out of the political cul-de-sac that has been created for us by the system.

Above all, we black people should all the time keep in mind that South Africa is our country and that all of it belongs to us. The arrogance that makes white people travel all the way from Holland to come and balkanise our country and shift us around has to be destroyed. Our kindness has been misused and our hospitality turned against us. Whereas whites were mere guests to us on their arrival in this country they have now pushed us out to a 13% corner of the land and are acting as bad hosts in the rest of the country. This we must put right.

Down with bantustans!!!

FRANK TALK

14

Black Consciousness and the Quest for a True Humanity

"Black Theology" is historically an American product, emerging from the black situation there. Its most articulate exponent there is Dr James H. Cone, Professor of Theology at the Union Theological Seminary, New York, author of Black Theology and Black Power (Seabury, 1969) and, most recently, of God of the Oppressed (Seabury, 1975; SPCK, 1977).

In mid-1970 UCM appointed Sabelo Stanley Ntwasa Travelling Secretary for 1971 with a special mandate to encourage thinking and writing on Black Theology. The book Black Theology: the South African Voice, edited by Basil Moore (C. Hurst & Co., London, 1973) is the result of that year's endeavours, and this paper by Steve is perhaps the most eloquent contribution to that book and, in the present writer's view, the best thing he ever wrote.

BLACK CONSCIOUSNESS AND THE QUEST
FOR A TRUE HUMANITY

It is perhaps fitting to start by examining why it is necessary for us to think collectively about a problem we never created. In doing so, I do not wish to concern myself unnecessarily with the white people of South Africa, but to get to the right answers, we must ask the right questions; we have to find out what went wrong – where and when; and we have to find out whether our position is a deliberate creation of God or an artificial fabrication of the truth by power-hungry people whose motive is authority, security, wealth and comfort. In other words, the "Black Consciousness" approach would be irrelevant in a colourless and non-exploitative egalitarian society. It is relevant here because we believe that an anomalous situation is a deliberate creation of man.

There is no doubt that the colour question in South African politics was originally introduced for economic reasons. The leaders of the white community had to create some kind of barrier between black and whites so that the whites could enjoy privileges at the expense of blacks and still feel free to give a moral justification for the obvious exploitation that pricked even the hardest of white consciences. However, tradition has it that whenever a group of people has tasted the lovely fruits of wealth, security and prestige it begins to find it more comfortable to believe in the obvious lie and to accept it as normal that it alone is entitled to privilege. In order to believe this seriously, it needs to convince itself of all the arguments that support the lie. It is not surprising, therefore, that in South Africa, after generations of exploitation, white people on the whole have come to believe in the inferiority of the black man, so much so that while the race problem started as an offshoot of the economic greed exhibited by white people, it has now become a serious problem on its own. White people now despise black people, not because they need to reinforce their attitude and so justify their position of privilege but simply because they actually believe that black is inferior and bad. This is the basis upon which whites are working in South Africa, and it is what makes South African society racist.

The racism we meet does not only exist on an individual basis; it is also institutionalised to make it look like the South African way of life. Although of late there has been a feeble attempt to gloss over the overt racist elements in the system, it is still true that the system derives its nourishment from the existence of anti-black attitudes in society. To make the lie live even longer, blacks have to be denied any chance of accidentally proving their equality with white men. For this reason there is job reservation, lack of training in skilled work, and a tight orbit around professional possibilities for blacks. Stupidly enough, the system turns back to say that blacks are inferior because they have no economists, no engineers, etc., although it is made impossible for blacks to acquire these skills.

To give authenticity to their lie and to show the righteousness of their claim, whites have further worked out detailed schemes to "solve" the racial situation in this country. Thus, a pseudo-parliament has been created for "Coloureds", and several "Bantu states" are in the process of being set up. So independent and fortunate are they that they do not have to spend a cent on their defence because they have nothing to fear from white South Africa which will always come to their assistance in times of need. One does not, of course, fail to see the arrogance of whites and their contempt for blacks, even in their well-considered modern schemes for subjugation.

The overall success of the white power structure has been in managing to bind the whites together in defence of the *status quo*. By skilfully playing on that imaginary bogey – *swart gevaar* – they have managed to convince even diehard liberals that there is something to fear in the idea of the black man assuming his rightful place at the helm of the South African ship. Thus after years of silence we are able to hear the familiar voice of Alan Paton saying, as far away as London: "Perhaps apartheid is worth a try". "At whose expense, Dr. Paton?", asks an intelligent black journalist. Hence whites in general reinforce each other even though they allow some moderate disagreements on the details of subjugation schemes. There is no doubt that they do not question the validity of white values. They see nothing anomalous in the fact that they alone are arguing about the future of 17 million blacks – in a land which is the natural backyard of the black people. Any proposals for change emanating from the black world are viewed with great indignation. Even the so-called Opposition, the United Party, has the nerve to tell the Coloured people that they are asking for too much. A journalist from a liberal newspaper like *The Sunday Times* of Johannesburg describes a black student – who is only telling the truth – as a militant, impatient young man.

It is not enough for whites to be on the offensive. So immersed are they in prejudice that they do not believe that blacks can formulate their thoughts without white guidance and trusteeship. Thus, even those whites who see much wrong with the system make it their business to control the response of the blacks to the provocation. No one is suggesting that it is not the business of liberal whites to oppose what is wrong. However, it appears to us as too much of a coincidence that liberals – few as they are – should not only be determining the *modus operandi* of those blacks who oppose the system, but also leading it, in spite of their involvement in the system. To us it seems that their role spells out the totality of the white power structure – the fact that though whites are our problem, it is still other whites who want to tell us how to deal with that problem. They do so by dragging all sorts of red herrings across our paths. They tell us that the situation is a class struggle rather than a racial one. Let them go to van Tonder in the Free State and tell him this. We believe we know what the problem is, and we will stick by our findings.

I want to go a little deeper in this discussion because it is time we killed this false political coalition between blacks and whites as long as it is set up on a wrong analysis of our situation. I want to kill it for another reason – namely that it forms at present the greatest stumbling block to our unity. It dangles before freedom-hungry blacks promises of a great future for which no one in these groups seems to be working particularly hard.

The basic problem in South Africa has been analysed by liberal whites as being apartheid. They argue that in order to oppose it we have to form non-racial groups. Between these two extremes, they claim, lies the land of milk and honey for which we are working. The *thesis*, the *anti-thesis* and the *synthesis* have been mentioned by some great philosophers as the cardinal points around which any social revolution revolves. For the *liberals*, the *thesis* is apartheid, the *antithesis* is non-racialism, but the *synthesis* is very feebly defined. They want to tell the blacks that they see integration as the ideal solution. Black Consciousness defines the situation differently. The *thesis* is in fact a strong white racism and therefore, the *antithesis* to this must, *ipso facto*, be a strong solidarity amongst the blacks on whom this white racism seeks to prey. Out of these two situations we can therefore hope to reach some kind of balance – a true humanity where power politics will have no place. This analysis spells out the difference between the old and new approaches. The failure of the liberals is in the fact that their *antithesis* is already a watered-down version of the truth whose close proximity to the thesis will nullify the purported balance. This accounts for the failure of the Sprocas* commissions to make any real headway, for they are already looking for an 'alternative" acceptable to the white man. Everybody in the commissions knows what is right but all are looking for the most seemly way of dodging the responsibility of saying what is right.

It is much more important for blacks to see this difference than it is for whites. We must learn to accept that no group, however benevolent, can ever hand power to the vanquished on a plate. We must accept that the limits of tyrants are prescribed by the endurance of those whom they oppress. As long as we go to Whitey begging cap in hand for our own emancipation, we are giving him further sanction

---

* Study Project on Christianity in an Apartheid Society. Set up by S.A. Council of Churches and Christian Institute in 1968. Editor's note.

to continue with his racist and oppressive system. We must realise that our situation is not a mistake on the part of whites but a deliberate act, and that no amount of moral lecturing will persuade the white man to "correct" the situation. The system concedes nothing without demand, for it formulates its very method of operation on the basis that the ignorant will learn to know, the child will grow into an adult and therefore demands will begin to be made. It gears itself to resist demands in whatever way it sees fit. When you refuse to make these demands and choose to come to a round table to beg for your deliverance, you are asking for the contempt of those who have power over you. This is why we must reject the beggar tactics that are being forced on us by those who wish to appease our cruel masters. This is where the SASO message and cry *"Black man, you are on your own!"* becomes relevant.

The concept of integration, whose virtues are often extolled in white liberal circles, is full of unquestioned assumptions that embrace white values. It is a concept long defined by whites and never examined by blacks. It is based on the assumption that all is well with the system apart from some degree of mismanagement by irrational conservatives at the top. Even the people who argue for integration often forget to veil it in its supposedly beautiful covering. They tell each other that, were it not for job reservation, there would be a beautiful market to exploit. They forget they are talking about people. They see blacks as additional levers to some complicated industrial machines. This is white man's integration – an integration based on exploitative values. It is an integration in which black will compete with black, using each other as rungs up a step ladder leading them to white values. It is an integration in which the black man will have to prove himself in terms of these values before meriting acceptance and ultimate assimilation, and in which the poor will grow poorer and the rich richer in a country where the poor have always been black. We do not want to be reminded that it is we, the indigenous people, who are poor and exploited in the land of our birth. These are concepts which the Black Consciousness approach wishes to eradicate from the black man's mind before our society is driven to chaos by irresponsible people from Coca-cola and hamburger cultural backgrounds.

Black Consciousness is an attitude of mind and a way of life, the most positive call to emanate from the black world for a long time. Its essence is the realisation by the black man of the need to rally together with his brothers around the cause of their oppression – the blackness of their skin – and to operate as a group to rid themselves of the shackles that bind them to perpetual servitude. It is based on a self-examination which has ultimately led them to believe that by seeking to run away from themselves and emulate the white man, they are insulting the intelligence of whoever created them black. The philosophy of Black Consciousness therefore expresses group pride and the determination of the black to rise and attain the envisaged self. Freedom is the ability to define oneself with one's possibilities held back not by the power of other people over one but only by one's relationship to God and to natural surroundings. On his own, therefore, the black man wishes to explore his surroundings and test his possibilities – in other words to make his freedom real by whatever means he deems fit. At the heart of this kind of thinking is the realisation by blacks that the most potent weapon in the hands of the oppressor is the mind of the oppressed. If one is free at heart, no man-made chains can bind one to servitude, but if one's mind is so manipulated and controlled by the oppressor as to make the oppressed believe that he is a liability to the white man, then there will be nothing the oppressed can do to scare his powerful masters. Hence thinking along lines of Black Consciousness makes the black man see himself as a being complete in himself. It makes him less dependent and more free to express his manhood. At the end of it all he cannot tolerate attempts by anybody to dwarf the significance of his manhood.

In order that Black Consciousness can be used to advantage as a philosophy to apply to people in a position like ours, a number of points have to be observed. As people existing in a continuous struggle for truth, we have to examine and question old concepts, values and systems. Having found the right answers we shall then work for consciousness among all people to make it possible for us to proceed towards putting these answers into effect. In this process, we have to evolve our own schemes, forms and strategies to suit the need and situation, always keeping in mind our fundamental beliefs and values.

In all aspects of the black-white relationship, now and in the past, we see a constant tendency by whites to depict blacks as of an inferior status. Our culture, our history and indeed all aspects of the black man's life have been battered nearly out of shape in the great collision between the indigenous values and the Anglo-Boer culture.

The first people to come and relate to blacks in a human way in South Africa were the missionaries. They were in the vanguard of the colonisation movement to "civilise and educate" the savages and introduce the Christian message to them. The religion they brought was quite foreign to the black indigenous people. African religion in its essence was not radically different from Christianity. We also believed in one God, we had our own community of saints through whom we related to our God, and we did not find it compatible with our way of life to worship God in isolation from the various aspects of our lives. Hence worship was not a specialised function that found expression once a week in a secluded building, but rather it featured in our wars, our beer-drinking, our dances and our customs in general. Whenever Africans drank they would first relate to God by giving a portion of their beer away as a token of thanks. When anything went wrong at home they would offer sacrifice to God to appease him and atone for their sins. There was no hell in our religion. We believed in the inherent goodness of man – hence we took it for granted that all people at death joined the community of saints and therefore merited our respect.

It was the missionaries who confused the people with their new religion. They scared our people with stories of hell. They painted their God as a demanding God who wanted worship "or else". People had to discard their clothes and their customs in order to be accepted in this new religion. Knowing how religious the African people were, the missionaries stepped up their terror campaign on the emotions of the people with their detailed accounts of eternal burning, tearing of hair and gnashing of teeth. By some strange and twisted logic, they argued that theirs was a scientific religion and ours a superstition – all this in spite of the biological discrepancy which is at the base of their religion. This cold and cruel religion was strange to the indigenous people and caused frequent strife between the converted and the "pagans", for the former, having imbibed the false values from white society, were taught to ridicule and despise those who defended the truth of their indigenous religion. With the ultimate acceptance of the western religion down went our cultural values!

While I do not wish to question the basic truth at the heart of the Christian message, there is a strong case for a re-examination of Christianity. It has proved a very adaptable religion which does not seek to supplement existing orders but – like any universal truth – to find application within a particular situation. More than anyone else, the missionaries knew that not all they did was essential to the spread of the message. But the basic intention went much further than merely spreading the word. Their arrogance and their monopoly on truth, beauty and moral judgment taught them to despise native customs and traditions and to seek to infuse their own new values into these societies.

Here then we have the case for Black Theology. While not wishing to discuss Black Theology at length, let it suffice to say that it seeks to relate God and Christ once more to the black man and his daily problems. It wants to describe Christ as a fighting God, not a passive God who allows a lie to rest unchallenged. It grapples with existential problems and does not claim to be a theology of absolutes. It seeks to bring back God to the black man and to the truth and reality of his situation. This is an important aspect of Black Consciousness, for quite a large proportion of black people in South Africa are Christians still swimming in a mire of confusion – the aftermath of the missionary approach. It is the duty therefore of all black priests and ministers of religion to save Christianity by adopting Black Theology's approach and thereby once more uniting the black man with his God.

A long look should also be taken at the educational system for blacks. The same tense situation was found as long ago as the arrival of the missionaries. Children were taught, under the pretext of hygiene, good manners and other such vague concepts, to despise their mode of upbringing at home and to question the values and customs of their society. The result was the expected one – children and parents saw life differently and the former lost respect for the latter. Now in African society it is a cardinal sin for a child to lose respect for his parent. Yet how can one prevent the loss of respect between child and parent when the child is taught by his know-all white tutors to disregard his family teachings? Who can resist losing respect for his tradition when in school his whole cultural background is summed up in one word – barbarism?

Thus we can immediately see the logic of placing the missionaries in the forefront of the colonisation process. A man who succeeds in making a group of people accept a foreign concept in which he is expert makes them perpetual students whose progress in the particular field can only be evaluated by him; the student must constantly turn to him for guidance and promotion. In being forced to accept the Anglo-Boer culture, the blacks have allowed themselves to be at the mercy of the white man and to have him as their eternal supervisor. Only he can tell us how good our performance is and instinctively each of us is at pains to please this powerful, all-knowing master. This is what Black Consciousness seeks to eradicate.

As one black writer says, colonialism is never satisfied with having the native in its grip but, by some strange logic, it must turn to his past and disfigure and distort it. Hence the history of the black man in this country is most disappointing to read. It is presented merely as a long succession of defeats. The Xhosas were thieves who went to war for stolen property; the Boers never provoked the Xhosas but merely went on "punitive expeditions" to teach the thieves a lesson. Heroes like Makana* who were essentially revolutionaries are painted as superstitious trouble-makers who lied to the people about bullets turning into water. Great nation-builders like Shaka are cruel tyrants who frequently attacked smaller tribes for no reason but for some sadistic purpose. Not only is there no objectivity in the history taught us but there is frequently an appalling misrepresentation of facts that sicken even the uninformed student.

Thus a lot of attention has to be paid to our history if we as blacks want to aid each other in our coming into consciousness. We have to rewrite our history and produce in it the heroes that formed the core of our resistance to the white invaders. More has to be revealed, and stress has to be laid on the successful nation-building attempts of men such as Shaka, Moshoeshoe and Hintsa. These areas call for intense research to provide some sorely-needed missing links. We would be too naive to expect our conquerors to write unbiased histories about us but we have to destroy the myth that our history starts in 1652, the year Van Riebeeck landed at the Cape.

Our culture must be defined in concrete terms. We must relate the past to the present and demonstrate a historical evolution of the modern black man. There is a tendency to think of our culture as a static culture that was arrested in 1652 and has never developed since. The "return to the bush" concept suggests that we have nothing to boast of except lions, sex and drink. We accept that when colonisation sets in it devours the indigenous culture and leaves behind a bastard culture that may thrive at the pace allowed it by the dominant culture. But we also have to realise that the basic tenets of

---

* Early nineteenth-century Xhosa prophet, sentenced to life imprisonment on Robben Island and drowned while escaping in a boat. Refusal by blacks to accept the truth of his death led to the mythical hope of his eventual return. Editor's note.

our culture have largely succeeded in withstanding the process of bastardisation and that even at this moment we can still demonstrate that we appreciate a man for himself. Ours is a true man-centred society whose sacred tradition is that of sharing. We must reject, as we have been doing, the individualistic cold approach to life that is the cornerstone of the Anglo-Boer culture. We must seek to restore to the black man the great importance we used to give to human relations, the high regard for people and their property and for life in general; to reduce the triumph of technology over man and the materialistic element that is slowly creeping into our society.

These are essential features of our black culture to which we must cling. Black culture above all implies freedom on our part to innovate without recourse to white values. This innovation is part of the natural development of any culture. A culture is essentially the society's composite answer to the varied problems of life. We are experiencing new problems every day and whatever we do adds to the richness of our cultural heritage as long as it has man as its centre. The adoption of black theatre and drama is one such important innovation which we need to encourage and to develop. We know that our love of music and rhythm has relevance even in this day.

Being part of an exploitative society in which we are often the direct objects of exploitation, we need to evolve a strategy towards our economic situation. We are aware that the blacks are still colonised even within the borders of South Africa. Their cheap labour has helped to make South Africa what it is today. Our money from the townships takes a one-way journey to white shops and white banks, and all we do in our lives is pay the white man either with labour or in coin. Capitalistic exploitative tendencies, coupled with the overt arrogance of white racism, have conspired against us. Thus in South Africa now it is very expensive to be poor. It is the poor people who stay furthest from town and therefore have to spend more money on transport to come and work for white people; it is the poor people who use uneconomic and inconvenient fuel like paraffin and coal because of the refusal of the white man to install electricity in black areas; it is the poor people who are governed by many ill-defined restrictive laws and therefore have to spend money on fines for "technical" offences; it is the poor people who have no hospitals and are therefore exposed to exorbitant charges by private doctors; it is the poor people who use untarred roads, have to walk long distances, and therefore experience the greatest wear and tear on commodities like shoes; it is the poor people who have to pay for their children's books while whites get them free. It does not need to be said that it is the black people who are poor.

We therefore need to take another look at how best to use our economic power, little as it may seem to be. We must seriously examine the possibilities of establishing business co-operatives whose interests will be ploughed back into community development programmes. We should think along such lines as the "buy black" campaign once suggested in Johannesburg and establish our own banks for the benefit of the community. Organisational development amongst blacks has only been low because we have allowed it to be. Now that we know we are on our own, it is an absolute duty for us to fulfil these needs.

The last step in Black Consciousness is to broaden the base of our operation. One of the basic tenets of Black Consciousness is totality of involvement. This means that all blacks must sit as one big unit, and no fragmentation and distraction from the mainstream of events be allowed. Hence we must resist the attempts by protagonists of the bantustan theory to fragment our approach. We are oppressed not as individuals, not as Zulus, Xhosas, Vendas or Indians. We are oppressed because we are black. We must use that very concept to unite ourselves and to respond as a cohesive group. We must cling to each other with a tenacity that will shock the perpetrators of evil.

Our preparedness to take upon ourselves the cudgels of the struggle will see us through. We must remove from our vocabulary completely the concept of fear. Truth must ultimately triumph over evil, and the white man has always nourished his greed on this basic fear that shows itself in the black community. Special Branch agents will not turn the lie into truth, and one must ignore them. In a true bid for change we have to take off our coats, be prepared to lose our comfort and security, our jobs and positions of prestige, and our families, for just as it is true that "leadership and security are basically incompatible", a struggle without casualties is no struggle. We must realise that prophetic cry of black students: "Black man, you are on your own!"

Some will charge that we are racist but these people are using exactly the values we reject. We do not have the power to subjugate anyone. We are merely responding to provocation in the most realistic possible way. Racism does not only imply exclusion of one race by another – it always presupposes that the exclusion is for the purposes of subjugation. Blacks have had enough experience as objects of racism not to wish to turn the tables. While it may be relevant now to talk about black in relation to white, we must not make this our preoccupation, for it can be a negative exercise. As we proceed further towards the achievement of our goals let us talk more about ourselves and our struggle and less about whites.

We have set out on a quest for true humanity, and somewhere on the distant horizon we can see the glittering prize. Let us march forth with courage and determination, drawing strength from our common plight and our brotherhood. In time we shall be in a position to bestow upon South Africa the greatest gift possible – a more human face.

15
What is Black Consciousness?

Extract from Steve's evidence in the SASO/BPC Trial given in the first week of May 1976. In the trial extracts printed in this book the defence lawyer is Advocate David Soggot assistant counsel for Defence. Cross-examination for the prosecution is by Mr L. Attwell, assistant counsel for Prosecution. The trial judge was Judge Boshoff.

The event leading to this Trial had been the pro-Frelimo rally at Currie's Fountain, Durban, in September 1974, planned by elements of BPC and SASO to celebrate the recognition of Frelimo as the de facto *government of Moçambique. Despite the fact that the South African Government had itself recognised Frelimo, when this rally was announced and a white businessman publicly declared that if it took place he and others would go and break it up, instead of dealing with the white businessman, the Minister of Justice banned the rally. At the same time a rally organised by Portuguese in Johannesburg to protest against Frelimo was allowed to take place without any official hindrance.*

The banning of the Currie's Fountain Rally was followed by the arrest of Black Consciousness leaders in Durban and all over the country, and their detention without trial and incommunicado for many months in Pretoria. Eventually charges were formulated against 13 of those detained (though 4 were subsequently discharged either before the Trial began or early in its course). The two most closely associated with Steve himself were Aubrey Mokoape and Strini Moodley. The all-embracing terms in which the indictment was framed made it clear that what was on trial was the Black Consciousness Movement itself: in fact this Trial may be said to have been for this Movement what the famous 'Treason Trial' was for the Congress Alliance of the 1950s.

The Trial dragged on through most of 1975 and all of 1976, and ended with all nine being found guilty of one or more charges under the Terrorism Act, which meant a mandatory minimum sentence of five years. Some have sentences of six years. All are now on Robben Island.

The last section of this chapter, "The Importance of Language", which is separate from the rest of the chapter, is included first as an

100

*example of Steve's conduct under hostile cross-examination, and
secondly for his perceptive understanding of the difference between
black and white uses of language. The incident referred to concerned
Mr Nthuli Shezi, then organiser of BPC. Confronting a white railway
worker who was molesting black women on Germiston station he was,
according to eye-witnesses, pushed onto the railway line by the worker
and killed by the oncoming train.*

Soggot: Now, I think that that brings us to the 1971 second GSC?*
Biko: Yes.
Soggot: Now I do not propose to take you through the whole of that
in any way, I merely want to refer you to certain aspects of the Resol-
utions passed at that GSC. If you look at paragraph 1: "SASO is a
black student organization" – have you got that?
Biko: Yes.
Soggot: Would you just read that please, paragraph 1?
Biko: "SASO is a black student organization working for the liber-
ation of the black man first from psychological oppression by themselves through inferiority complex and secondly from the physical
one accruing out of living in a white racist society".
Soggot: Now, the concept of Black Consciousness, does that link up
in any way with what you have just read?
Biko: Yes, it does.
Soggot: Would you explain briefly to His Lordship that link-up?
Biko: I think basically Black Consciousness refers itself to the black
man and to his situation, and I think the black man is subjected to
two forces in this country. He is first of all oppressed by an external
world through institutionalised machinery, through laws that restrict
him from doing certain things, through heavy work conditions,
through poor pay, through very difficult living conditions, through
poor education, these are all external to him, and secondly, and this
we regard as the most important, the black man in himself has developed a certain state of alienation, he rejects himself, precisely because he attaches the meaning white to all that is good, in other
words he associates good and he equates good with white. This arises
out of his living and it arises out of his development from childhood.

When you go to school for instance, your school is not the same as
the white school, and *ipso facto* the conclusion you reach is that the
education you get there cannot be the same as what the white kids get

* General Students' Council. Editor's note.

at school. The black kids normally have got shabby uniforms if any, or no uniform at school, the white kids always have uniforms. You find for instance even the organisation of sport (these are things you notice as a kid) at white schools to be absolutely so thorough and indicative of good training, good upbringing. You could get in a school 15 rugby teams. We could get from our school three rugby teams. Each of these 15 white teams has got uniforms for each particular kid who plays. We have got to share the uniforms amongst our three teams. Now this is part of the roots of self-negation which our kids get even as they grow up. The homes are different, the streets are different, the lighting is different, so you tend to begin to feel that there is something incomplete in your humanity, and that completeness goes with whiteness. This is carried through to adulthood when the black man has got to live and work.

Soggot: How do you see it carried through to adulthood, can you give us examples there?

Biko: From adulthood?

Soggot: Yes.

Biko: I would remember specifically one example that touched me, talking to an Indian worker in Durban who was driving a van for a dry-cleaner firm. He was describing to me his average day, how he lives, and the way he put it to me was that: I no more work in order to live, I live in order to work. And when he went on to elaborate I could see the truth of the statement. He describes how he has to wake up at 4 o'clock, half past four in order to walk a long distance to be in time for a bus to town. He works there for a whole day, so many calls are thrown his way by his boss, at the end of the day he has to travel the same route, arrive at home half past eight 9 o'clock, too tired to do anything but to sleep in order to be in time for work again the next day.

Soggot: To what extent would you say that this example is typical or atypical of a black worker living in an urban area?

Biko: With I think some variance in terms of the times and so on and the work situation, this is a pretty typical example, precisely because townships are placed long distances away from the working areas where black people work, and the transport conditions are appalling, trains are overcrowded all the time, taxis that they use are overcrowded, the whole travelling situation is dangerous, and by the time a guy gets to work he has really been through a mill; he gets to work, there is no peace either at work, his boss sits on him to eke out of him even the last effort in order to boost up production. This is the common experience of the black man. When he gets back from work through the same process of travelling conditions, he can only take out his anger on his family which is the last defence that he has.

Soggot: Are there any other factors which you would name in order to suggest that – to explain why there is this sense of inferiority, as perceived by you people?

Biko: I would speak – I think I have spoken a bit on education, but I think I must elaborate a little bit on that. As a black student again, you are exposed to competition with white students in fields in which you are completely inadequate. We come from a background which is essentially peasant and worker, we do not have any form of daily contact with a highly technological society, we are foreigners in that field. When you have got to write an essay as a black child under for instance JMB* the topics that are given there tally very well with white experience, but you as a black student writing the same essay have got to grapple with something which is foreign to you – not only foreign but superior in a sense; because of the ability of the white culture to solve so many problems in the sphere of medicine, various spheres, you tend to look at it as a superior culture than yours, you tend to despise the worker culture, and this inculcates in the black man a sense of self-hatred which I think is an important determining factor in his dealings with himself and his life.

And of course to accommodate the existing problems, the black man develops a two-faced attitude; I can quote a typical example; I had a man working in one of our projects in the Eastern Cape on electricity, he was installing electricity, a white man with a black assistant. He had to be above the ceiling and the black man was under the ceiling and they were working together pushing up wires and sending the rods in which the wires are and so on, and all the time there was insult, insult, insult from the white man: push this you fool – that sort of talk, and of course this touched me; I know the white man very well, he speaks very well to me, so at tea time we invite them to tea; I ask him: why do you speak like this to this man? and he says to me in front of the guy: this is the only language he understands, he is a lazy bugger. And the black man smiled. I asked him if it was true and he says: no, I am used to him. Then I was sick. I thought for a moment I do not understand black society. After some two hours I came back to this guy, I said to him: do you really mean it? The man changed, he

* Joint Matriculation Board, the governing body for secondary education. Editor's note.

became very bitter, he was telling me how he wants to leave any moment, but what can he do? He does not have any skills, he has got no assurance of another job, his job is to him some form of security, he has got no reserves, if he does not work today he cannot live tomorrow, he has got to work, he has got to take it. And if he has got to take he dare not show any form of what is called cheek to his boss. Now this I think epitomises the two-faced attitude of the black man to this whole question of existence in this country.

Soggot: The use of the word "black" in literature and as part of western culture, has that figured at all?

Biko: Sorry?

Soggot: The use of the word "black", what does black signify and how is it used in language?

Judge Boshoff: Is it a comprehensive term?

Biko: If I understand you correctly, the reference I think of common literature to the term black is normally in association also with negative aspects, in other words you speak of the black market, you speak of the black sheep of the family, you speak of – you know, anything which is supposed to be bad is also considered to be black.

Soggot: We have got that, now in that context . . . [*Court intervenes*]

Judge Boshoff: Now the word black there, it has nothing to do with the black man. Isn't that just idiom over the years because darkness usually, the night was a mystery for the primitive man? I mean I include the whites when I talk about primitive man, and when he talks about dark forces, he refers to forces that he cannot explain, and he refers to magic, black magic; isn't that the reason for this?

Biko: This is certainly the reason, but I think there has been created through history and through common reference – all the attitudes which are associated with exactly that kind of association – also go in regard to the black man, and the black man sees this as being said of magic, of the black market, precisely because like him it is an inferior thing, it is an unwanted thing, it is a rejected thing by society. And of course typically (and again in the face of this logic) whiteness goes with angels, goes with, you know, God, beauty, you know. I think this tends to help in creating this kind of feeling of self-censure within the black man.

Soggot: When you have phrases such as "black is beautiful", now would that sort of phrase fit in with the Black Consciousness approach?

Biko: Yes, it does.

Soggot: What is the idea of such a slogan?

Biko: I think that slogan has been meant to serve and I think is serving a very important aspect of our attempt to get at humanity. You are challenging the very deep roots of the Black man's belief about himself. When you say "black is beautiful" what in fact you are saying to him is: man, you are okay as you are, begin to look upon yourself as a human being; now in African life especially it also has certain connotations; it is the connotations on the way women prepare themselves for viewing by society, in other words the way they dream, the way they make up and so on, which tends to be a negation of their true state and in a sense a running away from their colour; they use lightening creams, they use straightening devices for their hair and so on. They sort of believe I think that their natural state which is a black state is not synonymous with beauty and beauty can only be approximated by them if the skin is made as light as possible and the lips are made as red as possible, and their nails are made as pink as possible and so on. So in a sense the term "black is beautiful" challenges exactly that belief which makes someone negate himself.

Judge Boshoff: Mr Biko, why do you people then pick on the word black? I mean black is really an innocent reference which has been arrived at over the years the same as white; snow is regarded as white, and snow is regarded as the purest form of water and so it symbolises purity, so white there has got nothing to do with the white man?

Biko: Right.

Judge Boshoff: But now why do you refer to you people as blacks? Why not brown people? I mean you people are more brown than black.

Biko: In the same way as I think white people are more pink and yellow and pale than white.

Judge Boshoff: Quite . . . but now why do you not use the word brown then?

Biko: No, I think really, historically, we have been defined as black people, and when we reject the term non-white and take upon ourselves the right to call ourselves what we think we are, we have got available in front of us a whole number of alternatives, starting from natives to Africans to kaffirs to bantu to non-whites and so on, and we choose this one precisely because we feel it is most accommodating.

Judge Boshoff: Yes but then you put your foot into it, you use black which really connotates dark forces over the centuries?

Biko: This is correct, precisely because it has been used in that context our aim is to choose it for reference to us and elevate it to a position where we can look upon ourselves positively; because no matter whether we choose to be called brown, you are still going to get reference to blacks in an inferior sense in literature and in speeches by white racists or white persons in our society.

Judge Boshoff: But would you still refer to black magic, if you refer to witchcraft?

Biko: Oh yes we do refer to black magic.

Judge Boshoff: Now do you use it in a good sense or a bad sense?

Biko: We do not reject it, we regard it as part of the mystery of our cultural heritage, we feel for ourselves it has not been sufficiently looked into with available scientific approaches as of this moment.

Judge Boshoff: But I am not asking you about witchcraft, I am referring to the term, would you refer to it as black magic?

Biko: Yes, we do refer to it as black magic.

Judge Boshoff: But now why do you use black there, in what sense do you use black?

Biko: Well we understand it to – when we talk of black magic in this country, unlike in London, for instance, people talk of black magic and it is supposed to be witchcraft, and there is no connotation that it comes from black society, but when you talk of witchcraft, superstition, in this country, automatically it is associated with black in the minds of most people. Whites are not superstitious, whites do not have witches and witchdoctors we are the people who have this.

Soggot: I am not so sure he is right there . . . [*Laughter*]

Judge Boshoff: Yes, we have a lot of witchcraft.

Biko: Well it is certainly not our type of witchcraft I must say, we have several cases, I am sure . . . [*Court intervenes*]

Judge Boshoff: Well how many whites go to witchdoctors?

Biko: You mean to our witchdoctors?

Judge Boshoff: Yes?

Biko: Oh well, this is fine, they go, but the witchdoctors and the witchcraft is ours.

Judge Boshoff: But you take it amiss, I mean the fact that the white man blames the witchcraft on the black man, or don't you take it amiss?

Biko: Well in certain instances yes, I think there tends to be a certain derogatory connotation to reference to blacks as superstitious beings in a certain point of our history especially during the time of Sir

George Grey when he spoke about the suicide of the Xhosas. This is blamed on witchcraft, superstition, and in a sense . . . [*Court intervenes*]

Judge Boshoff: But now does that not cause you people a lot of grief – witchcraft, I mean? When I go on Circuit and I do murder cases near Sekukuneland or even near Tzaneen, we always have witchcraft cases and they do the most terrible things. When a child dies they think that somebody must have bewitched the child and they just kill a few people. Well you cannot justify that?

Biko: No, we do not. We do not accept superstition. We do not accept witchcraft, but all we are saying is that there are certain things within this whole sphere of black magic which can be usefully investigated. I mean I would reject it as much as you do because I do not believe in it myself, but I do not have disdain for the people who believe in it like most of our society seems to have. I understand my exposure to so much more literature and other, I would say, cultures in the world, so I have decided that there is no place for this in my belief; but the person who believes in it, I can still talk to him with understanding. I do not reject him as a barbarian.

Judge Boshoff: But I suppose witchcraft is deprecated by reason of the fact that people do irresponsible things and harm people?

Biko: This is correct, yes.

Soggot: Is your concern not so much the restructure of the word "black" in the world of linguistics so much as to alter the response of black people to their own blackness?

Biko: It is certainly directed at man, at the black man.

Soggot: And I think you were talking about your understanding of the black man's own sense of inferiority and self-hatred and all that?

Biko: Yes.

Soggot: In the world of language, how does the black man figure, how does he feel?

Biko: Yes I think this is another area where experiences of well, let me say difficulties that I have experienced. We have a society here in South Africa which recognises in the main two languages, English and Afrikaans as official languages. These are languages that you have to use at school, at university I mean, or in pursuit of any discipline when you are studying as a black man. Unfortunately the books you read are in English, English is a second language to you; you have probably been taught in a vernacular especially during these days of Bantu education up to Standard 6; you grapple with the language to JC and matric,* and before you conquer it you must apply it now to learn discipline at university. As a result you never quite catch everything that is in a book; you certainly understand the paragraph, (I mean I am talking about the average man now, I am not talking about exceptional cases) you understand the paragraph but you are not quite adept at reproducing an argument that was in a particular book, precisely because of your failure to understand certain words in the book. This makes you less articulate as a black man generally, and this makes you more inward-looking; you feel things rather than say them, and this applies to Afrikaans as well – much more to English than to Afrikaans; Afrikaans is essentially a language that has developed here, and I think in many instances in it's idiom, it relates much better to African languages; but English is completely foreign, and therefore people find it difficult to move beyond a certain point in their comprehension of the language.

Soggot: And how does this relate to the black man or in particular to the black students as inferiority?

Biko: An example of this for instance was again during the old days of NUSAS where students would be something that you as a black man have experienced in your day to day life, but your powers of articulation are not as good as theirs; also you have amongst the white students a number of students doing M.A., doing Honours, you know, in particular quarters, highly articulate, very intelligent. You may be intelligent but not as articulate, you are forced into a subservient role of having to say yes to what they are saying, talking about what you have experienced, which they have not experienced, because you cannot express it so well. This in a sense inculcates also in numerous students a sense of inadequacy. You tend to think that it is not just a matter of language, you tend to tie it up also with intelligence in a sense, you tend to feel that that guy is better equipped than you mentally.

Judge Boshoff: But why do you say that? Isn't English the official language of SASO?

Biko: Yes, it is.

Judge Boshoff: Well now, but your complaint is against the language but it is just the very language that you are using?

Biko: No, no, I am not complaining against the language, I am merely explaining how language can help in the development of an

---

* JC is Junior Certificate, corresponding roughly to the Eleven Plus, and "matric" the highest qualification in the secondary system. Editor's note.

inferiority complex. I am not complaining against the language, the point in issue is that we have something like ten languages, we cannot speak all ten languages at one meeting, we have got to choose a common language. But unfortunately in the learning process this is really what happens, you do not grasp enough and therefore you cannot be articulate enough, and when you play side by side with people who are more articulate than you, you tend to think that it is because they are more intelligent than you, that they can say these things better than you.

Judge Boshoff: But your language is very idiomatic; well is it not easier for you people to speak Afrikaans because Afrikaans is like your language, it is very idiomatic?

Biko: This is true, actually, unfortunately again Afrikaans has got certain connotations historically that do provoke a rejection from the black man, and these are political connotations. I am not arguing for or against, but they are there.

Soggot: But your point as I understand it is that the black man feels a little bit of a foreigner in the linguistic field?

Biko: Right.

Soggot: Is that what you are saying to His Lordship?

Biko: Yes.

Soggot: You are not complaining about the language just as one does not complain about French when you are in Paris?

Biko: That is right.

Soggot: But it is something which you have got to master, is that what you are saying?

Biko: That is correct, yes.

Soggot: Mr Biko, still talking about the question of inferiority, you, if I may introduce this point in a certain way, an article "I write what I like by Frank Talk", Annexure 8 to the Indictment – "Fear – an important determinant in South African politics", who wrote that?*

Biko: I wrote that.

Judge Boshoff: You say you wrote it?

Biko: I wrote it.

Judge Boshoff: Is it Annexure 8? Is this by Frank Talk?

Biko: That is right.

Judge Boshoff: Isn't number 9 Frank Talk?

Biko: No, no, he was never Frank Talk, I was Frank Talk. [*Laughter*]

Soggot: M'lord, the Indictment alleged that he compiled and/or

* See Chapter 12.

wrote it, but in fact it was never ever suggested that number 9 wrote this. Annexure 9, Focus – "Ugandan Asians and the lesson for us"?
Biko: Yes.
Soggot: Who wrote that?
Biko: I wrote that.
Judge Boshoff: Just let me get that again, which is that?
Soggot: M'lord, Annexure 9. On page 11 of "I write what I like", you say: "Township life alone makes it a miracle for anyone to live up to adulthood". What do you mean by that?
Biko: This refers to the degree of violence that one gets in townships, which tends to introduce a certain measure of uncertainty about what tomorrow will bring. If I am in a different type of life and I spend a night at your place, somehow I feel unexposed to what I would call the elements, you know, I am not exposed to bad elements of society. When you are in a township it is dangerous to cross often from one street to the next, and yet as you grow up it is essential that kids must be sent on errands in and around the township. They meet up with these problems; rape and murder are very very common aspects of our life in the townships.
Soggot: And at night time what is the position?
Biko: It is especially at night time, I mean in the few days I have spent in Mabopane where I say . . . [*Mr Soggot intervenes*]
Soggot: That is near Pretoria?
Biko: Near Pretoria, I have seen two cases of grievous assault, one landed on our door and there is no relationship between the persons assaulted and the person assaulting. You see an old man being assaulted by a number of young men for apparently no reason whatsoever except that of course possibly it is the end of the month and possibly he might have some money around him, but this does not surprise me, it is a common experience, but I have never learned to accept it all the same, because it is a bitter reminder of the kind of violence that is there in our society. Now when I use that term there that it is a miracle to live to an adult age or whatever I said, the precise meaning of it is exactly that, that one escapes all these possible areas of pitfalls where one might die without any explanation. It is not because you are well kept, it is not because you are well protected, it is just a miracle, it happens.
Judge Boshoff: It would be interesting to know what your attitude here is. Isn't that a justification for influx control; isn't the difficulty that you have a lot of people seeping into such an area, and

you find your bad elements amongst those people because it is an uncontrolled element that comes in? To give you an illustration, years ago I was Counsel for the black people here when they wanted to move Newclare Black township, and at that time I think that 37,000 people were there who were not entitled to be there, that just came into the township, and they were there illegally. Now isn't that type of thing the cause of this type of crime that you get in a township?

Biko: I think, M'lord, that if one looks at it superficially yes; but there is a much more fundamental reason; it is absence of abundant life for the people who live there. With abundant life you get discipline, people get the things that they want. And because of course you do not get a society here which offers this to the people, they have got to introduce measures like influx control. One might say of course if you apply influx control laws you lessen crime, and this of course is correct.

Judge Boshoff: You see another point, you can continue but I just want to make this observation now. Usually influx control ensures that the people who are there in the township have employment?

Biko: Right.

Judge Boshoff: But now these people who are there illegally they are people without employment, and they probably have to steal to live. I mean otherwise they do not know how to exist?

Biko: I do not want to canvass the point of influx control too much . . . [*Court intervenes*]

Judge Boshoff: No, no, I am just asking you as a matter of interest because I see they make the point here of influx control being one of the reasons why the black man is oppressed?

Biko: Yes because I think the real point about influx control is that if it is necessary it must be applied equally to everybody. I don't think, you know – it is inconceivable that influx control may be necessary in society but where it is applied, it has got to be applied without reference to colour; it must be applied to everybody. It must not be that a white guy is free to move to Cape Town tomorrow, to Durban tomorrow, and some other place without being indexed, and I have got to go through a whole rigmarole of red tape in order to move from one area to another.

Judge Boshoff: But with the white people you do not have that situation in the sense that usually white people have (*sic*) rather full employment. Is that not so? You cannot say that unfortunately for the black man; so the position is that when black people come into an area where there is already conditions of overcrowding, then you find that crime comes with it?

Biko: Equally, M'lord, there are large sections of black people who do have full employment where they are going. When I had to be employed in Durban, I had to go through that whole system of influx control. Now in the first instance I had a job, I had no competitor, I was wanted, I was going to be assisted in getting a house, but somehow or other it was made difficult for me to move, and in the second instance, and this is part of the complaint about influx control, it is a very degrading system.

Judge Boshoff: Well usually it is the manner of application that usually causes difficulty?

Biko: Quite right, you are made in some instances to stand naked in front of some doctors supposed to be running pus off you, because you may be bringing syphilis to the town he tells you. Now it is inhuman the way it is done. Three people are lined up in front of him, all naked, and he has just got to look at all of you. Now I must feel that I am being treated as an animal, and as you enter the room where this is done in Durban there is a big notice saying: "Beware – Natives in a state of undress". Now one must feel that you know, it is not just the application of a good law; somehow there seems to be a certain infringement – calculation, you know, they are trying to put you in your place. I mean this is the problem, one does not want to argue always against the law as such; sometimes application counts a lot, and to whom it is applied. If it is applied equally, then fine.

Soggot: Whatever the causes, what you are saying is there is an insecurity in one's physical life in the townships; does this have an effect on the black man in relation to his sense of confidence or inferiority or whatever it is?

Biko: You mean the insecurity in the townships?

Soggot: The physical insecurity?

Biko: Yes, I think it has, I think it contributes to a feeling of – well, it helps to build up the sense of insecurity which is part of a feeling of incompleteness; you are not a complete human being; you cannot walk out when you like, you know, that sort of feeling; it is an imprisoning concept itself.

Soggot: Now, Mr Biko, I am coming back to the theme of this questioning namely conscientisation, but I just want to divert slightly; were you ever involved in actually monitoring people, ordinary people's conversations?

Biko: Yes . . . [*Mr Soggot intervenes*]

Soggot: Whether it was in the street, or – [*pause*]

Biko: You mean some form of research?

Soggot: That is correct?

Biko: Yes.

Soggot: Would you tell His Lordship briefly what that was?

Biko: M'lord, this was a research carried out, I think it was 1972; the purpose was literacy. Now the particular method we were using places a lot of emphasis on syllabic teaching of people; you do not just teach people the alphabet in isolation, you have to teach them syllables, and you have to start with words that have got a particular meaning to them, what we called generative terms. Now the preamble to it was some kind of research in a specific area where you are going to work, which carried you to several segments of the community, to particular places where the community congregates and talks freely. Your role there was particularly passive, you are there just to listen to the things that they are talking about, and also to the words that are being used, the themes being important; there we also used pictures to depict the themes that they were talking about. Now I was involved in this with a man called Jerry Modisane and Barney Pityana . . . [*Mr Soggot intervenes]*

Soggot: Was this in Durban?

Biko: In Durban.

Soggot: Who were you doing this research for?

Biko: We were doing it for ourselves. I had been asked to participate in a literary programme that was drawn up by SASO.

Soggot: Well whatever this was you listened to people?

Biko: That is right.

Soggot: In what circumstances?

Biko: Well we chose available circumstances. Now in this particular instance we listened to women in queues waiting to see a doctor or nurse at a clinic, some of them had babies on their arms or on their backs, we listened to people congregated in sports fields watching sport, we listened to people in shebeens; I did go around buying beer in a lot of shebeens, and we listened to people in buses as well, and trains.

Soggot: What was it that people were saying if anything at all about their condition of life? And the white man, if the white man or the white government came up at all?

Biko: The first thing to notice when observing such situations is the constant recurrence of what I would call protest talk about the situation of oppression that the black man is exposed to. Sometimes it is general, sometimes it is specific, but always contained what I would call a round condemnation of white society. Often in very very tough language, some of which is not admissible in Court. I remember for instance a specific bus in which I was travelling and in most instances the topic was dictated by the position of the bus on the way to town. As you are coming out of Umlazi you pass through a particular area which is a hostel in fact, called Gliblands; it is a hostel for adult male blacks. Now there are certain restrictions in hostels like they may not bring in women and so on, but each time we pass there in the morning of course there is a stream of women coming out of the hostel and people start talking about this, you know, . . . *[Mr Biko quotes in a Bantu language*]* . . . implying that these bachelors have got lots of women, and from there onwards the theme builds up almost automatically, why are they disallowed. Where does the white man think these guys are going to get their sex from, that sort of thing, and from there it blows up. And then again the bus goes through to the industrial area called Jacobs; you pass through the southern part of Jacobs, and there is a constant stream of people getting in and out of factories, and the talk centres around problems of labour and so on. I cannot quite remember specifically what was said, but they start from there again and always central to this theme is the condemnation of white society in general. You know when people speak in the townships they do not talk about the government; they do not talk about the Provincial Council, or City Councils, they talk about whites, and of course the connotation there is with reference to obvious structures, but to them it is just whites. And as I say the language is often hard, you know, sometimes to the point of not being admissible in Court because it is swear words really.

Soggot: And you yourself have lived for example in Ginsberg Location in Kingwilliamstown, is that right?

Biko: Yes, I have.

Soggot: And is that a rather poor rural location?

Biko: Yes it is a small township of about a thousand houses, very poor.

Soggot: So you are familiar with life there?

---

* i.e. African (cf. 118; witness 'in Xhosa'). Probably here, the language was Zulu as the place was Durban. Editor's note.

Biko: That is correct.

Soggot: Now the echoing of this sort of sentiment, did that take place there while you lived there?

Biko: Oh yes, very common.

Soggot: And you people talk of psychological and physical oppression, is there reference to oppression at all in any shape or form by people in their ordinary thinking?

Biko: Yes, often.

Soggot: Now, Mr Biko, when you set out to conscientise people, is that then to bring to them the ideas of Black Consciousness?

Biko: That is correct, yes.

Soggot: Can you tell us when you conscientise people do you refer at all, do you relate what you say to their condition and the various aspects which you have told His Lordship about, the question of starvation and labour and so on?

Biko: This is correct, we do make reference to the conditions of the black man and the conditions in which the black man lives. We try to get blacks in conscientisation to grapple realistically with their problems, to attempt to find solutions to their problems, to develop what one might call an awareness, a physical awareness of their situation, to be able to analyse it, and to provide answers for themselves. The purpose behind it really being to provide some kind of hope; I think the central theme about black society is that it has got elements of a defeated society, people often look like they have given up the struggle. Like the man who was telling me that he now lives to work, he has given himself to the idea. Now this sense of defeat is basically what we are fighting against; people must not just give in to the hardship of life, people must develop a hope, people must develop some form of security to be together to look at their problems, and people must in this way build up their humanity. This is the point about conscientisation and Black Consciousness.

Soggot: The question I want to put to you is this, haven't these people got used to and come to accept their, what you call, existential conditions, their grievances, insecurity, the absence of food or inadequate food and so on?

Biko: That is I think understating the position. I think it is possible to adapt to a given hard situation precisely because you have got to live it, and you have got to live with it every day. But adapting does not mean that you forget; you go to the mill every day, it is always unacceptable to you, it has always been unacceptable to you, and it remains so for life, but you adapt in the sense that you cannot continue to live in a state of conflict with yourself. You sort of accept, like the man who was working with the electrician was saying to me, you know, 'oh he talks in this way'. This is his explanation of it. This is his sort of glib adaptation to it, but deep inside him he feels it. He cannot keep on answering back to him every day: don't call me boy, don't shout at me, don't swear at me, because there is also the element of the job that he has got to keep. He had adapted but he does not forget it, and he does not accept it, which I think is important.

Soggot: The other question which is related is when in a document of BPC or SASO – we will come to BPC later, but take it as an example, you refer to the whites or the white government as oppressors. Does this not alter people's feelings or their attitudes in relation to the white government or the whites?

Biko: No, I think it only serves to establish a common basis for discussion; what is contained in that expression is usually what the black man himself normally says about the whole problem in even stronger terms. But when we talk about common problems or the problems that the black man faces, what you are merely doing is to establish a point of departure for what you are talking about, and the goal for BPC or SASO usually is that of a build-up of membership, especially for BPC.

THE IMPORTANCE OF LANGUAGE

Attwell: And this sort of language,* do you consider this as racially inflammable?

Biko: No, I think if you put this again – if you put this into Zulu, you would find that this is what any old man – if you pick up an old man from the village and ask him to speak about Nthuli, at his funeral, and tell him the facts, that he died through being pushed onto the rails, as we believe, by a railway worker at some station, and you tell him that the quarrel started when Nthuli Shezi was protecting the rights of women at the station who had been molested by this man, as we believe, if you ask any old man to go and talk, with that kind of background, that is precisely the kind of things he would say. Not necessarily the same words, but words like "soldier" and so on are going to come in there, and condemnation of that kind of man, that kind of mentality, that is what is being condemned here, not necessarily the specific man who pushed him, but the kind of society which

* This refers to a document allegedly circulated at the funeral. Editor's note.

gives that kind of mentality to a man to make him feel that he can freely push someone onto the rails, you must condemn the entire society because that man is not alone in developing this feeling against blacks. He is rooted in a society, a society which has got a particular history and a particular relationship with blacks, so he feels somehow that it is right when he does this. He might even feel in his own small mind that he is representing his people correctly by pushing this person onto the rails. Now when we talk about him therefore, you have got to reflect on the society, and that society is a white society. And I think that even an old man would be able to make that assimilation even within black society.

Attwell: The point is these are not in Zulu or in any other language, they are in English?

Biko: But they are understood by people who are rooted in that sort of culture, Zulu, Xhosa and so on. No matter what they are expressed in, in English or Afrikaans or what, but they are understood by people who are rooted in a particular culture.

Attwell: Would you say this . . .

Biko: They don't sit down to look at one word as such and say what does it mean, no, they listened to the whole paragraph. And understand the combined meaning. They are not analytical with the English, they listen to black words when you are talking.

Attwell: Is it only English which has this peculiarity of attaching a specific significance to the word?

Biko: I don't know other languages, I know a bit of Afrikaans, a bit of English, a bit of Xhosa; Zulu and all the other languages share one common factor, that of attaching not an analytical but some kind of emotional meaning to situations, whereas English tends to be analytical. You have got to use a precise word you know, to convey a precise meaning. And I think this is the problem we are having, one of understanding when we look at these documents.

Attwell: But isn't that one of the dangers that BPC was faced with? Portraying its precise meaning in this language? It shows out of its own free will that it adopted it as its official language?

Biko: I am saying both the drawers of this particular piece and the recipients will have no doubt about their communication. You in the middle who is an Englishman, who looks at words you know piecemeal, you may have problems, but the person who drew this up and the person who perceives it within a crowd has no problem. They are at one, they understand what they are talking about. You may not understand it because you are looking at the precise meaning of words.

Attwell: Are you suggesting that if I were to translate this into Afrikaans, word for word literally, that I would not get the same impression that I get from this document?

Biko: Literally?

Attwell: Literally word for word identical to Afrikaans?

Biko: Well, I don't know; let us think about Zulu and think about Xhosa then I will be an expert there, but certainly I have got a vague impression that even in Afrikaans you would not be able to convey the same meaning if you translate that word for word.

Attwell: Why did BPC choose this language to convey its meaning?

Biko: It is communication with a lot of people who speak several languages, right, but at least they can commonly speak English. Not to any degree of sophistication but to some degree.

Attwell: Will they necessarily each interpret this back into their own language to see whether this is . . .

Biko: You don't have to interpret it back into your language because your values as a person, whether you speak English or not, your values are affected by your culture, so your perceiving – you perceive a document in terms of your general make-up, in terms of your understanding and what I am saying to you is that not one black person looks at this thing in terms of the precise meaning of each word. After this has been read for instance, if you ask a black person how will whites – how were whites described in that document, he will not remember the precise words. He will just have a vague idea. This is all I am trying to say to you, about the meaning of language.

Attwell: Allright, now he reads that document and all he is left with is a vague or general impression?

Biko: Of the precise words, the meaning is there.

Attwell: What is the meaning of this?

Biko: Well, . . .

Attwell: In BPC J.2? Look at J.1 and J.2?

Biko: It is a description of white society, specifically of this man in terms of the role which he was playing, right. He stands in the middle. On one hand he is portraying the rights of women, on the other he is portraying them against a particularly violent society, okay, which is white society. And what happens is he dies. Now symbolically he dies like a soldier, a soldier dies fighting for a cause. His cause was to protect the rights of women, this is basically what the document is saying. No matter what individuals are saying, that is what the man catches that they are talking to.

Attwell: I would agree with you that is made here a symbol of the black community and that this white official whoever he may have been is made a symbol of the white system?

Biko: I have explained why.

Attwell: And what impression is the man going to have of the white system who reads this? Whether he be a Zulu or a Xhosa or an Indian or anything else?

Biko: It is the same old thing, you know, it is again what he knows okay. Now at the funeral the focus of course is on the man who is being buried. Now if you go to any black funeral the trend is the same. We attempt to bring to light the good facts about the person who is dying, we are paying our last respects to him. Secondly we talk about how he died. This is you know the average conduct of any funeral amongst the blacks. They are just held in that context. The man, who is he, what does he believe in, and so on, what does he stand for? And what caused him to die? We normally say in Xhosa for instance there will be a speaker about the life of the person – [*the witness quotes in Xhosa*]. There will be a speaker about the sickness of the person, okay, that is now – [*witness again quotes in Xhosa*]. It is done that, in any funeral, so that as a speaker you must find – if I am called upon to speak at somebody's funeral I must go out of my way to trace his life and bring out what is good in him. So this is quite logical, besides it is an African funeral.

Attwell: I submit to you that they brought out all the good in Mr Shezi, whatever good there may have been, and neglected any weak points that he may have had?

Biko: This is done.

Attwell: And brought out all the evil nasty possible things they can about the whites, and ignored all the good that there may or may not be. Would you agree with me?

Biko: I think they have not finished all the evil.

Attwell: They have not finished all the evil yet?

Biko: No, no.

Attwell: Would you have gone further than this?

Biko: You could have gone further if you wanted to.

Attwell: Would you have gone further?

Biko: Who is that?

Attwell: You?

Biko: Not necessarily me, but I am saying anybody could have gone further if he wanted to. If the intention was to try and portray white society as bad, and use that to make everybody who was there angry, you could have produced a whole litany of evil if you cared to. This just shows the selflessness of the death in that someone in view of the mentality which he has got from a society, which has got no respect for black people, killed Shezi. It could have been prevented, that is all that this thing is saying.

Attwell: If I understand you correctly then, that to portray or to cause racial hostility, you consider that one of the possible ways to do so would be to list a whole lot of all the things that the whites do against you?

Biko: I said that if really the intention is to cause that kind of feeling, to come out to the fore amongst blacks, you can again use their concession of language, you have got to use very colourful language. Take a simple event, not describe it now in concrete terms, but play around the nastiness of the various aspects of the event, you can carry many across to the blacks and they can become angry. It is thus necessarily enough to make anybody angry in black society. This is really regarded as a description of the circumstances in which the man died. All right, we must blame that guy who pushed him, okay, we have got to, and we have got to explain that it is not as if he personally hated Shezi. He is portraying a mentality which he has borrowed from his society, but if one had to make society angry at that funeral, there would be a whole litany of things we can pick up, and we would describe them in precise language calculated to you know, bring out the emotion of the black man, would make people angry. It is not difficult to make people angry if you want to. Thus this was not the intention here. It was purely to describe the circumstances in which the man died. That is all.

Attwell: You say it is not difficult to make the black man angry?

Biko: If you want to, you have just got to draw up whatever you say in very beautiful floral language, concentrate on the detail, you can, assuredly.

Attwell: What more do you think the man who drew up this document should have done? If that had been his intention?

Biko: This is all fair comment on the factual evidence, at least on the factual situation of what happened at that funeral, I mean at that station, a fair comment.

Attwell: You consider this fair comment?

Biko: Completely fair comment.

16
"The Righteousness of our Strength"

If, as has been indicated in the introduction to chapter 13, the Black Consciousness Movement is implacably against the Afrikaner's "Divide and Rule" policy of the bantustans, what is its own vision for the future of South Africa? "One Azania, one Nation" is the BPC motto. Azania is the name adopted by blacks for South Africa, as Zimbabwe for Rhodesia, and Namibia for South West Africa. In these extracts from Steve's evidence at the Trial he spells out, in response to leading questions from Defence Counsel Advocate Soggot, what this means in terms of "one man one vote", the place of whites in an open society, the modifications in a shared society demanded by the insights of African culture and experience, and finally how to achieve the aim of one shared open society. Steve's advocacy of peaceful means was based on the Movement's realistic assessment of the power it was up against, and also on his own unquenchable optimism in the power of persuasion if your cause was just. At the moment at least in May 1976, he still believed that "this government is not necessarily set on a Hitlerised course". It is no comfort to us sadder, but not necessarily wiser men to know he was wrong. It should be added that Steve always recognised the relevance of a guerilla warfare strategy, but that this alone was not enough.

One interesting effect of Steve's evidence, and particularly of his courage under hostile cross-examination, has been told me by Mr Ben Khoapa. Steve gave his evidence and was cross-examined during the whole first week of May 1976. The proceedings were fully reported in the Rand Daily Mail. *Overnight Steve became the toast of the Soweto shebeens (pubs). Here at last was the authentic voice of the people, not afraid to say openly what all blacks think but are too frightened to say. For example, in answer to a question from Counsel for the Prosecution, "What do you think of Africans who work for the Security Police?" came straight and clear, "They are traitors", and this in a courtroom ringed by armed Security Police, black and white!*

Can the example of this one man's courage have inspired the boys and girls of Soweto to face death, as they so bravely did just six weeks later? This is not to suggest that Steve was "responsible" for the spontaneous uprising of 16 June; but perhaps the close association of these two events is not just an unrelated coincidence. Courage is infectious.

Soggot: Mr Biko, would you refer to Resolution 42 on page 249. In paragraph (2) there you have referred to the definition of black people which I will not trouble you with, but paragraph (3) I should like you to deal with. "SASO believes" – if you will read (a) please?

Biko: Yes. "SASO believes that (a) South Africa is a country in which both black and white live and shall continue to live together."

Soggot: Now what does that mean?

Biko: Well, this means that we accept the fact that the present South African society is a plural society with contributions having been made to its development by all segments of the community, in other words we speak of the groupings both black and white. We have no intention of – of course we regard ourselves as people who stay here and shall stay here. And we made the point that we've got no intention whatsoever of seeing white people leave this country; when I say leave, I mean leave this country.

Soggot: Leave?

Biko: Yes.

Soggot: L-e-a-v-e?

Biko: That is right. We intend to see them staying here side by side with us, maintaining a society in which everybody shall contribute proportionally.

Soggot: I wonder, in this context, would you please have a look at SASO G. 1, Resolution 45? On page 206.

Biko: Right?

Soggot: Would you read from: "This country belongs . . . ."?

Biko: "Therefore we wish explicitly to state that this country belongs to black people and to them alone." Whites who live in our – who live in this country on terms laid down by blacks and on condition that they respect the black people. This should not be construed as anti-whitism. It only means that in as much as black people live in Europe on terms laid down by Europeans, whites shall be subjected to the same conditions. "We further wish to state that in our opinion it shall always be . . . .".

Soggot: Can you explain what SASO meant by that resolution?

Biko: Well, I must explain I was not at this particular meeting but from reading this document, what I understand it to mean is that this country is essentially a country in Africa, a continent which is inhabited always naturally by black people, and that whites – it is conceived that whites are here and that they may live in the country, or they may leave the country, depending on their relationship with blacks, and their acceptance of whatever conditions blacks in this country shall lay at a certain time. I don't know what time the resolution is referring to.

Soggot: You yourself as you understand the position, on the accession to an open society, how will people be able to vote? What rights for example will the white man have to vote?

Biko: Well, we view the voting as strictly being on a one man, one vote, basis. That is the current theme in our talking.

Soggot: Was this the current thing at that time?

Biko: It was a current thing at the time, we took the policy manifesto, I am not aware that it has changed.

Soggot: Yes, then 3(b) please, that is on SASO A.1, page 249: Back to the second . . .

Biko: Oh, I see. "That the white man must be made aware that one is either part of the solution or part of the problem".

I think this statement is self-explanatory. In a situation where you have a hiving of privileges within society for the sole enjoyment or for the major enjoyment by one section of society, you do get a certain form of alienation of members who are on opposite sides of the line, and that the white man specifically has got to decide whether he is part of the problem – in other words whether he is part of the total white power structure that we regard as a problem – or he accedes and becomes part of the black man, that is the target of the problem. I think this is what that particular statement is saying.

Soggot: Then 3 (c)?

Biko: "3(c) That in this context because of the privileges accorded to them by legislation and because of their continual maintenance of an oppressive régime whites have defined themselves as part of the problem."

Again this I think speaks for itself. Generally speaking it is white society who votes at election time; it is them who return a government into power, be it Nationalists, the party, the United Party, the Progressive Party, and it is that government which maintains legal provision that creates problems for black people – problems of oppression, problems of poverty, problems of deprivation, and problems of self-alienation as I said earlier on. It is white society on the whole. Some may vote one way, some may vote another, but all of them belong to an electoral college if one may speak in those terms, of the whole society, which is jointly responsible for the government that does all these things, or that makes all these provisions applying to black people. And in this sense therefore they lose the natural right to speak as co-planners with us in our way of determining our future. This is what that resolution is saying. They define themselves in other words as the enemy.

Soggot: 3(d)?

Biko: "That therefore we believe that in all matters relating to the struggle towards realising our aspirations, whites must be excluded." – I think that speaks for itself.

Soggot: Once the struggle is over, what is the attitude of SASO?

Biko: The attitude is a simple one, an open society, one man, one vote, no reference to colour.

Soggot: And what do you mean by the phrase "the open society"?

Biko: We regard an open society as one which fulfils all the three points I have mentioned just now. Where there can be free participation, in the economic, social and all three of the societies by anybody, you know, equal opportunity and so on.

Soggot: Then 3(e), have you any comment on that?

Biko: "That this attitude must not be interpreted by blacks to imply anti-whitism, but merely a more positive way of attaining a normal situation in South Africa."

Now again this is a warning to the membership that it is not our intention to generate a feeling of anti-whitism amongst our members. We are merely forced by historic considerations to recognise the fact that we cannot plan side by side with people who participate in their exclusive pool of privileges, to make sure that both privileges are shared. We don't believe – we don't have faith in them anymore, that they are willing to share with us without any form of . . .

Soggot: What sort of whites were you thinking of at that stage?

Biko: When we spoke of . . .?

Soggot: Of this attitude to whites, and in the struggle and . . .?

Biko: Whites in general.

Soggot: What sort of whites had participated in the struggle with you as did the blacks?

Biko: Mainly the Liberals, mainly students, left-wingers if one may call it that, and to some extent the Progressives.

Soggot: Yes, now 3(f), Mr Biko?

Biko: "That in pursuit of this direction therefore, personal contact with whites, though it should not be legislated against, must be discouraged especially where it tends to militatè against ... [?] ... hold dear."

Now we did not intend making ourselves a policeman organisation over the formation of friendships between one individual and another. We did not intend discouraging any particular black student or a member of SASO at that time, from forming a friendly relationship with either his mother's employer or his father's employer or another fellow student or any white person within society, but we felt that where there was a possibility – and this was strictly within the political arena, of such a friendship militating against the beliefs that we hold dear, we must warn those who are involved.

Soggot: Now Mr Biko, I will return to this document in the context of dealing with some of the more overriding features of BPC as well. My Lord, with Your Lordship's permission, may I then leave this document for the moment. I think it might be more convenient to deal collectively with certain of the themes. It might save time.

Judge Boshoff: Just before you leave that document, now you say you people stand for one man, one vote?

Biko: Yes.

Judge Boshoff: Now is it a practical concept in the African set-up? Do you find it anywhere in Africa?

Biko: Yes, we find it, even within this country.

Judge Boshoff: Now apart from this country, I mean now let us take any other country in Africa. Do you have one man, one vote in any other country?

Biko: Yes.

Judge Boshoff: Which country?

Biko: Here in Botswana, . . . not to go far.

Judge Boshoff: Yes, those are under the influence of the South African background and traditions. Now take it away from the South African traditions?

Biko: Where to My Lord, for instance?

Judge Boshoff: Well, now anywhere outside South Africa?

Biko: You have it in Ghana. The one man . . .

Judge Boshoff: What parties are there in Ghana?

Biko: I would not know what parties are there now.

Judge Boshoff: Well, why do you say there is one man, one vote there?

Biko: There was at the time . . .

Judge Boshoff: Oh yes, that is so, there was. Didn't that disappear in Nkrumah's day already?

Biko: It didn't disappear, what has happened is that in Ghana now there is a military régime, but the concept of elections, be it for city council, be it for provincial council, or any of the governmental structures that they have, is on a basis of one man, one vote.

Judge Boshoff: Well, that may be the subordinate bodies, but now when it comes to the important vote, affecting the country, is there any country in Africa where you have one man, one vote?

Biko: Yes, My Lord, let us take the Kenya situation for instance, where there has been a natural dealing [?] of the opposition.

Judge Boshoff: But I thought that disappeared when Odinga Oginga (*sic*) was assassinated?

Biko: No, Oginga Odinga has not been assassinated, he is still alive.

Judge Boshoff: Tom Mboya?

Biko: Tom Mboya was with the governing party, and the governing party is still governing up until now.

Judge Boshoff: Yes, but then they found out that he had a certain adherence amongst the people and. . . .

Biko: I think My Lord, you are mistaking Tom Mboya with Kariuki. It was Kariuki who was murdered, and it was Kariuki who had generated amongst the people a certain thought, but Kariuki was also operating from inside the governing party. You see, in Kenya there is a very good demonstration of what a one-party state can achieve by way of differing thought within the party. Kariuki was the advocate on the one hand of the common man, the worker, the servant in Kenya, against this whole development in Kenya, of a bourgeoisie within the ruling party. You had Kenyatta on the other hand who felt constantly attacked by Kariuki. Okay, Kariuki was allowed to air his views in parliament, he was allowed to hold meetings throughout the length and breadth of the country, but still operating from within KANU, which is the ruling party. This is the essence of a one-party state. That there is no need to divide your men and let them lead other parties to . . .

Judge Boshoff: Yes, but Kariuki didn't survive all this?

Biko: Oh well, My Lord, several politicians don't survive, it seems like Verwoerd didn't survive. [*Laughter*]

Judge Boshoff: But now you see, it is not his own people who killed him, it is not his own party people who killed Verwoerd?

Biko: We don't know who killed Kariuki. It has not been established.

Judge Boshoff: Well, who did they accuse of having killed Kariuki?

Biko: Well, there are rumours there that it is probably Kenyatta, it is probably so and so, it has not been established, My Lord. But we know that in politics this sort of thing happens. Like I mean I could make an allegation here which would be preposterous. Amongst the black society there is a very strong belief that Mr Verwoerd's murder was generated from within the Nationalist Party and that a particular politician is named. This is the kind of belief which can sometimes go out and is believed by the outside world. The same thing applies to Kariuki.

Judge Boshoff: Yes, but now you have only been able to mention the one country, Kenya of '46.

Biko: Well, I happened to discuss that with two Kenya Quakers who visited this country recently; that is why I know, it came to me. I have also discussed Botswana with people from Botswana who visited this country. The point in issue is that there isn't much interchange of ideas between Africa and South Africa, because it is not so easy from Africa to visit South Africa and vice versa, as they have not been allowed to move around the country, so I cannot from our own experience and dialogue with people quote other instances in Africa.

Judge Boshoff: Well, are you prepared to say that there is one man, one vote in the other countries?

Biko: Yes, I am. I want to say quite frankly that the military in Africa tends to play a very important part in politics. The military in Africa tends to often decide to declare the election and the election is some kind of coup, okay, but then you get situations throughout the world where there is chaos. You get in Italy a government resigning virtually every two months. You can't help it.

Judge Boshoff: Yes, because there you have one man, one vote? You see, that is the trouble.

Biko: Now I think we share the belief of one man, one vote, with the government, because when they set up the bantustans they gave one man, one vote, to the Transkei, to Zululand, to Bophuthatswana and so on. They don't say to people only those who can . . . [?] . . . may vote. It is a one man, one vote. Suddenly they are mature enough to . . .

Judge Boshoff: I am interested in whether it is going to work, that is why I am asking you, do you think it is going to work?

Biko: It seems to be working, it seems to be working in the Transkei.

Judge Boshoff: Well, the Transkei is just starting. It has just started. But do you think it will work in the Transkei?

Biko: I think one man, one vote, could work. I doubt if the Transkei itself will work. [*Laughter*]

Judge Boshoff: Yes, but now why do you say that?

Biko: I think that . . .

Judge Boshoff: Why do you say one man, one vote will work, and that the Transkei won't work? I mean it is inconsistent ideas?

Biko: No, you may find that My Lord, if Matanzima decides to take the issue of the Transkei Independence to a referendum, there will be a beautiful vote, well-controlled vote, people voting earnestly without force, but they may reject the concept of an independent Transkei.

Judge Boshoff: They may reject it?

Biko: They may reject it, yes.

Judge Boshoff: Yes well, that is another matter, and you will say that is – will you blame one man, one vote for that?

Biko: I will blame – no, I will blame apartheid. I will say the Transkei has not worked, one man, one vote has worked.

Judge Boshoff: Democracy, doesn't it pre-suppose a developed community, democracy where you have one man, one vote?

Biko: Yes, it does, it does, and I think it is part of the process of developing the community. You cannot – My lord, people in voting, when allowing them to vote, I think you have got to give them the vote, I think you may devise [?] as the government in a way the means of ensuring a proper exercise of that vote, but certainly you give them the vote.

Judge Boshoff: Yes, but democracy is really only a success if the people who have the right to vote can intelligently and honestly apply a vote?

Biko: Yes, My Lord, this is why in Swaziland for instance where they have people sometimes who may not read the names of the candidates, they use signs.

Judge Boshoff: Yes, but do they know enough of the affairs of government to be able to influence it by a vote? I mean surely you must know what you are voting for, what you are voting about? Assuming now they vote on a particular policy, such as foreign investment, now what does a peasant know about foreign investment?

Biko: I think My Lord, in a government where democracy is allowed to work, one of the principles that are normally entrenched is a feedback system, a discussion in other words between those who formulate policy and those who must perceive, accept or reject policy. In other words there must be a system of education, political education, and this does not necessarily go with literacy. I mean Africa has always governed its peoples in the form of the various chiefs, Chaka and so on, who couldn't write.

Judge Boshoff. Yes, but the government is much more sophisticated and specialised now than in those days?

Biko: And there are ways of explaining it to the people. People can hear, they may not be able to read and write, but they can hear and they can understand, the issues when they are put to them. And I think this is happening in fact in . . .

Judge Boshoff: Well, take the Gold Standard, if we have to debate whether this government should go on the Gold Standard or go off the Gold Standard, will you feel that you know enough about it to be able to cast an intelligent vote about that?

Biko: Myself?

Judge Boshoff: Yes?

Biko: I think probably much better than the average Afrikaner in the street, My Lord.

Judge Boshoff: Yes well, that may be so, now do you think you know enough about it to be able to cast such an intelligent vote that the government should be based on that vote?

Biko: Yes, I think if – I have a right to be consulted by my government on any issue. If I don't understand it, I may give over to someone else that I have faith in to explain to me.

Judge Boshoff: Well, how can you? I mean that is your vote, and what about the ten other people who have votes?

Biko: The same applies to everybody else, and this is why we have the political process whereby things are explained. I mean the average man in Britain does not understand on his own accord the advantages or disadvantages of Britain becoming involved in the whole economic market, but when it becomes an issue for referendum, political organisers go out to explain and canvass their points of view, and the man in the middle listens to several people and decides to use what he has, the vote. But in the meantime he has got no particular equipment to understand these technicalities of the whole of society.

Judge Boshoff: But isn't that one of the reasons why Britain is probably one of the most bankrupt countries in the world?

Biko: I think I prefer to look at it more positively and say it is one country which is most democratic.

Judge Boshoff: Yes, but now it is bankrupt?

Biko: I think it is a phase, My Lord. Britain has been rich before, it may still get, you know, up on the ladder. I think it is a phase in history.

Judge Boshoff: Yes, but something went wrong somewhere along the line, and is it because of its different democracy probably?

Biko: I don't think so, I don't think so personally. I think it has been partly the whole decolonisation process which has robbed Britain of a very fixed life, of what they used to get before. Now they are forced back on their resources and they don't have much. It is a small country, smaller than Natal. What can you get? It has got 56 million people, no land to cultivate, very few factories unless by . . .

Judge Boshoff: Yes, but now capitalism really develops and wasn't Britain powerful and because she was powerful she developed, she became an empire and then that is how capitalism, it is like a snowball, it just grows and grows?

Biko: Yes.

Judge Boshoff: But she must have had good government at one stage?

Biko: I think she could have had good resources at one stage and she could have tightened the belt such that the distribution of wealth did not touch the lower man at some stage; like during the time of Adam Smith, even the time of the laissez-faire policy when you know, the few people who controlled industry in Britain went rampant throughout the country, manufacturing . . . [*inaudible*], making themselves rich, and of course the government got rich, but the people didn't get rich. The people got poorer, and this is why in Britain now more than in any other country . . . [*intervention*]

Judge Boshoff: They had a vote?

Biko: They had a vote then, and they have been gradually returning a more socialist government which is against exploitation of people. People are you know restoring the whole process, the wealth must come back to the people.

Judge Boshoff: But doesn't that all go to show that one man, one vote is not the "clear all"?

Biko: I think this is a debate which is going on in the world now, the debate between Democracy and Communism, between Capitalism and . . .
Judge Boshoff: Yes, they all have disadvantages?
Biko: Yes, they all have.

Steve led by Mr Soggot now expounds some of the modifications required in an open South African society to express black experience, black culture and black values.

Biko: I think what we need in our society is the power by us blacks to innovate, we have got the very system which – from which we can expand, from which we can innovate to say this is what we believe, accept or not accept, things that are thrown at us, and it is society that is a constant physical . . . *[witness speaks very indistinctly]* . . . you know, cultures affect each other, you know like fashions and you cannot escape rubbing against someone else's culture. But you must have the right to reject or not anything that is given to you. At the moment we exist sort of as a limb of the white culture. You know we form what we must call a subculture, precisely because of a situation that forces us to behave in a certain way. For instance if you look at the sub-culture of drinking at a shebeen, now this is very common in black society, you know; everybody drinks at a shebeen; I drink at a shebeen. Now it cannot be traced back *per se* to our tribal life because we didn't have shebeens in our tribal life. But it is a sub-culture aris-ing out of the fact that we don't have bars, we don't have hotels where we can drink, so what do we do? We are either a genius to invent a shebeen and to drink at the shebeen, and out of this a sub-culture de-velops you know, what I am trying to suggest here my Lord, is that . . . *[Court intervenes]*
Judge Boshoff: It is evolution, the shebeen fact just happens?
Biko: But the primary important thing is that you must have the right to reject or accept any new trend.
Soggot: The question I think which is of greater interest to us is on the first day of the open society, on the following day, is there going to be general destruction – any destruction or proscription of existing culture and cultural values?
Biko: I think a modification all round.
Soggot: Now what sort of modifications are envisaged?
Biko: I think again it would depend very much on the bargaining

processes and the result thereof. I think SASO in its documents, and certainly in the many speeches delivered by its members, all that they insist on is primarily a culture that accepts the humanity of the black man. A culture that is basically sufficiently accommodative of African concepts, to pass as an African culture. What we are saying now is that at the present moment we have a culture here which is a European culture. This country looks, My Lord, like a province of Europe. You know, to anybody who perceives the behaviour pattern it looks like a province of Europe. It has got no relationship rootwise to the fact that it happens to exist in Africa, and when Mnr* Pik Botha says at the United Nations *"We are Africans"*, he just doesn't know what he is talking about. We don't behave like Africans, we behave like Europeans who are staying in Africa. So we don't want to be just mere political Africans, we want to be people living in Africa. We want to be called complete Africans, we – social Africans – . . . [*inaudible*] . . . said I must understand Africa and what Africa is about. And we don't have to go far. We just have to live with the man here, the black man here, whose proportionate contribution in the joint culture is going to sufficiently change our joint culture to accommodate the African experience. Sure, it will have European experience, because we have whites here who are descended from Europe. We don't dispute that. But for God's sake it must have African experience as well.

Finally Steve spells out the means by which the Movement intends to achieve the aim of one shared and open society in South Africa.

Soggot: Now Mr Biko, still while we are dealing with overall themes, can we now get onto the question of the achievement of your freedom? I would like you to – I know this is short-circuiting your evidence, but I would like you in this context to deal with BPC as well. We will look at the BPC documents tomorrow.
Biko: Right.
Soggot: But I think they can usefully be dealt with in the same breath as the SASO documents. Would you have a look on the same page at paragraph 4(c)?
Biko: Yes.
Soggot: Would you read that please?
Biko: "SASO accepts the premise that before the black people

* "Mnr" is an abbreviation for "Meneer". The English equivalents are "Mr." and "Mister". Editor's note.

should join the open society they should first close their ranks to form themselves into a . . . [inaudible] . . . group, to oppose the definite racism that is meted out by the white society, to work out their direction clearly and bargain from a position of strength. SASO believes that a truly open society can only be achieved by blacks . . .".

Soggot: Yes, now I wonder if you would pause there. Now I think – without troubling you with actual documents, in BPC A.1 there is in a resolution the following phrase – it is on page 2, and that is – "A political movement be formed that shall consolidate" – paragraph 4 – "consolidate the different sections of black community with an aim towards forming a power bloc."

Have you got that, and you know what I am talking about? Paragraph 5, – "The primary objective the total liberation of all blacks."

Now would you indicate to His Lordship your conception, SASO's conception of the forming of – here it is referred to as "a solid group", and in BPC as a "power bloc". And how you visualise the generation of this so-called bloc as leading towards your liberation?

Biko: First of all I accept that in our analysis the cardinal point is the existence in our society of white racism which has been institutionalised, and also cushioned with a backing of the majority of whites. In other words a white child does not have to choose whether or not he wants to live with the white, he is born into it. He is brought up within white schools, institutions, and the whole process of racism somehow greets with him at various levels and he attempts to have an attitude against blacks, so whites are together around the privileges that they hold, and they monopolise this away from black society.

Soggot: Yes?

Biko: Now then comes the analysis. Can we in fact crack this cocoon, you know, to get whites away from the concept of racism, away from the concept of monopolising the privileges and the wealth of the country onto themselves without necessarily being together? Can you preach to them in other words as individuals? Now our belief is that white society will not in fact listen to preaching. They will not listen to their Liberals. The Liberal Party has not grown within white society, and certainly we as black people are unable to stand idle watching the situation.

Soggot: Yes?

Biko: Now we can only generate a response from white society when we as blacks speak with a definite voice and say what we want. The age of the Liberal was such that the black voice was not very much heard except in echoing what was said by Liberals. Now has come the time when we as blacks must articulate what we want, and put it across to the white man, and from a position of strength begin to say – "Gentlemen, this is what we want". "This is where you are, this is where we are, this is what we want." Now putting . . . [*inaudible*] . . . there is a specific moment at which bargaining you know will be entered into. In fact this is not true. All that BPC wants is to gain a majority of black support so that it can authentically sound a . . . [*inaudible*] . . . on behalf of the black people. You know, we must be able to say tomorrow that we don't want a Transkei as black South Africans, and know also that it is known by the white society that we are speaking for the majority of blacks in this country. Now the bargaining process again is not anything which will clear that particular point in history. It starts now when we take a resolution at a conference and we say we are going to communicate the contents of this resolution to the people concerned, whether it is a university, in the case of SASO, or whether it is a sporting body, a governing body in the case of BPC, all of this is bargaining. We are beginning to say this is what we are thinking.

Soggot: Yes?

Biko: Now at this given moment our strength is such that we have got to deal with issues that are very very low-key. Now as you develop strength you begin to pick up issue after issue and it is all over a course of time, and it is all not as clearcut as perhaps it might be suggested by this term here which says: "Form yourself into a solid bloc and then begin to bargain". It is not as clearcut as all that. This is a frivolity, this is a way of putting the process into one paragraph. The process in fact may take well over 20 years of dialogue between blacks and whites. We certainly don't envisage failure. We certainly don't have an alternative. We have analysed history. We believe that history moves in a particular logical direction, and in this particular instance the logical direction is that eventually any white society in this country is going to have to accommodate black thinking.

Soggot: Yes?

Biko: Now we believe that we are mere agents in that history. There are alternatives, on the one hand we have groups that are known in this country, who have opted for another way of operation, who have opted for violence. We know that ANC and PAC have done this in the past; they have taken this step. Now we don't believe it is the only alternative. We believe that there is a way of getting across to where we want to go, through peaceful means. And the very fact that we decided to actually form an above-board Movement implies that we accepted certain legal limitations to our operations. We accepted that we are going to take this particular course. We know that the road to that particular truth is fraught with danger. Some of us get banned, like I am. Others get arrested like these men who are here, but inevitably the process drives towards what we believe history also drives to, an attainment of a situation where whites first have to listen.

I don't believe that whites will be deaf all the time. We believe that this is, you know, a last ditch stand so to speak. There are signs right now of Mr Vorster going to Smith to face issues. Inevitably he must know in his own mind that at some stage I must speak to everybody. Okay, but for the moment it is only a plan dismissed. Even the whole idea of bantustans being given freedon, this is a way of accommodating political aspirations of the people which is an inevitable accommodation of what the blacks want eventually. But we reject this, what we want is a total accommodation of our interests in the total country, not in some portion of it. So we don't have a side programme, we don't have any alternative. We believe ultimately in the righteousness of our strength, that we are going to get to the eventual accommodation of out interests within the country.

Soggot: Your rejection of the bantustan solution, do you consider that it has any political significance? At this moment?

Biko: Yes, it has.

Soggot: Is BPC a strong organisation at the moment?

Biko: Well, I would not say it is strong; I mean I don't know what strength you are using; for instance, I would not compare it to the Nationalist Party. It certainly has a following. It probably has got much more following than it has got members in the country. But part of what you are trying to kill has not quite died, the whole concept of fear, and black people are steeped in fear. We want to get them away from this.

Soggot: Black people are steeped in fear?

Biko: In fear, yes; they are afraid of existing structures and reactions you know, from the System*, so that they may not come forth. You do get in fact within bantustans people coming from – coming to you to tell you that they agree with you, 'you guys, we know we must work for

* The South African security network. Editor's note.

our bread.' One man who advocates propaganda in Radio Bantu here at home every day, it is some sort of current affairs programme, he came to me one time and said – "You know, I don't believe in what I am saying, but I am paid to say it." And I quite believe him.

Soggot: Mr Biko, you say that your present rejection has a political meaning.

Biko: Yes.

Soggot: Would this have a greater or a lesser meaning if your organisation were taken as in fact representative of the black people?

Biko: It would have much greater meaning.

Soggot: Could you just tell us how you see that?

Biko: At present the – let us refer to the whole Transkeian institution. I believe that if BPC were an established organisation that is known to represent the majority interest of black people, and if BPC were to say – "we are not going to accept the kind of independence which is being given to the Transkei", there would be resulting action in the Transkei, in the form of people saying to their Matanzima, that we don't want this. But right now black people are operating under a veil of silence, and their operational uses are not known. And because BPC has not quite got to that position where it can be regarded by everybody, all and sundry, speaking for the majority of black people, even when they speak about the Transkei independence, it is not sufficient for the people to come and say they don't want this independence, because BPC hasn't developed this kind of complexion of speaking for the majority of black people.

Soggot: Now assuming that it had developed that, what effect do you visualise it would have on the government?

Biko: In . . . ?

Soggot: In the bargaining process?

Biko: I believe it would have a softening process. I believe that inevitably this government will listen to black opinion. In my view this government is not necessarily set on a Hitlerised course. I think it is buying time. From their interpretation of the situation at the moment, the situation is such that they can continue. Mr Vorster can postpone some problems and say – well, the Coloured issue will be solved by the next generation. Because he can see his way clear, even given the kind of timidity to which black people have been pushed; but I believe that as the voice which says "no" grows, he is going to listen, he is going to begin to accommodate the feelings of black people, and this is where the bargaining starts. You know, any issue that you win because of your "no" implies that you are being listened to by those in power.

Soggot: I think the suggestion which may be made is that you are building up a power bloc; you will then confront Mr Vorster and force on him the decision of war or peace?

Biko: Yes, I said to you we don't have an alternative. We believe that – in fact the whole process of bargaining is then damaged in our operation, we are not interested in armed struggle. We have stated clearly in our own documents that we are not interested either in confrontation methods, by that meaning demonstrations which lead to definite breaking of existing laws, such that there is reaction from the System, what you call the System.

Soggot: Yes?

Biko: Now our operation is basically that of bargaining and there is no alternative to it. It is based as I say mainly on the fact that we believe we have interpreted history correctly, that the white man anyway is going to eventually accept the inevitable.

Soggot: My Lord, I think that I would not start on the theme of the BPC. Perhaps your Lordship might find this a convenient stage . . .

Judge Boshoff: I just want to ask him one question and then we can take the adjournment. I think what Mr Soggot is trying to say to you is this; assuming now that one doesn't find any fault with your aims and politics as such, but can it not be said that you are trying to achieve your end in such a way that you are building up a hostile power bloc, which is sort of oriented for action, and if you don't get your – if you are not satisfied when it comes to, well, bargaining, that your power bloc will then react and then you will have no control over the power bloc?

Biko: My Lord, I don't . . .

Judge Boshoff: Perhaps I should put it in a different way. When I say that you are preparing it in such a way it means I am trying to convey that the means that you adopt in order to build up the power bloc and to conscientise people, has the effect, of antagonising the black people, and eventually you have a situation where you will not be able to control this bloc if they don't get their claims met by the white group?

Biko: If I contest the first point, My Lord, I don't think the means [that] are used for conscientisation have that effect at all – of making – of antagonising black people, or of creating antagonism within black people. On the contrary, what I would say is that our methods do in fact give hope. I think it must be taken in the context of a situation where black people don't have any hope, don't see any way ahead, they are just defeated persons, they live with their misery and they drink a hell of a lot because of the kind of misery. . . .

Judge Boshoff: Well, that is why I say. . . .

Biko: Now when you speak to them, conscientising them, what you are in fact doing is to rekindle their hope.

Judge Boshoff: Yes, but the objection is not against conscientisation as such, it is the manner of conscientisation pointing out to them what enemies they have in the white people?

Biko: Again as I said earlier on, this is just a common starting point. You are speaking about what that man knows; you are moving from there to talk about ways you go from here. You are giving him some kind of home within a group called the Black People's Convention; if you are in trouble go to the Black People's Convention . . . [*indistinct*] . . . You are saying this is what BPC is all about. You stand squarely on the side of the black man, we understand the problems to be these. And they know the problem. No matter what you say to them they know the problem. As I say they can express their problem stronger than you can but now you move from there to create some kind of hope, some kind of opportunity, and in fact I think you are giving them some kind of psychotherapy to move away from being a defeated society to being a hopeful society; and you are not dealing out some kind of juggernaut that is going to get out of hand. When you are speaking of black solidarity all you are talking about really is just that feeling that you are speaking for the majority of blacks. You are not going to have every individual placed in a room and taught point 1 to 20 which he can decide . . . No, he is just going to believe that BPC speaks for me, BPC is my Movement, right, and now my leaders are bargaining and this is what they are saying, you know, and when we consult him he . . . says we want this or we don't want this. This is all. In a sense, in the same way that one is a member of the Nationalist Party. There is nothing sinister in it. You are just a member, you just support the party that to you gives you the best hope in a given society. This is what black solidarity is all about.

17

American Policy towards Azania

This is a memorandum for U.S. Senator Dick Clark.* It was prepared hurriedly, as Steve had been released from 101 days in detention under Section 6 of the Terrorism Act less than a week before his meeting with Clark.

When one considers that an important element in sec. 6 detention is the total isolation of the detainee in solitary confinement, with access to no books except the Bible, still less to newspapers or radio, the coolness and lucidity of this memorandum becomes the more remarkable.

The reader will not fail to notice that, in the second of Steve's "minimum requirements", he comes as close as he legally can to calling for "trade boycotts, arms embargo, withdrawal of investments etc." from Mr Carter. This was and is by no means an irresponsible statement by a powerless black who is unaware of the hardships such a policy will bring on his fellow blacks. Steve and his comrades in the Black Consciousness movement are fully aware that the black suffering will increase if America and her allies implement that policy. Their argument, however, is that the people cannot suffer more materially than they are already suffering psychologically (and, in the majority of cases, materially as well); that the white electorate can still be reached through such a non-violent weapon as a trade boycott; and that this is for them an acceptable alternative to the escalating guerilla conflict, which the whites cannot win, but which can only lead to a more protracted state of suffering and bloodshed for blacks, with its legacies of hatred and bitterness.

Thus Steve, speaking this time with mature and conscious authority as leader of the real opposition to the Nationalists in Pretoria, makes his penultimate plea to those who alone can bring about a relatively non-violent end to the tyranny of apartheid. His final word would be his death itself. A year later it appears that still the West has not heard.

---

* Chairman of the Senate Sub-Committee for Africa. Senator Clark was in Lesotho for a Conference at the African-American Institute. Editor's note.

MEMORANDUM
To: SEN. DICK CLARK
From: B. S. BIKO
On: AMERICAN POLICY TOWARDS AZANIA (SOUTH AFRICA)

May I start off by saying how grateful I am that you have decided to grant me this opportunity to see you? By way of clarification I should point out that I am not speaking only on my behalf but also on that of many followers of the Black Consciousness movement in and out of jail.

It has become pretty obvious to us that these are crucial years in the history of Azania. The winds of liberation which have been sweeping down the face of Africa have reached our very borders. There is no more doubt about the inevitability of change – the only questions now remaining are *how* and *when.*

At this stage of the liberation process we have become very sensitive to the role played by the World's big powers in affecting the direction of that process. In a sense America – your country has played a shameful role in her relations with our country.

Given the clear analysis of our problems, the choice is very simple for America in shaping her policy towards present day South Africa. The interests of black and white politically have been made diametrically opposed to each other. America's choice is narrowed down to either entrenching the existing minority white regime or alternatively assisting in a very definite way, the attainment of the aspirations of millions of the black population as well as those of whites of good will.

We are looking forward to a non-racial, just and egalitarian society in which colour, creed and race shall form no point of reference. We have deliberately chosen to operate openly because we have believed for a very long time that through process of organised bargaining we can penetrate even the deafest of white ears and get the message to register that no lie can live forever.

In doing this we rely not only on our own strength but also on the belief that the rest of the world views the opression and blatant exploitation of the black majority by a minority as an unforgiveable sin that cannot be pardoned by civilised societies.

While many words and statements to this effect have been made by politicians in America, very little by way of constructive action has been taken to apply concerted pressure on minority white South African regime. Besides the sin of omission, America has often been positively guilty of working in the interest of the minority regime to the detriment of the interests of black people. America's foreign policy seems to have been guided by a selfish desire to maintain an imperialistic stranglehold on this country irrespective of how the blacks were made to suffer.

The new American administration must however take to account that no situation remains static for ever. Through their political intransigence and racial bigotry, the South African white minority regime has increased the level of resentment amongst blacks to a point where it now seems that the people are prepared to use any means to attain their aspirations.

Equally obvious is the fact that alliances will be sought where they can be meaningfully obtained from. Whereas this was merely a threat a few years ago, it has now become imminent because of the fast changing situation in Southern Africa.

All this underlines the importance of the role America can play in shaping the future of the things to come. Because of her bad record America is a poor second to Russia when it comes to choice of an ally in spite of black opposition to any form of domination by a foreign power. Heavy investments in the South African economy, bilateral trade with South Africa, cultural exchanges in the fields of sport and music and of late joint political ventures like the Vorster–Kissinger exercise are amongst the sins with which America is accused. All these activities relate to whites and their interests and serve to entrench the position of the minority regime.

America must therefore re-examine her policy towards South Africa drastically. The last minute Kissinger-type conferences will not work because a mediator needs to have clean hands.

A few minimum requirements can perhaps be outlined at this stage:

- Mr Carter should reverse the policy whereby America looks to the South African government as a partner in diplomatic initiatives in Africa
- Mr Carter should immediately develop a new approach to in-volvement by America in the South African economy – whether in so-called bantustans or in metropolitan "white" South Africa.

Whilst it is illegal for us to call for trade boycotts, arms embargo, withdrawal of investments etc., America herself is quite free to decide what price South Africa must pay for maintaining obnoxious policies.

– Where American firms do not on their own withdraw, the least that can be expected is for their government to set rigid rules on questions like remuneration, rate for the job, job reservation, trade unions etc. to completely make sure that America is not involved in the exploitation of South African blacks.

– America should cease showing any form of tolerance to bantustan leaders who are operating as a model and platform obviously designed for the perpetual subjugation of black people. Invitations to people like Gatsha Buthelezi, Matanzima, Mangope and granting of any form of official or semi-official recognition to them is gross insult to the black people of this country.

– America must insist on South Africa recognising the need for legitimate non-government-initiated platforms like the Black People's Convention. Equally organisations banned in the past like the African National Congress should be re-allowed to operate in the country.

– America must call for the release of political prisoners and banned people like Nelson Mandela, Robert Sobukwe, Steve Biko, Govan Mbeki, Walter Sisulu, Barney Pityana and the integration of these people in the political process that shall shape things to come.

– American official visitors to this country should insist on seeing authentic black leadership as represented by the people mentioned above and refuse to be involved in the kind of one-sided political circus that Kissinger seemed to have accepted.

– Mr Carter must move fast on the Namibian question. SWAPO is recognised by us black people as an indispensable organisation in the formulation of any independence plans for Namibia.

The direction in which allegiances will go will obviously be affected by the role played by the various world powers. If America goes for a full-scale support of the struggle for the black man's liberation then she stands a chance of influencing political trends and being regarded as a genuine friend. Otherwise so far her role has been seen as that of bolstering the minority regime all at the expense of the black man.

Mr Carter will therefore no doubt be aware that he takes up power at a time when American influence in Africa has become of particular significance. If he stands on the sides of those whose righteousness may not be doubted – he shall have used the tremendous influence that America has legitimately and usefully. If on the other hand he assists those who are trying to keep the clock still, then America will have irreparably tarnished her name in the eyes of black people in this country.

STEVE BIKO
1/12/76

18
Our Strategy for Liberation

*In this important interview Steve sums up the core thinking of the Black
Consciousness Movement. The BCM philosophy states that the white
man in South Africa has carefully constructed a political system which
ensures continued white domination by the use of psychological
pressure and physical violence against the black majority. Thus BCM
leaders such as Steve realised that even the opposition process within
the white system was designed to frustrate black aspirations.*

*White psychological and physical violence meant that by the late
1960s black opposition was in disarray with those who organised either
in exile or prison and white-induced fear so pervasive that many
aspirant middle-class blacks began to look to white-created institutions
such as "homelands" and "universities" as a solution to their desire for
comfort.*

*But the BCM rejected the idea of white societal standards as the
norm. They rejected black fear of white power. The BCM calls for
black unity in the face of which white domination must crumble and fall.
Steve never publically pronounced himself or the BCM as being in
favour of "violent change" but this must be looked at in the context
within which he was forced to speak. He accepted that white
domination was maintained by violence and accepted that a degree of
black violence would be needed to counter white violence. He believed
that, however violent white South Africa was prepared to be, this would
be most easily overcome or averted by solid black unity in a struggle
which would be mainly political rather than mainly military.*

OUR STRATEGY FOR LIBERATION
Stephen Biko: A number of our organisations are operating at different levels. The history of it starts off after 1963–4. If you remember,
there were many arrests in this country which stemmed from under-
ground activities by PAC (Pan Africanist Congress) and ANC (African National Congress); this led to some kind of political
emasculation of the black population especially, with the result that

there was no participation by blacks in the articulation of their own aspirations. The whole opposition to what the government was doing to blacks came in fact from white organisations, mainly student groups like NUSAS (National Union of South African Students), the Liberal Party, the Progressive Party. Blacks who were articulating any sense were far fewer by comparison to the olden days, and they were dispersed amongst these particular organisations.

When I came to varsity [Durban University], which was some time in 1966, in my own analysis and that of my friends there was some kind of anomaly in this situation, where whites were in fact the main participants in our oppression and at the same time the main participants in the opposition to that oppression. It implied therefore that at no stage in this country were blacks throwing in their lot in the shift of political opinion. The arena was totally controlled by whites in what we called "totality" of white power at that time.

So we argued that any changes which are to come can only come as a result of a programme worked out by black people – and for black people to be able to work out a programme they needed to defeat the one main element in politics which was working against them: a psychological feeling of inferiority which was deliberately cultivated by the system. So equally, too, the whites in order to be able to listen to blacks needed to defeat the one problem which they had, which was one of "superiority".

Now the only way to bring about this of course was to look anew at the black man in terms of what it is in him that is lending him to denigration so easily. First of all, we said as black students we could not participate in multi-racial organisations which were by far white organisations because of the overwhelming number of white students at universities in this country.

Second, these organisations were concentrating mainly on problems which were affecting the white student community.

Third, of course, when it came to political questions they were far more articulate than the average black student because of their superior training and because of their numbers – they could outvote us on any one issue. Which meant that NUSAS as an organisation gave political opinions which were largely affected by the whiteness of that particular organisation.

So in 1968 we started forming what is now called SASO – the South African Students Organisation – which was firmly based on

Black Consciousness, the essence of which was for the black man to elevate his own position by positively looking at those value systems that make him distinctively a man in society.
Like what?
First of all, we were of the view that this particular country is almost like an island of Europe in Africa. If you go through the whole of Africa you do find aspects of African life which are culturally elevated throughout the continent. But in this country – somehow any visitor who comes here tends to be made to believe almost that he is in Europe. He never sees blacks except in a subservient role. This is all because of the cultural dominance of the particular group which is now in power.

DIMINISHING FEAR
To what extent have you been successful?
We have been successful to the extent that we have diminished the element of fear in the minds of black people. In the period '63–'66 black people were terribly scared of involvement in politics. The universities were putting out no useful leadership to the black people because everybody found it more comfortable to lose himself in a particular profession, to make money. But since those days, black students have seen their role as being primarily to prepare themselves for leadership roles in the various facets of the black community. Through our political articulation of the aspirations of black people, many black people have come to appreciate the need to stand up and be counted against the system. There is far more political talk now, far more political debate and far more condemnation of the system from average black people than there has ever been since possibly 1960 and before.

I'm referring here to the whole oppressive education system that the students are talking about. After complaining about it, the government wants to further entrench what the students are protesting about by bringing in police and saracens [armoured cars] and dogs – almost soldiers, so to speak.

Now the response of the students then was in terms of their pride. They were not prepared to be calmed down even at the point of a gun. And hence, what happened, happened. Some people were killed. These riots just continued and continued. Because at no stage were the young students – nor for that matter at some stage their parents – prepared to be scared. Everybody saw this as a deliberate act of op-

pressive measures to try and calm down the black masses, and everybody was determined equally to say to the police, to say to the government: we shall not be scared by your police, by your dogs and by your soldiers. Now this is the kind of lack of fear one is talking about which I see is a very important determinant in political action.
Since last June something like 400 young blacks were killed.
499 actually.
Do you think this will not be a deterrent?
No. I think it has been a very useful weapon in merging the young and old. Before then there was a difference in the outlooks of the old generation and the younger generation. The younger generation was moving too fast for the old generation. The old generation was torn between bantustan politics on the one side – old allegiances which were not progressive alliances, to groups like ANC, PAC, without any result in action – and there were those simply too scared to move.
Do you condemn bantustan leadership?
Yes, of course. We condemn bantustan leaders, even the best of them like Gatsha Buthelezi.
Just say a few words on that.
Our attitude here is that you cannot in pursuing the aspirations of black people achieve them from a platform which is meant for the oppression of black people. We see all these so-called bantustan platforms as being deliberate creations by the Nationalist government to contain the political aspirations of the black people and to give them pseudo-political platforms to direct their attention to.

Now men like Gatsha Buthelezi, Matanzima, Mangope and so on are all participants in the white man's game of holding the aspirations of the black people. We do not feel it is possible in any way to turn such a platform to useful work. We believe the first principal step by any black political leader is to destroy such a platform. Destroy it without giving it any form of respectability. Once you step in it, once you participate in it, whether you are in the governing party or the opposition, you are in fact giving sanctity to it, you are giving respectability to it.

So in a sense people like Buthelezi, like Matanzima, like Mangope, are participants in a white man's game and they are participants at the expense of the black man. They are leading black people to a divided struggle – to speak as Zulus, to speak as Xhosas, to speak as Pedis – which is a completely new feature in the political life of black people in this country. We speak as one combined whole, directing ourselves to a common enemy, and we reject anyone who wishes to destroy that unity.

We are of the view that we should operate as one united whole toward attainment of an egalitarian society for the whole of Azania. Therefore entrenchment of tribalistic, racialistic or any form of sectional outlook is abhorred by us. We hate it and we seek to destroy it. It is for this reason therefore that we cannot see any form of coalition with any of the bantustan leaders, even the so-called best of them like Gatsha Buthelezi, because they destroy themselves by virtue of the kind of arguments that one has put up.

THE RED MENACE

The government of course has said that all this unrest really is due to communist agitation. Are you a communist?

We are by no means communist. Neither do I believe for a moment that the unrest is due to communist agitation. I do know for a fact that there has been participation, it would appear anyway from signs, by a lot of people in the unrest. But the primary reason behind the unrest is simple lack of patience by the young folk with a government which is refusing to change, refusing the change in the educational sphere, which is where they [the students] are directing themselves, and also refusing to change in a broader political situation.

Now when these youngsters started with their protests they were talking about [exclusive use of] Afrikaans [in black schools], they were talking about Bantu education, and they meant that. But the government responded in a high-handed fashion, assuming as they always have done that they were in a situation of total power. But here for once they met a student group which was not prepared to be thrown around all the time. They decided to flex their muscles, and of course, the whole country responded. . . .

There are lessons to be gleaned from this whole unrest situation of last year. In the first instance, I think blacks have flexed their muscles a bit – and they now know the degree of dedication they can find among their own members when they are called to action. And they now know the kind of responses they will get from the various segments of the population – the youth, the older ones and so on.

The second lesson is of course the response from the government and the white population at large. The government responded in one way, and the white population also in another way. One doesn't want to get into details here but reading these newspapers you get some kind of idea of the extent of fear that was prevalent in white society at a particular time, especially just after the first onslaught in Soweto, where there was a real fear throughout the community, throughout the country. Nobody knew just where something would happen next.

So how will these lessons express themselves in the future?

I am of the view that any recurrence of disturbance of that nature can only result in more careful planning and better calculation, thereby achieving the desired results to a greater extent than this spontaneous situation we had last year, for instance.

Do you believe that by these means you will bring about a real change of this society?

I see this as only one form of expression of discontent inside. I am of the view that the whole change process is going to be a protracted one in this country. It depends entirely on the degree to which the Nationalist government is prepared to hold on to power. My own analysis is that they are wanting to hold on to power and fight with their backs to the wall.

Now, conflict could only be avoidable if they were prepared to avoid it. Those who are at the seeking end, that is those who want justice, who want an egalitarian society, can only pursue their aspirations according to the resistance offered by the opposition. If the opposition is prepared to fight with their backs to the wall, conflict can't be avoidable.

Now we as BPC – I am a member of the Black Consciousness movement, I was a member of BPC before I was banned, and now I've been, I'm told, appointed honorary president of BPC – now the line BPC adopts is to explore as much as possible non-violent means within the country, and that is why we exist.

But there are people – and there are many people – who have despaired of the efficacy of non-violence as a method. They are of the view that the present Nationalist Government can only be unseated by people operating a military wing.

I don't know if this is the final answer. I think in the end there is going to be a totality of the effect of a number of change agencies in operating in South Africa. I personally would like to see fewer groups. I would like to see groups like ANC, PAC and the Black Consciousness movement deciding to form one liberation group. It is only, I think, when black people are so dedicated and so united in their cause that we can effect the greatest results. And whether this is going to be through the form of conflict or not will be dictated by the future. I don't believe for a moment that we are going to willingly drop our belief in the non-violent stance – as of now. But I can't predict what will happen in the future, inasmuch as I can't predict what the enemy is going to do in the future.

NO TIMETABLE
Can you guess at all at the number of years the change might take?
That is a very difficult exercise. I don't want to get involved in that kind of exercise. Some people say five years, others say ten years. I think that we are not at the stage yet where it is possible to fix a precise timetable.
You speak of an egalitarian society. Do you mean a socialist one?
Yes, I think there is no running away from the fact that now in South Africa there is such an ill distribution of wealth that any form of political freedom which does not touch on the proper distribution of wealth will be meaningless. The whites have locked up within a small minority of themselves the greater proportion of the country's wealth. If we have a mere change of face of those in governing positions what is likely to happen is that black people will continue to be poor, and you will see a few blacks filtering through into the so-called bourgeoisie. Our society will be run almost as of yesterday. So for meaningful change to appear there needs to be an attempt at reorganising the whole economic pattern and economic policies within this particular country.

BPC believes in a judicious blending of private enterprise which is highly diminished and state participation in industry and commerce, especially in industries like mining – gold, diamonds, asbestos and so on – like forestry, and of course complete ownership of land. Now in that kind of judicious blending of the two systems we hope to arrive at a more equitable distribution of wealth.
Do you see a country in which black and white can live amicably on equal terms together?
That is correct. We see a completely non-racial society. We don't believe, for instance, in the so-called guarantees for minority rights, because guaranteeing minority rights implies the recognition of portions of the community on a race basis. We believe that in our country there shall be no minority, there shall be no majority, just the people. And those people will have the same status before the law and they will have the same political rights before the law. So in a

sense it will be a completely non-racial egalitarian society. *But will the vast number of blacks after all their experiences be able to live their life without giving vent to feelings of revenge, of. . . .*

We believe it is the duty of the vanguard political movement which brings change to educate people's outlook. In the same way that blacks have never lived in a socialist economic system they've got to learn to live in one. And in the same way that they've always lived in a racially divided society, they've got to learn to live in a non-racial society. They've got many things to learn.

All these must be brought to them and explained to the people by the vanguard movement which is leading the revolution. So that I've got no doubt in my mind that people – and I know people in terms of my own background, where I stay – are not necessarily revengeful, nor are they sadistic in outlook. The black man has got no ill intentions for the white man. The black man is only incensed at the white man to the extent that he wants to entrench himself in a position of power to exploit the black man. But beyond that, nothing more.

We don't need any artificial majorities, any artificial laws to entrench ourselves in power because we believe once we come into power our sheer numbers will maintain us there. We do not have the same fear that the minority white government has been having all along, which has led to his many laws designed to keep him there.

FREE FRANCHISE
As you know the main argument of the government is always that the black man just isn't on a civilisation level at present to pull his full weight politically. Do you think of a one-man, one-vote franchise?

Yes, we do think so. Entirely. Entirely one-man, one-vote, no qualification whatsoever except the normal ones you find throughout the world.

Don't you think that the black man in fact is perfectly well able. . . .

The black man is well able – and the white man knows it. The irony of that kind of situation is that when the white government negotiates so-called independence for the so-called Transkei, they don't speak in terms of a qualified franchise. In the Transkei, every Transkeian votes. You get white nationalist politicians arguing that this is a system that is going to work for the Transkei. But somehow, when it comes to the broader country, the blacks may not vote because they do not understand the sophisticated economic patterns out here. They understand nothing. They need to operate at a different level. Now this is all nonsense. It is meant to entrench the white man in the position in which he finds himself today. We will do away with it altogether. There will be a completely non-racial franchise. Black and white will vote as individuals in our society.

This is all fascinating. As an outsider, as a visitor, I can only say that my feeling is that this is bound to be a very long and probably very bloody road.

There is that possibility. There is that possibility. But as I said earlier on, it will be dictated purely by the response of the Nationalist party. If they have been able to see that in Rhodesia Smith must negotiate with the leaders of the black people of Rhodesia. . . .

I think conflict is unavoidable given the predictable response from the present system. And this conflict can be pretty generalised and extensive and protracted. My worst fears are that working on the present analysis, conflict can only be on a generalised basis between black and white.

We don't have sufficient groups who can form coalitions with blacks – that is groups of whites – at the present moment. The more such groups which come up, the better to minimise that conflict.

Mr Biko, thank you.

19
On Death

These words, extracted from an interview with an American businessman given some months before Steve's final detention and death, but not printed in The New Republic *until 7 January 1978, need no further comment.*

You are either alive and proud or you are dead, and when you are dead, you can't care anyway. And your method of death can itself be a politicizing thing. So you die in the riots. For a hell of a lot of them, in fact, there's really nothing to lose – almost literally, given the kind of situations that they come from. So if you can overcome the personal fear for death, which is a highly irrational thing, you know, then you're on the way.

And in interrogation the same sort of thing applies. I was talking to this policeman, and I told him, "If you want us to make any progress, the best thing is for us to talk. Don't try any form of rough stuff, because it just won't work." And this is absolutely true also. For I just couldn't see what they could do to me which would make me all of a sudden soften to them. If they talk to me, well I'm bound to be affected by them as human beings. But the moment they adopt rough stuff, they are imprinting in my mind that they are police. And I only understand one form of dealing with police, and that's to be as unhelpful as possible. So I button up. And I told them this: "It's up to you." We had a boxing match the first day I was arrested. Some guy tried to clout me with a club. I went into him like a bull. I think he was under instructions to take it so far and no further, and using open hands so that he doesn't leave any marks on the face. And of course he said exactly what you were saying just now: "I will kill you." He meant to intimidate. And my answer was: "How long is it going to take you?" Now of course they were observing my reaction. And they could see that I was completely unbothered. If they beat me up, it's to my advantage. I can use it. They just killed somebody in jail – a friend of mine – about ten days before I was arrested. Now it would have been bloody useful evidence for them to assault me. At least it would indicate what kind of possibilities were there, leading to this guy's death. So, I wanted them to go ahead and do what they could do, so that I could use it. I wasn't really afraid that their violence might lead me to make revelations I didn't want to make, because I had nothing to reveal on this particular issue. I was operating from a very good position, and they were in a very weak position. My attitude is, I'm not going to allow them to carry out their program faithfully. If they want to beat me five times, they can only do so on condition that I allow them to beat me five times. If I react sharply, equally and oppositely, to the first clap, they are not going to be able to systematically count the next four claps, you see. It's a fight. So if they had meant to give me so much of a beating, and not more, my idea is to make them go beyond what they wanted to give me and to give back as much as I can give so that it becomes an uncontrollable thing. You see the one problem this guy had with me: he couldn't really fight with me because it meant he must hit back, like a man. But he was given instructions, you see, on how to hit, and now these instructions were no longer applying because it was a fight. So he had to withdraw and get more instructions. So I said to them, "Listen, if you guys want to do this your way, you have got to handcuff me and bind my feet together, so that I can't respond. If you allow me to respond, I'm certainly going to respond. And I'm afraid you may have to kill me in the process even if it's not your intention".

Martyr of Hope:
A PERSONAL MEMOIR
by Aelred Stubbs C.R.

ONE

I first met the Biko family in the person of Kaya, Stephen's elder brother. In May 1963, with more than 40 of his comrades, Kaya was expelled from Lovedale Institution, Alice, and then arrested and charged with membership of an unlawful organisation, POQO, the militant wing of the banned Pan Africanist Congress (PAC). Four months earlier our Community had moved St Peter's Theological College from Rosettenville, Johannesburg, to Alice, Cape Province, to form the Anglican constituent college in the ecumenical Federal Theological Seminary of Southern Africa.

When these boys were arrested the priest-guardian of one of them telephoned us from the Transkei and asked us to engage legal defence for this boy and to try to secure bail for him. The member of the Community who located him in the Fort Beaufort prison, where all the boys were being held, subsequently discovered another five boys of Anglican families, of whom Kaya was one.

As the Biko family lived in Kingwilliamstown, only 37 miles from Alice, it fell to me to visit Kaya's mother and ask if she wanted us to arrange legal defence for him. At that time Mrs Biko was still working at the Grey Hospital, in unpleasant conditions and for miserable pay. Stephen's existence was still unknown to me.

Some features of the trial, which took place in Alice at the beginning of August, are worth recording here, both as an example of South African justice and for the formative influence these events had on my education in the "South African way of life". On the eve of the trial the attorney chosen by the majority of the boys, Mr L. L.

Mtshizana, was detained under the '90-day Law' by the Security Branch. During the trial Sgt Hattingh, at that time head of the Security Branch in Alice, kept the boys who had turned State evidence in a place where they could hear what was being said by each one as he gave evidence, until this was pointed out to the Magistrate. The Court was ringed by armed police. One felt "this is war". The Magistrate bullied the witnesses called by the Defence in a manner which evoked strong condemnation by the Judges in the Supreme Court when the case went on appeal. All but three of the boys were convicted. Having come to know the family reasonably well I gave evidence in mitigation for Kaya, pleading that in view of his age, previous lack of convictions, and the poverty of the family he be given a suspended sentence or strokes rather than be sent to gaol. He was given two years, 15 months of which were conditionally suspended. He was released from Fort Glamorgan Prison, East London, on 12 May 1964. After the trial another member of the Community and myself received threatening anonymous letters and telephone calls.

I continued to visit Mrs Biko both before and after Kaya's release, and occasionally her brother would visit me at Alice; but I had still not met Stephen. Then either in 1964 or 1965 one day I received a very long letter from him. After introducing himself as Kaya's brother he launched into a long series of questions about the Christian faith. The school where he was in Natal was run by Roman Catholic monks and nuns, and Stephen found a good number of their teachings either unintelligible or unacceptable. I answered his questions as best I could, invited him to visit us at Alice during his next holidays, and remember thinking that the letter showed an unusual facility of expression, as well as a sharp and enquiring mind. I cannot now remember if he took up my invitation. The acquaintance did not blossom; but the Biko family remained in my prayers because of my admiration for his mother, struggling to give her four children a better education than she could afford, and becoming prematurely aged in the process. For their part the family, Stephen included (as I only learned ten years later), now regarded me as a father in Christ, to whom they could turn in time of need.

TWO

The years 1963–67 were years of demoralisation for the African people generally in South Africa and for the students especially. The savage repression launched after Sharpeville in March 1960 continued. There were no above ground political organisations. At the University College of Fort Hare for example, next door to our Seminary at Alice, the remaining ANC and PAC elements were winkled out by the Security Branch who had the entrée to the College and access to the students' files. Militant resistance to the hated Bantu Education system was succeeded by an apparent apathy and students' resentments and frustrations were expressed by some in heavy drinking and sexual promiscuity. It seemed that at Fort Hare, once the intellectual heart of black South Africa, the authorities had won, if only in bludgeoning the students into a defeated acquiescence with the system.

During those years the multi-racial Liberal Party was on the defensive: it ultimately dissolved itself in 1968 rather than obey legislation which made a multi-racial political party illegal. Thus NUSAS (the National Union of South African Students founded more than 50 years ago by a great Afrikaner, the late Leo Marquard) was left as the only nation-wide expression of the liberal tradition. It was banned on the Fort Hare campus, but at the Seminary it flourished – a situation which did not sweeten relations between the two neighbouring institutions, at least at official level. At considerable risk to themselves committed students at Fort Hare and other non-white campuses retained their links with NUSAS.

Stephen seems to have attended a NUSAS Conference while still at Mariannhill. After matriculating, he entered the medical school at Wentworth, Durban (UNNE – University of Natal Non-European, as it was then called), at the beginning of 1966 and immediately joined NUSAS, and became active and indeed prominent in that organisation during the period 1965–7.

THREE

1968, as you will remember, was 'the year of the students'. In South Africa as far as NUSAS was concerned it was the beginning of the end of the organisation as a union genuinely national and multi-racial. But for the non-white campuses, as they were still called even then, it was a year of miraculous renaissance.

Nowhere was this more dramatically expressed than at Fort Hare. A new Rector was appointed, J.J. de Wet, whose academic field was Statistics. Although there was no Students' Representative Council, and therefore no recognised student leadership, the students demanded to see the new Rector in an attempt to persuade him to treat them as responsible human beings, not as a lower form of human life. Yielding to the negative advice of a senior African Professor, a notorious "sell-out", the Rector refused. There ensued a well-disciplined and entirely non-violent strike, in which nearly 500 out of a total of about 550 students took part. Beginning at the end of the third term it was resumed after the short break, and was only broken up when police were asked by the Rector to come on to the campus with dogs and teargas, and to escort the striking students, who were all suspended, to the railway station. Each student had to re-apply for admission in person with his father, or a parent – a punitive device which not only fell heavily on the family purse, but was also calculated to get the parents on the side of "law and order". One father even brought a sjambok (whip) and thrashed his son in the Rector's presence in order to persuade the Rector to re-admit him! Twenty-two students were told they could not re-apply. Despite the strike's anonymous leadership these 22 were regarded by the administration, probably on the advice of informers, as the ring-leaders. One of these was Barney Pityana, due in two months' time to complete his first degree.

The unquenchable spirit displayed in this whole operation was not only miraculous, coming out of the deadness of the mid-1960s Fort Hare; it also boded well for the nascent all-black students association, which had been conceived by Stephen and others at the University Christian Movement Conference at Stutterheim in July. Next year the South African Students' Organisation (SASO) was born, and Steve was elected first President. Barney succeeded him in July 1970, and when his term of office expired he was made general secretary, a paid full-time post.

Barney was and is a deeply committed Christian, and I had known him well through the Fort Hare Anglican chaplaincy. Now I came to see Steve occasionally, through visits he paid to the Seminary to encourage the growth of SASO at Fort Hare and the Seminary. Ironically the Organisation was immediately accorded official recognition by the Fort Hare Administration, who liked its segregated appearance! Although SASO's strategy in confining its membership to blacks was one of 'withdrawal' in order to regroup, build up confidence, a sense of identity and a power base, and then to re-emerge to confront the white power structure, the latter saw it initially (as indeed SASO was clever enough to portray itself) as conforming to the segregationist "separate development" policy of the Nationalists. Only later did the Fort Hare and other bantu, Coloured and Indian university authorities realise what a viper they were nursing in their bosoms! At the Seminary on the other hand it appeared at first to negate all that the Seminary stood for – a resolute opposition to apartheid in all its manifestations, and positively a Christian witness to non-racial brotherhood and reconciliation. Even the students in an institution like ours were confused to begin with. But by 1970 we at St Peter's Anglican College in the Seminary, both staff and students, were sufficiently at home with the new ideology to cope with a strike when it erupted in the Seminary. The students made it clear, by an unusual zeal in keeping the College devotional rule, that they had no quarrel with the St Peter's administration. At the same time we, the staff, had to respect the solidarity they had to show with their fellow black students in the rest of the Seminary.

Largely through the compelling eloquence of Steve, who even before July 1969 had travelled extensively speaking for the nascent organisation, and who spent a great deal of his Presidential year 1969–70 touring the campuses, SASO began to make progress even on a liberal campus like the Seminary at Alice. He had at that time an extraordinary magnetism. His hold on his all-black audiences was almost frightening; it was as if they were listening to a new 'messiah'. Yet the Organisation was not only democratic, but from the outset set its face against a leadership cult.

Despite having precipitated the break with NUSAS which had to be made if SASO was to get off the ground, Steve insisted upon maintaining personal friendships. He was always too big a man to put ideology before persons. Besides which he enjoyed company and he loved to shock. A Roman Catholic priest remembers this large 'surly-looking youth' frequently hanging around the Christian Workers' Office in Durban. Once the priest came in to find Steve sitting in the office with a white girl on his lap! Towards the end of 1970 I planned to bring together a group of friends at an informal house-party on Hogsback, near Alice, centring round a quartet of radical young blacks whom I hoped would attend. Barney Pityana was one. He had already attended a similar house-party which I had organised in September 1969. Stephen was another, invited because I knew him to be the outstanding leader in SASO, and had sufficient familiarity with him to be able to extend an invitation. Sabelo Stanley Ntwasa from Kimberley, a student at St Peter's and an eloquent exponent of Black Consciousness and Black Theology, was a third. The last was Lindelwe Mabandla, a Fort Hare student whom I had come to appreciate through our common love of English literature; he was Vice-President of SASO.

I had come to realise that these young men had the key to the future in South Africa, that I was almost uniquely privileged in having gained their confidence, and that I ought to enable other whites to meet my young friends in the kind of relaxed atmosphere that prevailed at Innisfree. Unfortunately Stephen and Barney received a late invitation to attend an important student conference in Cape Town (see chapter 11), so had to cry off, and we could not find an alternative date which all could manage: so the meeting took place without those two.

But I remember so well the physical presence of Stephen at that time. Tall, and big in proportion, he brought to any gathering a sense of expectancy, a more than physical vitality and power. He was not unusually dark in complexion – Barney is much darker. His forehead was high and prominent, his nose long and slightly up-tilted towards the end, with wide, flared nostrils. But his soul was in his eyes, which were brown liquid and infinitely expressive; and in his whole body, which communicated him more directly than is normally the case. I never saw him naked; yet in another sense I always saw him 'naked', even when he was clad in the old army greatcoat he affected in the winter. There was a burning inner spirit which filled his limbs, so that he always met you with his own powerful presence. His clothes simply did not matter. When first greeting the young black friends I visited we normally embraced with a warm hug. In the later years of our friendship Stephen and I tacitly dropped this practice; there was a deeper understanding of which the hug could no longer be adequately sacramental. He was even at that time, despite uncertainty as to his choice of profession, to an unusual degree, whole. He was a proper man. No wonder the girls fell in love with him, and the young men gave him their unstinting loyalty. He never changed physically during all the time I knew him, except that the sedentary life consequent on his banning led to his putting on weight. A photograph taken on his release from 101 days in detention in 1976 gives a poignant glimpse of his earlier self.

At about the same time, i.e. at the turn of the year 1970–1,

Stephen married Ntsiki Mashalaba, a young woman from Umtata who was training as a nurse in Durban. I had not met her at that time, but a student of ours who knew her well said she was an exceptionally sweet and gentle person, and he wondered if she would want to see her husband engaged in a political career. However that may be, Steve was later to tell me that she was the one person in his life with whom he could share the whole of himself, from whom he needed to withhold nothing. At that time, in any case, Steve was still training to be a doctor: and it was perhaps not until he was expelled from Wentworth in 1972, allegedly for poor academic performance, that the decision to devote himself full-time to Black Consciousness activities was taken, and he began to work for BCP (Black Community Programmes) in Durban.

In 1972 my own life changed. After 12 years as Principal of St Peter's, I left Alice early in July and returned to our Community Priory in Johannesburg at Rosettenville. Before that, however, an event important for the development of my own vocation and ministry had taken place. In March the Security Branch had served a banning order on one of our own students, Stanley Ntwasa, and had removed him from the College to his home in Kimberley, where he was put under house arrest. A passionate advocate of Black Consciousness, he had been permitted to interrupt his ministerial training for a year in 1971 to act as travelling secretary of the radical University Christian Movement, with special responsibility for promoting the growth of "Black Theology" on the seminary and university campuses all over the Republic. There is no doubt that it was because of this "subversive" activity that Stanley was now given this cruel punishment without trial, and it became my duty to continue to give him all the pastoral care I could when living 300 miles away. This was my initiation into a ministry to the banned, which was to become my chief service and joy in the next five years.

During my last year at the Seminary I did not see much of Stephen, but I remember entering the students' common room at St Peter's one day and seeing him sprawled in an armchair, as usual the centre of attention. He looked like one of the larger feline animals – a tiger maybe – with an animal grace and an insolent ease and a sense of immense latent power. "Hallo, there!" he greeted me, not rising from his chair, but with a relaxed friendliness which was virtually irresistible. It was only much later that I understood that this spontaneous informality masked his deep respect for me as his "dear priest".

FOUR

But then it was only much later, and after a serious row, that we really came to know each other. All through the period I have so far covered he revered me as an elder, a "missionary", about whose family, antecedents, education, even Christian name he was not free to ask. For my part I was fascinated by this extraordinary young man who came from a background I knew, yet seemed possessed of a charisma I could not account for, a power which might be for immense good or, possibly, for destruction; a person dangerous to know, and yet, to me, even then, so vulnerable that it would have been impossible, even had I wished it, to close my heart to him.

The circumstance which served to transform this unequal relationship – although not at once – was his banning in February 1973. In that month the Nationalist Government banned eight NUSAS leaders; and then, while the uproar over that in the press and overseas was still at its height, it also banned eight SASO leaders including Steve himself, Barney Pityana, Harry Nengwekhulu and Strini Moodley.

What did this involve for Steve? First he must leave Durban where he had lived to all intents and purposes since 1966, and where he was currently working for BCP, and return to his home town of Kingwilliamstown. There he was confined to the magisterial district: no visits to East London, Alice, Fort Hare, Grahamstown, Port Elizabeth – let alone Durban, Cape Town, or Johannesburg. He could not enter an educational institution. He could write nothing for publication. He could not speak in public. He could attend no gathering of any kind except a *bona fide* Church service. He could not be quoted in the press or in any publication (this ban included all he had written up to that point). No one could visit him at his home, where he had to reside, except a doctor. He could never be in the company of more that one person at a time; even a chance meeting in the street would constitute a 'gathering' if protracted beyond the most formal exchanges.

The intention of a banning order – served on a person at the sole discretion of the Minister of Police, with no previous trial– is to restrict its subject at his or her own expense to a particular geographical area, to silence him, hence to hope that he will be forgotten. In cases where the Minister is satisfied that the person has had a "change of heart" and "seen the error of his ways" the ban can be lifted, again at the sole discretion of the Minister. Normally a banning order lasts for five years but it can then be extended for a further five years. Steve's would have expired in February 1978.

When Steve returned to King (as Kingwilliamstown is known all over South Africa) he was just 26, and it must have seemed that he was returning to his home town as a failure. He was not qualified for any profession; he had a wife and child to support; the chances of employment for a banned "bantu male" in a "dorp" like King, with the Security Branch everywhere, were slender indeed. But more than that, he would seem to the local community to have failed in every respect. He had not qualified as a doctor, which would have been a great honour for the Ginsberg community and a special pride to his mother, who had sweated for his education. The movement he had founded had been dealt a seemingly mortal blow with eight of its leaders banned. "A prophet is not without honour except in his own country". In all the main black educational centres of the country Steve had attained an almost messianic status. But his own community, close to the harsh realities of poverty and unemployment, looked more for deeds than words. They were now to see them.

Three years later Steve had not only built up BCP in the King area to be a showpiece of community development unsurpassed anywhere in the country; he had been instrumental in getting another organisation, the Zimele Trust Fund, established on a nation-wide basis; he had transformed King itself, on the black side, from depressed apathy into some semblance of militant solidarity, at least in Ginsberg, his home location; and he had made this little market town in the Border area of the Ciskei a place of pilgrimage for leaders both within and outside South Africa, who wished to learn from the man best qualified to tell them what young black South Africans wanted for the future of their country. How this happened is what I want to tell: how his very restrictions were utilised and transcended in such a manner as to entrench the claim often made that he was the legitimate successor to Nelson Mandela and Robert Sobukwe.

It took time. First it was necessary to establish BCP in the Eastern Cape. Steve was made Branch Executive, responsible to the Executive Director in Durban, Ben Khoapa, and to the Branch Board of Directors, a group of mostly professional men united in their opposition to the government policy of "separate development" and bantustans. During 1973 Steve was assisted by having nearby the Reverend David Russell, a young Anglican priest only a few years older than himself, fluent in Xhosa and dedicated to the service of the poor and the oppressed. He helped Steve not only in practical terms, but more in that here was someone close at hand, of commitment equal to himself and able to provide intellectual stimulation. That was a fine friendship, which mitigated the hardship of the first months of banning.

Closer at home, his mother provided from the first an indomitable base of support. Unlike the parents of one or two of Stephen's contemporaries Mrs Biko had never had a chance to be a political activist even if she had had the inclination. She had been too poor, and had had to work too unsparingly to bring up four children after the early loss of her husband. But she now showed that she knew how to cope with the "system", as the Security Branch is everywhere called in the black world. She stood no nonsense from them: enquiries as to the whereabouts of her son were met with vacant stares and blank denials. Even if she felt fear, she never showed it. Nor, on the other hand, was she rude to them; she simply treated them with a cold, polite correctness. Very soon the "system" had to acknowledge defeat on this front, and all through the four and a half years of his banning Steve had anyone he wanted into his mother's house, which continued to be home for him and his family (Ntsiki, his wife, could only find employment as a nursing Sister at the Anglican mission hospital at St Matthew's 35 miles out if King). It seems to me in retrospect that his mother's courage was all the more heroic in that it was not her natural disposition. Her son made it clear from the first that he was in no way going to be subjugated by his restriction order. Out of love for him she complied. Her strong Christian faith helped her; whatever his spoken criticisms of the Church might be Stephen never denied being an Anglican, and this was due chiefly to loyalty to his mother, and to admiration of the quality of her faith. And this home was a warm and friendly place, the best place for his children's formative years. Even though Ntsiki had to work 35 miles away and could only come home once a week, it really was home for them – as only those who know African family life can understand. Always Steve was at home between five and eight each evening, to be with Nkosinathi and, later, Samora. Sometimes he would break his banning order to drive Ntsiki back to St Matthew's, far outside the permitted magisterial district of King. Life was to be as normal as possible.

FIVE

Distances in South Africa are formidable. King is about 600

miles from Johannesburg, and Port Elizabeth another 150 miles beyond King. An opportunity came to visit Steve and Barney in their two places of banning in May 1973, less than three months after the serving on them of their restriction orders. By this time I had visited Stanley three or four times in Kimberley, and Jerry Modisane, President of SASO 1972–3, and restricted at the same time as Steve and Barney, who was now also there, so I was well acquainted with the drill in visiting a banned person. The golden rule is to observe whatever precautions the person himself wants you to observe. The Church hierarchy in Kimberley was at first so scared of getting Stanley into more trouble that with the best intentions they added a dimension of further restriction to his already curtailed freedom of movement and association.

Granted that the system in King was less oppressive that in Kimberley, and considerably less vicious than that at Port Elizabeth, it was interesting to notice how much in control of the situation Stephen seemed to be after less than three months' residence. A modicum of precaution was taken when he and David Russell and I wanted to talk together (three constitutes a 'social gathering', i.e. it was a breach of the banning order). This was not only for his protection but also for ours; if he had been caught and charged we should have been subpoena'd to give evidence. Had we refused, as both of us would have, Stephen would not have been able to be convicted, but we should have been liable to imprisonment for contempt of Court (this actually happened to Peter Welman, a reporter on the *Rand Daily Mail*, who got six months for refusing to give evidence against his banned friend, Cosmas Desmond, on a similar charge). As time went on, however, Steve's ascendancy in King became so marked that one increasingly found it difficult to remember that he was banned.

Everyone who is banned has to come to terms with his restriction order in his or her own way. I noticed that on the whole my white friends were more scrupulous in observing precautions than the blacks. Some of them compensated for this by making constant applications for relaxations of their restrictions, on the principle of the parable of the importunate widow. Whether their applications were successful or not – and sometimes they were – they certainly succeeded in making a nuisance of themselves with the authorities. An exception to this was Cos Desmond, who refused to ask permission to leave his house on Sunday morning to attend Mass (he was under house arrest from 6pm to 6am each day, and throughout the week-end from 6pm Friday to 6am Monday). He just went. A few weeks later the unasked-for permission arrived in the post!

Most blacks in South Africa tend to live on the wrong side of the law anyway. They have a contempt for the law as it manifests itself in their daily lives, whilst retaining a passion for justice. The obvious response of the black banned person, therefore, is to see how he can get round the law or break it without being caught. How careful he will be depends on how much he has to fear the system's enforcement of his restriction order. In the case of Barney Pityana in Port Elizabeth the system was from the outset relentlessly repressive towards him and intimidating to anyone who maintained contact with him. Two days after my first visit to him in May 1973 they had discovered who I was and where I was staying, and came to warn me not to go on visiting him. My response was to get into the car at once and go and see him at his mother's house in New Brighton, the old location of Port Elizabeth. We agreed to pay no attention to such behaviour. Barney was already well on the way to becoming a lawyer. He knew what his rights were, but he also needed to be exceptionally careful to avoid a conviction which, however unjust, might prejudice his acceptance by the Law Society. Steve understood this and was always careful not to involve Barney in anything that could get him into big trouble. On the other hand he knew the depth of Barney's commitment, and how oppressive his situation was; he therefore took equal care to see that Barney was kept informed of what was going on. As the unofficial but tacitly recognised leader he was prepared to take calculated risks himself, and he continued to maintain contact with and be sensitive to the needs of the other restricted members.

Because of the distances involved, and my duties in Johannesburg, I do not recall visiting Stephen again until March 1974, but a letter from him dated 4 December 1973 indicates that he was heavily engaged with BCP, and also struggling with a law degree by correspondence through UNISA (University of South Africa). His intention was to complete the junior degree, and then take on a senior one (i.e. in Law). He also wrote in the same letter

> King is quite pleasant despite the sometimes savage near-assaults from the Branch. One has learnt not to bother too much about them. I no more think they are as much of a threat as they are reputed to be and I suspect they know this too. Still they are trying very hard to pin a charge on me. One such case is still "under

investigation". It so happens that it's one of those fairly innocent occasions that look highly suspicious. I don't think they will lay a charge on this alone anyway. If they do, they will be providing us with a fairly welcome break

He continued:

> . . . If possible I intend finding expression for my skills in the context of the present job. Over the years I have developed a strong liking for the kind of work done by the Black Community Programmes. One admits that there are many unfulfilled missions to work on. These will need longer experience and much better training than some of us have at the moment. All this of course is dependent on an accident-free atmosphere. Should there be too many problems I may have to re-assess my own future.

"Accident-free" and "problems" refer, probably, to keeping free from the kind of convictions on charges of breaking his banning order referred to in the foregoing paragraph. Letters are always liable to be opened; hence the use of indirect terms such as "accident-free".

After giving me the names of the Board of Directors of BCP, now a registered non-profitmaking company, he concluded cheerfully:

> . . . The one thing about them is that they are highly unified through having had to suffer severe assaults on their staff in the past few months. Ironically with most of the BCP staff being now banned we seem to be facing a much more stable future.

Lastly he wrote:

> . . . The rest of the folk at home except for Ntsiki, Kaya and myself, are going on a short holiday to the Natal South Coast for a week in December. This is meant to be a special treat for my mother who has not travelled outside the Cape since she was born! I just felt Natal will do well for her. The South Coast is easily at its best in mid-summer and it shall have to be a really troubled mind indeed that can resist the relaxing and soothing effect of a holiday spell in that part of the world.

He also alluded to the imminent departure from King of Father David Russell, but did not then reveal what a gap it would leave in his own life. It was only ten months later, at a time when he and I were at last moving into a deeper and more human relationship with each other, that he admitted:

David's going away left a gap which cannot be closed. The evenings we spent together were very good palliatives to the mental decay which so easily sets in. Besides this he was a person full of life and always with something new to pursue. He was strong and reliable and made life purposeful. I am aware that I must have served a purpose in the many consultations we had, and this was good to know. Often I think of him, but have never written to him since he lift King. I thought he needed to be relieved of good old King's problems.

During the first year of BCP's work in King, Stephen had secured excellent premises for their offices and show-room. Through the co-operation of the Anglican Rector and Parish Council in Zwelitsha, BCP was able to rent a disused church right in the middle of King. Besides the administrative office there was a research and publishing department, and a showroom for displaying the clothing procured at the local home industry centres run by the Border Council of Churches, and also the leatherwork from Njwaxa, a cottage industry started by BCP in co-operation with Father Timothy Stanton, C.R., then Rector of St Bartholomew's, Alice, in whose parish Njwaxa fell.

But the most ambitious project which took shape in 1974 was the Zanempilo Community Health Clinic established at Zinyoka, five miles outside King. Stephen wrote in the preamble to the initial budget proposals of R30,000:

The creation of Zanempilo Community Health Clinic is part of a wider and more general health project introduced by the Black Community Programmes in the Eastern Cape. The aim of this project is to provide the Black Community with essential services of a medical nature, both curative and preventative, which are often sadly lacking especially in the "resettlement areas".

Through the establishment of such a clinic Stephen and his fellow workers hoped to show a typical "grass-roots" rural community what their own people could do in the way of providing essential health services, independent of government control except for such health inspection as was common all over the Republic. They planned to instil a sense of community, to "conscientise" people to the facts of their situation, not so much by talking as by doing, that is by example. In a letter dated 25 September 1974 he wrote:

> The work at Njwaxa Home Industry and on the Clinic Front at Zanempilo has brought forth a lot of promise, that is, of proper footholds in useful community development work. I am thrilled at the progress.

Support for this and the Njwaxa project was to be sought from within South Africa as far as possible:

> ... I am of the opinion and determination that I should raise as much support for these projects as possible from South African sources. Hence I would like to urge you to do all in your power to see that some support is given to these projects by any friends you have that have not the means.

With the help of Cosmas Desmond (at that time still banned and under house arrest), who worked for the Chairman's Fund of Mr Harry Oppenheimer's vast mining corporation Anglo-American, I did what I could, and in fact, mainly through the generosity of a personal donation from another source, most of the money spent in building and equipping Zanempilo was South African money. This was important, not only in terms of possible government action against BCP, but much more positively to show that a Black Consciousness organisation could support itself from within the South African community. Some people asked how Steve, an avowed radical and communalist, could take money from a capitalist organisation like 'Anglo', to which Steve replied that the money belonged to the people anyway, as the earth from which the metal was extracted was for the benefit of *all* South Africans, by virtue of the sweat of the black workers who extracted it from the soil. He was merely giving Anglo the opportunity to put back into the service of the people a tiny fraction of what belonged properly to them rather than to the shareholders of the Corporation (it is true that 70% of Anglo-American profits go in tax to the Government, but only a minute proportion of that goes to the welfare of the black people).

The building was carried out at an extraordinarily low cost by Mr Flask, a local contractor, who as far as possible employed local labour. Thus the entire enterprise was a community project from start to finish.

Despite the obstructive hostility of the local bantustan government of the Ciskei the project went ahead, began work on 1 February 1975 and was officially opened in April of that year, being christened the Zanempilo Community Health Centre. Dr Mamphela A. Ramphele, whom Steve had known well at Medical School in Durban, was appointed the first Medical Officer.

Looking back now I find it hard to believe that that Clinic operated for only two and a half years under the aegis of BCP. From the beginning it was utterly different in spirit from any other clinic or hospital in the country – even the great Charles Johnson Memorial Hospital at Nqutu, Zululand, built up by Doctors Anthony and Margaret Barker. It was, more than any other institution or project, the incarnate symbol of Black Consciousness. And because it was *incarnate*, that is to say because the spirit was expressed in the black-designed, black-built buildings, but above all in the staff who serviced it, there was no need to shout the message in words. Only deeds can be heard by the poor and oppressed. They came, they paid something if they could possibly afford it, they were properly examined, treated with dignity and respect as full human beings, given the best medication available, hospitalised if necessary, taught how to feed and care for their new-born infants, given lessons in hygiene and diet, helped with family planning – and all this was being done for them *by their fellow blacks*, and not for personal gain but in a spirit of sacrificial devotion. When I met Mr Sebe, Chief Minister of the Ciskei Bantustan, with the Anglo-American executives mentioned in the next paragraph, one of the criticisms he made of the Clinic was that the staff "talked politics" to the patients. In fact he made this criticism of "Mrs Biko" – who was nursing at St Matthew's, 35 miles away! But the real point is that there was no need to "talk politics", even if there had been time or inclination. The *spirit* of Zanempilo, which informed all its work, proclaimed the gospel of Black Consciousness far more effectively than any "political talk" could have done. These people knew what conditions were like at the Grey Hospital* in King, and at Mount Cook Mission

* This hospital, founded by Sir George Grey in the 1850s, has not always been as it is

Hospital. At Zanempilo they entered a different world from these institutions, *their own true world*. This was the point.

I persuaded two senior executives in Anglo to come down and see the 'baby' which they had helped to bring to birth, but really so that they could meet the young man whose vision and energy had been behind it all. This meeting took place in the middle of June. I confess I was slightly apprehensive. I was introducing two great personal friends of mine to each other. The one, though certainly not the conventional picture of a "bloated capitalist", was nevertheless dedicated to that economic philosophy. The other, whilst not a fanatical socialist, had never disguised the fact that in any take-over of government by blacks the mining industry must as a matter of fundamental principle be nationalised. I need not have worried. With the help of a little whisky the ice was quickly broken; the only person Bill Wilson got cross with at any point was myself, and the two of them, Bill and Steve, with the rest of us mostly silent, went at it with increasing mutual appreciation until 2.30 the following morning. That was the beginning of an acquaintance which would have undoubtedly ripened into a friendship but for Steve's restrictions. As it was they only met once again when the latter managed to visit Bill's home in Johannesburg when he came up the following year for legal consultations in connection with the forthcoming BPC – SASO Trial in Pretoria. This is the kind of personal impoverishment, on both sides, which makes living in South Africa such a heart-breaking business.

SIX

If this memoir is to be the personal document of the title, it is time to say something of our own relationship. At first as I have already written, I came into Stephen's life through my involvement with his elder brother.

I got to know you [he wrote late in 1974] through Kaya and my mother. I got on to conducting some correspondence with you . . .

today. Writing of its early years, Professor Monica Wilson notes that "under an inspired and devoted superintendent J.P. Fitzgerald . . . it accommodated both white and African, who were treated identically, and Fitzgerald (unlike most whites) was careful to cultivate traditional diviners whom he received as "colleagues', and invited to view his hospital (Oxford History of South-Africa, ed. L. Thompson and M. Wilson, vol. I, p. 263). Editor's note.

During that time I learnt to develop a strong faith in God and this was not completely unrelated to your role. Your letters to me and my personal reflections about things in general. Some things you said to me formed the basis of such reflections. As a result I have always held you in high esteem as a committed Christian with whom I would like to maintain close ties for a long time. Significantly then the "missionary" element has never completely disappeared in my regard of you.

To analyse this a bit further [he wrote, in answer to a query from me as to why, after so long, he continued to call me "Fr Stubbs" and not "Fr Aelred" or, as Barney and several others of that generation do, "Fr A."], I'll compare your relationship with me to one I have with Dave. I got over the Fr Russell story pretty quickly because our relationship did not really stamp this aspect. He is not much older than me – he is more of a political person, a friend, an equal, a schlenterer, a comrade, than a pastor, a "missionary", an elder and my dear priest. My self-consciousness in his presence could never be the same as in your presence. Equally so my respect towards him in the traditional sense of respect towards an elder could never be the same. I could easily ask him about his family – father, mother, sisters, brothers, family wealth and property etc. and adopt freely any attitude I like towards this, but I've never felt free to ask you and indeed do not know anything about your family – father, mother, sisters, brothers, home, or for that matter even where you were born, educated, what qualifications you have etc. Indeed what I know about you is dangerously little in terms of background. I know that you are Fr Stubbs, and over and above that I know what little I have gleaned of your personality, your leadership qualities etc.

There was also the friendship he had with two young blacks who were already dear to me, Stanley Ntwasa and Barney Pityana. On the other hand, while priding myself on my tolerant attitude towards modern student mores, I found distasteful the stories which clustered around him and his Durban colleagues of heavy drinking and excessive womanising. Such distaste had found expression after a long talk with Mr Robert Sobukwe in Kimberley on one of my visits to Stanley.

Sobukwe was the leader of the Pan Africanist Congress. He had spearheaded the PAC Anti-Pass Law Campaign, and had been convicted of incitement and burning his 'pass' and given three years, the last year of which was spent on Robben Island. On completion of his sentence, instead of being released, a special Act of Parliament was passed 'in the interests of the security of the state' to keep him detained on the Island. As he was no longer a convicted prisoner he could not be kept with his fellow convicts Nelson Mandela, Walter Sisulu, and all the other great black patriots in that most distinguished island prison. For six years, therefore, he endured a solitary confinement which was renewed by Act of Parliament each year, the indomitable Mrs Helen Suzman being the only M.P. to register a protest each year. At length his health deteriorated and he was 'released', which meant that he was banished to Kimberley where he was under the same restrictions as Steve in King. Robert, or "Prof." as he was called by Steve's generation, was a hero and an elder to this new generation of political activists, who admired his unflinching integrity as they did his intellectual pre-eminence, his perception of the need in the South African situation to keep leadership in black hands without in any way being anti-white, and his legendary eloquence.*

During this talk in 1972 Robert had told me he did not like the stories he was hearing about the social habits of the SASO leaders. He said it would lead to a loss of respect from the rank and file for the leadership. On his campaigns in the late 1950s round the country he had always put himself in the hands of the local PAC Committee and accepted whatever hospitality he was given. African men might have different standards to Christian norms as far as drinking and women were concerned (Robert was a deeply committed Christian), but they expected the leadership to be beyond reproach in these areas.

I repeated this first to Barney, and found support; but when I taxed Stephen with it he reacted vigorously, saying that theirs was a student movement, which was true; that student mores had changed over the past 20 years, which was only partly true; and that in this respect "Prof" was out of date; to which I dissented. I remembered this when 18 months later a mutual friend told me that Steve's relationship with a certain person was giving cause for concern and might soon damage his image. One of the difficulties at this time was that, because of my work in Johannesburg, I was only able to visit him and Barney for short spells at long intervals. Unwisely I brought the matter up during a very short visit, and left before we could give the topic the length of time its seriousness demanded. On my return

* Robert Sobukwe died in Kimberley in March 1968. Editor's note.

to Johannesburg I received a long letter from him.

I thought our parting was not the best ever [he began], and I felt
like writing to you about the matter you raised just as you were
going. First let me say I raised the issue with both parties
concerned and with a mutual friend of ours in P.E.* Our initial
reaction is simply that it was unfortunate that you raised this in the
way you did. I am in no way ashamed to talk about that matter
with anyone, and indeed I find aspects of it very good illustrations
of the complexities of the human nature. Often an observation of
myself in the context of the relationships involved there offers a
good basis for a study of my own personality. However the point
about the way you raised it is that it presupposed a very thorough
discussion of myself and my emotional relationships with others
by friends none of whom had ever had the guts to raise the issue
with me directly first. The tendency then with the human mind is to
ask an endless string of "whys". I have resolved even this aspect of
it finally – which is why I am now writing to you. I have assumed
that your motives are completely altruistic – that you see a
situation which is potentially explosive and you wish to share with
your friend your fears about the possible outcome and if possible
help in the formulation of some kind of solution. My response of
course is that I regard topics of this nature as being extremely
private. I am in many instances aware of the complexity that can
be introduced by a willingness to accommodate the feelings of
friends in a matter that is essentially private between two – or in
this case three – parties. I have never, ever, found it necessary to
reflect on my friends' private activities except in so far as I thought
they affected at any one stage their political standing and their
performance. Similarly I could never wish to ask you about your
love life, your sexual life, etc. because I regard that as strictly
speaking your business. If I have confidence in your general
leadership qualities I must have a basis to believe you will
adequately take care. On the other hand if you do experience
problems and you wish to share I will only be too ready to do that.
Or for that matter if you experience success I will share with you in
that as well. But otherwise I restrict my friendship even with my
best of friends to topics that are generally voluntarily declared by
both parties.

* Port Elizabeth. Editor's note.

This brings me to an analysis of your own contribution in situations of this nature . . . There is a profound difference in the way Westerners basically believe in character analysis to that adopted by us here. In many discussions I used to have with David [Russell] I agreed with him in comparing our attitude on the whole to that of the European working-class approach to life. When you guys talk about a person, you tear him apart, analyse the way he speaks, looks at someone, thinks; you find a motive for everything he does; you categorise him politically, socially, etc. In short you are not satisfied until you have really torn him apart and have really parcelled off each and every aspect of his general behaviour and labelled it.

. . . Now most blacks do not indulge in reflection upon the self or upon others. They never form therefore any cut and dried opinions that thereafter govern their relationship with others. Of course this tendency is wrong in that on the whole for evaluation and redirection of oneself in life, a bit of reflection and self-analysis is necessary. But this has to be checked and not allowed to reach excesses . . .

. . . When you talk to me about my own relationship do not operate on the assumption that I am not aware of the "imminent dangers" involved. When I brush aside what I regard as undue inquisitiveness with the comment: "things will be sorted out" do not labour the point with a backhander "just like in the political situation, these things do not sort themselves out, someone has to do something about them". Allow a friend to subtly close a topic when he does not see any value in discussing it. . . . I would not like you to continue with any aspect of this debate as I believe there is nothing to be served by it and it remains a private matter.

I have in some parts of this letter spoken very frankly – not to kill my friendship with you but rather to preserve it . . .

To this letter I replied, thanking him for his frankness, apologising for the clumsy timing of my approach, and respecting his right to emotional privacy. Soon after this exchange came the recognition of Frelimo by the world (including South Africa) as the *de facto* government of Moçambique, and the abortive attempt by BPC and SASO to hold pro-Frelimo demonstrations all over the country. This gave the system an excuse to round up Black Consciousness leaders, and over 30 were detained and taken to Pretoria including Barney, Jerry,

Mapetla Mohapi, Lindelwe and Cele Mabandla, Aubrey Mokoape, Strini Moodley, Saths Cooper, Aubrey Mokoena, Muntu Myeza, Mosioua Lekota, Zitulele Cindi, Johnny Issel, Steve Carolus – a representative collection of the successive SASO leadership from 1972 onwards. Steve alluded to these mass detentions in his next long letter, as well as to the matter that had been between us:

> I will not further debate aspects of the other matter with you. I prefer to take up your views seriously as those of a friend who is concerned. I don't think an intellectual argument can help here. Though I reacted to your concern and the way it was expressed I do feel it is one way or the other good that it came. Some things have been sorted out.
>
> Arrests have broken out all over the country and all of us are speculating on what is afoot. I have remained calm and will do so in any eventuality. I am much more sorry for Barney and Jerry's relatives because unlike most of the other guys they have been pretty aloof. It just goes to show that in this country it's no use saying "I'll play it cool" in the absolute sense. One's history often is just as good as the present for an excuse towards repression. What I think, however, is that something is being cooked up against the organisations through their successive hierarchies starting from the Barney–Strini–Jerry group right down to the present group. Even this still does not make complete sense with me however. We hope guys will be freed. I learn most of them are in Pretoria. We'll see what happens!

Evidently this long letter did not satisfy him as far as our own relationship was concerned, for shortly afterwards I received this, written in the small hours:

> It's an odd hour for me to be writing a letter (1 a.m.) but I could not resist the temptation. My little son who is sleeping next to me now has kicked me awake and during the resultant insomnia I found myself thinking about the letter I wrote to you this afternoon. That was a rushed affair during lunch hour and it left out a few things I would have liked to say. Besides, in the regular hustle of office hours one tends to be a bit dry. You will hopefully excuse me if I use this type of paper – I have nothing better next to me and I did not want to lose the kind of comprehensive, orderly

and creative style that is normally associated with night time (i.e. in my case: Stanley can bear me out on this).

I've been reflecting on the two letters I wrote to you – today's and the previous one – and cannot help feeling that I have been unkind to you, if nothing else, just in allowing myself to drop a lot of things together. I do not for a moment believe that in a dual relationship only one side should be blamed and I have sounded as if I'm heaping all sorts of blame on you. I hope you have a big enough heart – and I think you do – to complete the gaps and to take everything I've said in context. A lot of friends of mine believe I am arrogant and they are partly right. Often what I call a critical frankness sounds much sharper than was intended and tends to assume holier-than-thou proportions. The problem with me is that I often take friends for granted and do not cater for the protective subjectivism that we all suffer from. I cannot say I do not mean what I say but I can point out the honest fact that whatever I've said is 100% devoid of malice or intention to hurt.

I want to be a little more constructive now and to ask you to do me two favours. Firstly – following up on what I wrote this afternoon, I would appreciate your writing at length to me about *yourself*. I had a laugh this afternoon just when we were about to send away our mail. Thami Moletsane (Moses) saw the letter addressed to you and insisted that I add "C.R." behind your name because this is how you would like it. I don't think he was completely serious but it reminded me of the basic African attitude to things and persons of reverence. We tend to shy away from extreme familiarity. When the Catholic Church decided to do away with Latin liturgy in their services (I was in Mariannhill at the time) the African Catholics there made the greatest noise. They could not understand how the dignity of the liturgy could be so heavily prostituted by the substitution of Latin with Zulu. Some of them argued that God was being made commonplace – this is true. They seemed to prefer the non-intelligible Latin gabble simply because it was consistent with the theory that God cannot be fully comprehended. Somehow Latin seemed a holier medium. I also felt personally disappointed a little with the change though for poetic reasons. I am not comparing you to God but I cannot help recalling this when I ask you to write to me about yourself. Probably my sub-conscious reluctance to get to know you too well at a personal level could be traceable to this attitude. You will recall that I used to express quite strongly my regard of you in Christ-like or God-like terms some time back.

The second request is that you would, when you pass through this way, come and see me so that we can talk about those things you cannot write about – basic political beliefs, your view of our world, your contribution, etc. All these must sound a little belated in a relationship which has been going on for years but I believe that the rude way in which they were brought out to the fore suggests that the necessary adjustments have to be made. Besides this of course now that the questions have been asked I am genuinely and naturally curious.

Then came a rare admission of the difficulties of his situation:

You know I am (so I think) a reasonably strong person but quite often I find the going tough under the present restrictions. I am nowhere near despair and frustration but can understand only too well why some of our guys are. I have been much luckier than most blokes. I live with a very supportive family, one which is fully committed to my commitment if not to the cause itself. The township I am in is supportive and defensive. I still work relevantly and in a reasonably fulfilling and challenging situation, but in spite of all this it's quite tough.

There was not only the strain of living under a restriction order. He now had also to live with the knowledge that nearly all his comrades in the movement were in detention under the dreaded section 6 of the Terrorism Act, which meant indefinite detention in solitary confinement, with the knowledge that the system stopped at nothing, including beating people to death, to extort the "confessions" they were after. It was anguish to me to think of Barney, Jerry and Lindelwe (the three I at that time knew best of those detained) in the hands of these ruthless men; but on Steve fell a more crushing weight. So that the same letter from which I have been quoting ends:

My major problem at the moment is a strange kind of guilt. So many friends of mine have been arrested for activities in something that I was most instrumental in starting. A lot of them are blokes I spoke into the movement. And yet I'm not with them. There's nothing we can do about this really because neither they nor I know why some people have been arrested – nor is there anything in the activity trend of the movement warranting the terror act being invoked. Anyway the problem remains. One does not think this way in political life of course. Casualties are expected and should be bargained for. An oppressive system often is illogical in the application of suppression.

I think I'll stop. I may find myself going out of bounds. I hope to hear from you soon.

In response to his invitation I visited him at the end of the following month – November. I suggested that possibly the system had not taken him in, in order to try to discredit him with the movement as a whole. He agreed that this was a possibility, but he had made more of an analysis of the backgrounds and positions of the various detainees and decided that, whilst they had taken in men like Barney and Strini Moodley who were his exact contemporaries in the movement, these, together with Jerry Modisane, had been on the SASO Executive in 1972–3, and it looked as if questioning as well as the external event provoking the detentions were centring round contact with student movements in independent countries further north. Steve himself had not served on the SASO Executive in 1972–3 because of his new work with BCP.

This period August–November 1974 proved to be decisive in our relationship, though there was nothing very dramatic about it. From now on we understood each other, and there was no further need for the kind of correspondence from which I have been quoting. I remained "Fr Stubbs". I had also for him become a human being. He remained a son; and he had become a friend and a brother. More and more in the remaining two and a half years he was also to become a leader.

SEVEN

On 31 January 1975, 13 of the detainees appeared in court in Pretoria. From this appearance dated the mammoth BPC-SASO Trial – the Trial of Black Consciousness – which continued until the conviction of the nine on 16 December 1976. Most of the remaining detainees remained inside until the end of March or beginning of April.

Meanwhile at King life continued to be full, and 1975 was, in retrospect, a golden year, marred only by the savage vandalism of an attack on the BCP offices in Leopold Street in September, and by the tragically sudden death of Steve's elder sister at about the same time. Already during my visits in 1973–4 I had met a number of the other folk in the community there, and been accepted by them. This really came home to me when on one visit he and I spent a good deal of time together, and some of the others felt – and told him! – that I was neglecting to spend time with them! It did not happen again. But Johannesburg, my so-called home, and King were so far apart, and my visits so short, it was difficult to do justice to all the demands made upon one.

The first time I stayed in King – as distinct from the May 1973 visit when I was merely passing through – Stephen arranged for me to stay with a young white friend of his, who had a business in the town and was being useful to Steve in BCP matters. But on all other visits I either stayed with an Anglican curate in town, the Reverend John Williams, or at the Clinic at Zanempilo. Because of the Church's acquiescence in the social structures imposed by apartheid John had no formal responsibility whatever for local African Anglicans. His duties lay with the white congregation and with little pockets of whites 35 miles away in Peddie and Alice, and even as far as Hogsback, 60 miles from King. How could I in conversation with my young black friends attempt to justify such an institution? I could not, and did not. In any case, there were more important things to talk about. But John enjoyed the occasional contacts he had with them, and they appreciated his sensitive courtesy. Two worlds were existing side by side and never meeting; the great joyous world of the blacks, true heirs of the South Africa to come; the narrow joyless ghetto of the whites, clinging with increasing desperation to their tribal privileges.

On one visit Steve asked me to help two of the community who were having trouble in their marriage. Privately I was amazed and wondered if they would want to share their difficulties with a white middle-aged stranger who could not even speak their language. But each separately agreed to see me, and through this almost impromptu counselling I found my bonds with the community deepening.

Another time we had a party at the Clinic on a Saturday evening. As I look back now, life at Zanempilo seems to have been one continuous party! But this was not in fact the case. People, and Steve most of all, at his own job as BCP Branch Executive (not to speak of his other commitments), worked very hard. Because of this he encouraged me when possible to time my visits for week-ends (easier once I had given up the Rosettenville parish) as there was leisure then for long talks. And for parties! On this particular Saturday evening I forget all the folk who were there, but certainly they included Malusi Mpumlwana, Nohle Mohapi, Thoko Mbanjwa, Phumla Sangotsha, and probably a few visitors from outside King. Towards midnight Steve suggested that we might have a Eucharist next morning. I was startled; I knew by this time his views about the Church. But I could see that he was quite sober enough to know what he was asking for, so I manifested no surprise and agreed. It was his way both of saying that he guessed that he and many of the community wanted a Eucharist as a community, and also of signifying that I was now acceptable not only as a person but also as a priest. I had neither vestments, wafers, wine nor vessels, and only one book; nor had I permission from the priest-in-charge. The latter, however, was one of our old St Peter's students, and a good friend both to myself and the BCP (The Rev. James Gawe, instrumental in BCP renting 15 Leopold Street in town, and also in their leasing from the Church the site on which the Clinic had been built). I knew I could put it right with him later. So I asked Mamphela to bake a scone; we used brandy (fermented juice of the grape after all), well diluted with water; Malusi Mpumlwana and Sister Moletsane led the singing; and we had our Eucharist in the lounge of the doctor's house the following morning. It was the only time I was ever able to give Stephen the Sacrament of the Body and Blood of Christ.

During this year especially, King became a centre for all those committed to the Black Consciousness movement. The BPC (Black People's Convention), the political wing of the movement, was growing in strength, and the branch at King was one of the strongest in the country. In 1976 Mxolisi Mvovo, Steve's brother-in-law, became National Vice-President. BPC (Black People's Convention), must be distinguished from BCP Black Community Programmes, despite the similarity of the initials. BPC was the nearest thing to a national political party for blacks – *all* blacks, including Indians and Coloureds – to exist since the banning of ANC and PAC. BCP was a community development organisation and embraced in its adherents blacks who could not have identified themselves with BPC. Equally some of the more militant members of BPC thought

Steve and the others were wasting their time with BCP! Steve recognised the vital need to conscientise and thus politicise the masses
by community development action. Through BCP and Zimele the
Black Consciousness movement acquired almost accidentally a
grass-roots support that those who knew the elder Congress movements say they never quite attained.

Although Steve could hold no office in BPC because of his
banning order he was constantly being consulted. It was amazing
how much he knew. Sometimes he would pass on information to
me, which he thought might be useful in my particular spheres of
influence. More than once he warned me not to get too close to
certain people, white or black, whose contacts were less than desir-
able. He was always right. He never spoke against anyone if he could
possibly help it. Even when he did, it was always in a particular context. Bantustan politicians were of course witheringly dismissed.
When he learned that money I was offering him for petrol came from
a church organisation whose integrity he doubted he refused to take
it. He did not want to be beholden to anyone he mistrusted. Thereafter my trips were always financed by my own Community; he
accepted us and in particular admired Father Timothy Stanton with
whom he had worked over the Njwaxa project. There was this fierce
integrity about them all. If you were with them you were in, and
everything was given and taken. If in any way you were furthering
your own ends, or trying to run with the hare and hunt with the
hounds, you were out. Even the beloved Beyers Naude, in an ill-
advised but mercifully short-lived flirtation with a bantustan
leader, was treated somewhat distantly for a while; but that was a
single aberration, and the man's shining integrity and personal goodness meant there could be no serious or lasting rift. BCP owed a great
deal to the Christian Institute in the early stages (in more ways than
one), and Steve did not forget that. It was fitting that the CI should
have been banned at the same time as all the Black Consciousness
organisations on 19 October 1977. They were the only Christian
body to have given unstinting support to SASO, BCP and BPC from
the beginning.

There was then a rigour and discipline about the movement. It was
accepted that many would break under 'interrogation' and make
statements; that was OK. But you must not stand by your statements
in court. Better to go to gaol for "perjury", as not a few have done. A
student who made a statement not even under duress was out. He

was an intelligent young man and a valued member of the community, but he could no longer be trusted. I pleaded privately with Steve and one or two others to find some way of disciplining such an offender without, as it were, "excommunicating" him altogether; but they and their colleagues were those who suffered from the consequences of such lapses. One was back in the atmosphere of the early, persecuted Church, that mingle of exhilarating communion and rigorous discipline; one deadly sin after baptismal rebirth, and you were out!

Despite the rigour there was no breath of fanaticism. One could not imagine Lenin or Trotsky being at home with them. Herein lay the weakness of the movement: it was too much the movement of an idea, too little a ruthless, organised force. Its weakness, yes; but also its ultimate strength! Being the movement of an idea, almost a mood, it was, and is, extraordinarily infectious. Individuals could be banned, detained, banished; wherever they were they continued, almost by the quality of their breathing, to spread this new mood of inner freedom, this refusal any more to acknowledge the rule of a minority group, the tyranny of a tragically lost, calvinist tribe. I predict that the same will be found to be true of the banning of the Black Consciousness organisations. Given the circumstances he faced of a strongly entrenched, powerfully armed minority on the one hand, and a divided, defeated majority on the other, perhaps the political genius of Steve lay in concentrating on the creation and diffusion of a new *consciousness* rather than in the formation of a rigid *organisation*.

I remember one day attending the Trial in Pretoria with a nun. The court was bristling with system guys and with SAP (South African Police). There they stood, the uniformed police with revolvers, the system in safari suits and concealing their guns; all of them with set, tense, joyless and, yes, frightened expressions. The nine on trial came up from the cells underneath the court room singing a freedom song as they came, with arms raised in the clenched fist salute. Dead silence, except for the rustle as the crowd rose to its feet. Then, at the end of the song, a roar from the nine, AMANDLA: and, from the crowd, a forest of arms shooting up and the deafening response of NGAWETHU (strength . . . is ours). "There's not much doubt who's in power here, is there?" whispered the Little Sister to me.

When Mapetla Mohapi was released from detention at the end of March 1975 I saw him about six weeks later in King. We had barely met before he was taken in the previous October, but he was willing to talk to me about his experience inside. He said that what hurt him more than the physical torture – though there was some of that – was the total lack of humanity in his warders. Black warders (though they can be just as brutal as whites) are never allowed to guard political detainees, so during his six months in Pretoria Mapetla only saw white faces, and they would only speak to him in Afrikaans, a language he did not understand. But they did not even speak to him in sentences. A warder would open the grille in his cell door and shout at him in Afrikaans *"Bucket!"* This meant that he must put his sanitary bucket outside. *"Shower!"* and if he didn't understand what the word meant, he missed his chance of a shower. That a fellow human being should beat him up, though unpleasant and illegal, was intelligible, but that he should be systematically treated like a dog, a member of another species, a non-human being, this was profoundly shocking. And of course it was the warders themselves who were dehumanised. One is reminded of the comment of Athanasius on the arian heretics of the fourth century who denied the divinity of Christ: "Human nature is prone to pity and sympathises with the poor. But these man have lost even the common sentiments of humanity". What the Christian deviants of Pretoria share with the arians is a denial of the central verity of our Faith, that God has a human face.

The release of Mapetla from detention more or less coincided with a decision by Steve and others to launch a new organisation to be called the Zimele Trust Fund (*Zimele* means "Stand on your own feet!"). When political prisoners come off Robben Island they are more often than not banished from their old home in towns such as Port Elizabeth to one of the notorious resettlement camps like Dimbaza, Ilinge or Sada. The system of influx control and the lack of work in these places means that there may be no opportunity of employment as they will not be able to move out of their restricted area into a town. Even if they do get employment the system will come along and advise their employers that this man is a dangerous communist agitator. Thus the long misery of imprisonment on the Island is followed by a living death in a resettlement camp. The only organisation set up to alleviate their distress was the "Dependents' Conference" of the South African Council of Churches. This had done good work earlier, while the men were still on the Island, in providing some support for the men's dependents. Rents were paid, children's educational fees, and money paid for the occasional trip to the Island by the wife of nearest relative of the prisoner. The handling of released prisoners was less satisfactory, and there was real danger of making the man and his family "dependent" in another sense, with consequent demoralisation. Besides this the organisation, which was controlled from Johannesburg (although by far the greater number of the families, for historical reasons, were in the Eastern Cape) was too white-dominated.

The idea which Steve, Mapetla and the others associated with the foundation of Zimele had was to create a fund which could not only parallel the existing work of Dependents' Conference (never able to cope adequately with the vast needs of political prisoners and their families), but could also provide loans or grants to enable ex-prisoners – if possible working in groups as a small 'collective' – really to stand on their own feet again. Steve knew that they were dealing here with a true élite – men hardened by years of oppression into an unconquerable determination for freedom; but also men who could quickly become permanently embittered unless they were given a chance to rehabilitate themselves. In Dimbaza a small collective of ex-prisoners from the Island was enabled to start a brick-making business. A hidden motive behind the launching of the Fund was to attempt to forge closer human links between the young Black Consciousness movement and its banned elder brothers, the African National Congress and Pan Africanist Congress. Virtually all the ex-prisoners were either ANC or PAC. Zimele could well act as a solvent to out-dated rivalries, and forge a new solidarity, with the militant young generation.

By this time, despite more than two years' restriction under his banning order, Steve's reputation was so high with certain organisations overseas that it was not difficult to get such a fund launched. All the same, both BCP and Zimele were in desperate need of money, very few organisations within South Africa having the vision or courage to give support. Barclays Bank, for example, when an appeal was made to them, gave R100 (about £66)!

For this reason Steve asked me, when I visited King in September 1975 if I would be interested in doing some speaking for BCP in Europe. I said that I would if it were OK by Ben Khoapa, the Executive Director. He said he would speak to Ben, and I should arrange to visit him, which I did early in November. Ben is a man rather older than the rest of the Black Consciousness leaders, who did not come in through SASO but was "converted" when already a qualified social worker who had spent years working for the "Y" (YMCA). He is an impressive character, cool, shrewd, practical, yet deeply committed. He was now not only restricted to the black urban area outside Durban called Umlazi, but also under house arrest.

It was agreed that I should speak for BCP and leave Zimele for others, but later I was asked to speak for Zimele also in one or two places on my itinerary. In fact, although there was no formal connection between the two organisations, their fundamental ideals were the same, and often the same persons were involved in both. Most of my seven weeks were spent with my Community and family, but I made contact with a number of organisations in England, and then on the last week of my trip I visited Holland, Norway, Germany and Switzerland. It was very encouraging to note the warmth shown towards organisations which were entirely in the hands of blacks and which were committed to radical but non-violent change. Although it would obviously have been better if one of the officials of the organisations had been able to do the trip, the very reason why this was not possible was authentic testimony to the creative work of BCP and Zimele. It is a fairly safe bet with South Africa to say that the degree of restrictions a person or organisation suffers is a measure of his or its effectiveness. Fortunately the system, as Steve never tired of saying, is in many ways extremely stupid, so sometimes a really effective programme escapes their attention for a significant interval.

It was also interesting to note how much naiveté there was in organisations committed to development, about conditions in South Africa, and a very widespread ignorance about the scope and vision of the Black Consciousness movement. There was over-simplification. I met a few from a left-wing background for whom it was a matter of faith that there could be *no* above ground resistance within South Africa, that the *only* hope lay in the freedom fighters and in urban guerillas drawn from ANC and PAC. This strategy of despair was the delight of BOSS (Bureau of State Security, the external equivalent of the Security Branch), knowing as they did that for a long time to come the Republic had the military strength to deal with this kind of attack. What BOSS and its government lack are creative ideas, and it is in this area that the strength of Black Consciousness lies. But I only visited one organisation which displayed this kind of naiveté. Most of the people I was dealing with were guilty rather of an under-estimation of the malignant ruthlessness of the Vorster régime. "Were not things really getting better?" I was asked, and certain cosmetic changes in the field of sport, as well as of external relations with black Africa, were adduced (for this was the era of Vorster's "Give us six months" and the détente policy). Very often one had to persuade respectable church bodies that an entirely black-run organisation was neither chaotic nor committed to violence. Fortunately there were in most places one or two informed individuals who already knew of the stature of Steve; and the success of the trip was largely due to the spread of his reputation. It was not that he was at this time widely known, certainly not in the sense that today his name is a household word. But through NUSAS particularly, with its influential contacts in the Western world, and to a lesser extent with Christian bodies and organisations devoted to development work, he was now an accepted and trusted figure. There was moreover a strong desire in such circles to aid black-run organisations, and so avoid the stigma of "paternalism".

This fact was not unknown to the system, and at about the same time as my trip to Europe an extra clause was inserted into Steve's banning order prohibiting him from working for BCP. Fortunately this came at a time when he was already getting more and more involved with Zimele, and when also the demands on his time from a constant stream of "pilgrims" were increasing. BCP as a matter of principle continued to pay his salary – a practice it and other Black Consciousness organisations continued to follow whenever any of its employees were banned or detained. Dr Mamphela Ramphele succeeded him as the Eastern Cape Branch Executive, doubling this with her work as Medical Officer at Zanempilo, where there was now, however, a second doctor on the staff. One of the most impressive features of BCP was its capacity to survive the removal of apparently key personnel, and to continue to function with a minimum loss of effectiveness, and no loss at all of spirit. The most conspicuous example was in the second half of 1976 when at least 13 of the staffs of BCP and Zimele in King were detained under the Internal Security Act, yet both organisations continued to function, and shortly afterwards Zimele greatly expanded its field of operation to meet the needs of detainees and their dependents in Johannesburg, Cape Town, Port Elizabeth and Durban. If Steve had been the kind of leader who kept everything in his own hands the organisation would have collapsed. But full scope was given to every individual for initiative, and the supportive spirit of the King community buttressed whatever shortcomings an individual might be afraid of in him or herself. When Mamphela and Dr Siyolo Solombela (the second doctor at Zanempilo) were detained in August 1976, within five days another doctor, Dr "Chappie" Phalweni, had arrived from Kuruman about 600 miles away! Thanks to the assistance of two local doctors, one white and one Indian, the main Clinic never ceased to operate, and on only two days was it not possible to visit the outstations.

EIGHT

But we are going ahead too fast: and perhaps this is the moment to expand on the last sentence of Section Six concerning my own relationship to Steve "more and more in the remaining two and a half years he was also to become a leader". Section Seven has given examples of how, in fact, Steve "used" me – as a priest to the little community at King, as an envoy for BCP and Zimele. To what extent was I merely "obliging" him? How far was I committing myself to serve the Black Consciousness movement with him as its leader? This memoir is about him, not about me; but an exploration of these questions will perhaps reveal much about his extraordinary gift of leadership.

It should be clear from what I have already written that I was strongly in favour of "Black Consciousness" long before I left Alice. After initial confusion I had welcomed the coming into being of SASO and its ascendancy on the Seminary campus. We had made St Peter's available for the SASO formation school in 1972. The banning and house arrest of Stanley Ntwasa had strengthened my conviction of the essential rightness of the black consciousness analysis of the situation in the country. Visits to him and Robert Sobukwe, and then to Barney and Steve, confirmed this. But it was Steve who brought me actually *into* the movement, so that almost insensibly I grew to evaluate everything that happened in South Africa – and beyond its borders – by the canons of the Black Consciousness movement.

There was a conflict going on in my life, which a long-standing functional weakness, as I shall tell in more concrete detail below, made more acute. On the one hand there was my official work which was at this time expressed in two main forms: First, as parish priest to the domestic workers in the southern suburbs of Johannesburg: second, as theological educator of the self-supporting ordinands of the Johannesburg diocese (i.e. men who were offering themselves for the ordained ministry of the Church while continuing in their secular occupations). The first job was like that of a doctor who has no remedy for a wound that will not heal. One can go on cleansing the wound and making the patient comfortable, cure is impossible. The social, political and economic situation of these workers was so crushing that nothing we could do for them in the Church could more than alleviate their pain. Most of them did view the "homelands" as their home; they looked forward to retiring there. Meantime they endured the drudgery of their daily lives for 11 months of the year, living in squalid back rooms separated by law from their employers' houses. Their only opportunity for real joy lay in having children by men who, even if they wanted to, could rarely afford to marry them – and then they were compelled by law to send the child away to Grannie in the "homeland". Ministering to such a congregation, of whose languages I was ignorant, was so distressing (despite the love of the people) that after enduring it for nearly two years I welcomed the chance to get back into theological education – even though when I left Alice I had vowed to stay out of it! This was at least more stimulating and thanks to the imagination of my younger colleague, the Reverend John de Beer, and to my own experience, we built up one of the best programmes of this new kind of theological education in the Anglican Church in South Africa, moulding into a unity a truly representative non-racial group through monthly training weekends, with assignments and tutorials in between. All the same one was to a considerable degree training men to be efficient servants of one more facet of "the system", the institutional Church.

That was one part of the dialectic. The other was my ministry to the banned which, beginning with Stanley Ntwasa in Kimberley, reached out to include others all over the country. Talking and even more listening to them, all of them (except Mr Sobukwe) young men of Steve's generation, observing the conditions under which they lived, I could not but be increasingly dissatisfied with the way in which I was forced to spend the greater part of my time. The one advantage of my position as an officer of the institutional Church was the protection it gave me from deportation – "your front organisation", as a friend called it.

The tensions caused by this unnatural existence were compounded by having to live in the all-white environment of the Priory at Rosettenville, after the extraordinary privilege of the years in the black world of the seminary at Alice. In the end I realised that I only really 'came alive' in my rare visits to Stanley, Steve and Barney. At the most these added up to a month in the whole year, so that I too in a way had become like my former parishioners – enduring a frustrating existence for 11 months of the year in order to enjoy the 'home' freedom of one month.

All this made me ill. Since 1963 I have suffered from a malfunction of the middle ear called "Meniere's disease", the symptoms of which are a noise in the ear, partial deafness, and, in an acute attack nausea, giddiness and vomiting. After a prolonged bout of this in the early part of 1976, in which I had partially kept my feet through drugs, I was ordered a complete rest and went for a fortnight to friends in the Eastern Cape. At the end of the fortnight, though rested, I was still on the powerful sleeping pill I had had to take for the past three months. I was by no means cured. Western medicine has no cure for this disease except surgery: one can contain it by drugs, and that is all.

Before returning to Johannesburg I spent a long week-end at Zanempilo. Whilst I had been in the Eastern Cape convalescing Steve had been giving evidence for the defence in the mammoth BPC-SASO Trial in Pretoria (see chapters 15 and 16) but now he was back. Mamphela gave me her bedroom in the doctor's house. The record-player in her sitting room next door, which was normally kept on non-stop from 5 p.m. onwards each working day, and all day at week-ends, was muted lest it trouble my ear (they all knew and were to a rare degree tolerant of my monastic need of silence!).

We talked, laughed, drank. Steve was there most of the time. They talked about my condition – "So and So wouldn't be able to stand it for more than five minutes" (naming a certain black politician). Steve and I visited his mother. We went out to the Dam, our favourite place for a private walk and talk. White fishermen were there as it was a Saturday; they looked at us curiously, but without hostility. He told me a little about the Trial; he was quite satisfied with his "performance", but said it had been exhausting. The experience of being in Johannesburg and Pretoria again had been stimulating. There had been consultations with the lawyers during the past six months which had enabled him to move around the townships; and he was relieved to discover that three years of banning in Kingwilliamstown had not caused him to be forgotten in Soweto and elsewhere. He had renewed old contacts, made new ones. Interestingly, he gave me no hint of the explosion that was to erupt in Soweto only a month later. We spoke of myself, my life in the Community. He understood the enduring loyalties – was only concerned lest they be deadening. We returned to King, had a drink with John Williams. I was to say Mass for the white congregation next morning.

Back to the Clinic. Who else was there? Besides Steve and Mamphela (and here I am bringing together recollections of many Saturday night parties) there might be Siyolo Solombela, the assistant doctor; Pinkie, a young lady from Fort Hare whom he married after his detention: Mzoxolo Ndzengu, of course, the indefatigable driver-clerk. He doesn't smoke, doesn't drink goes early to bed: how he slept through the noise of one of our parties I do not know. He never grumbled to my knowledge; was also ready to turn out at any time for an emergency ambulance case, usually a woman needing to be delivered. Malusi Mpumlwana might be there, also banned but so irrepressible, so always on the move that you couldn't accept the fact of his banning. Malusi does everything with the whole of himself even to playing cards. Watching Malusi play cards with two or three others was far more entertaining than most white theatre shows in Johannesburg could be. Thoko Mbanjwa, who married Malusi after their detention, might be there; the austere Mapetla and his radiant wife Nohle might come in – but only if they were specially asked, as Zwelitsha was far from Zanempilo, and they had no transport. Mxolisi Mvovo, Steve's brother-in-law, would certainly be there if he was not travelling – dark, saturnine, deeply sensitive, a true friend and an implacable enemy; he loved my cigars, and I loved his company, as I did that of his turbulent, extrovert wife Nobandile (Steve's younger sister). Probably Thenjiwe Mtintso, reporter on the *Daily Dispatch*, was there. Maybe also Zweli Simanga and Phumla Sangotsha (the latter the secretary for the Clinic) who completed the trio of marriages that took place at the end of the year; perhaps Silumko Sokupa ("Soks"), a devoted SASO worker.

Being a weekend there were sure to be visitors from other parts of the country; medical students from Wentworth, maybe, BPC and SASO representatives from anywhere in the country. Drink appeared after supper. My partiality for whisky was known; I usually tried to bring a little myself, but what was one bottle among so many?

Talk centred mainly on the Pretoria Trial, on the imbecilities of the
Prosecution, the disposition of the Judge – very hard to determine –
the subtly differing stances and underlying unity of the nine accused.
Nearly always the talk was entirely in English, but sometimes there
would be an exchange in Xhosa, which I could not understand.
"How long have you been out here, Father Stubbs? Seventeen years?
And you still can't speak Xhosa? It's an absolute disgrace!" This
from Steve.

Later in the evening – but on this occasion I went early to bed – he
might reminisce about his childhood, often with Church stories to
tease me. He had been a server at the little church in Ginsberg.
During the sermon he and his pals would retreat under the altar
where, concealed from view by the frontal, they would tuck into the
Communion wine, emerging for the Sanctus with swaying candle-
sticks.

Next morning I was up early to celebrate Mass in the white church
in town. It was impossible to believe one was on the same continent
as Zanempilo, let alone in the same neighbouring small town.
Almost certainly none of the congregation, except the Rector's wife,
would even have heard of the name Biko, which was now known all
over black South Africa and even, in certain circles, all over Africa
and the western world. If they had, they would think of him as a "ter-
rorist", "Communist" or at best "agitator". The only white man I
ever met in four years of visiting Steve in King who really appreciated
him was significantly not a church-goer. And this was the institution
of which I was an official representative. The credibility gap was a fis-
sure reaching down almost to the roots of one's being.

Have I written enough to indicate how it was that I came more and
more to accept the leadership of this black? Since the eclipse of
NUSAS by SASO there was no white organisation that offered any
promise of radical change. But in any case I was not a politician: I
was a priest. The Church, then? Ah, the Church! Indeed I believed in
the Church, in a way impossible for Steve, as a divine-human organ-
ism enduring through time and space. But the Church in South
Africa – and here I refer to all the "historic" churches imported into
Africa from the West – these white-dominated institutions would
have to be completely broken up and re-fashioned by true blacks on
true black lines. Not that whites should be excluded – God forbid!
But we must first be humbled to the dust. This was already happening with comparative ease in the Anglican diocese of Damaraland in

Namibia, where an overwhelmingly black Synod ironically still voted to keep as their bishop the charismatic figure of the deported Colin Winter. It was happening in a more halting manner in Zululand, thanks to the presence of one of the truly great Christians of this century, Bishop Alphaeus Zulu. But in Johannesburg and Grahamstown, the two dioceses which I had served since 1959 – there nothing but a revolution in the country itself, it seemed to me, would remove the entrenched attitudes in the Church of white superiority and white values. A superficial 'blackening' of the church there might be, through the appointment of a black archdeacon here, a black dean or even assistant bishop there, through arranging racial parity of representation on synods, provincial committees and so on. None of this changed the fundamental attitudes, purpose or direction of these Churches and to my radical black friends many (though by no means all) of the blacks in high ecclesiastical positions were witheringly dismissed as "non-whites" (one of the most contemptuous terms in the Black Consciousness vocabulary, used to describe a person who, calling himself black, by his behaviour or lifestyle shows he hankers after or accepts white values). I would not leave the Church. God forbid! It is His Church, and He knows what He is about. But except by prayer, prayer embraced as a whole way of life, I could do nothing to change it.

On the other side there was my friendship with this amazing man, whose gift of leadership consisted pre-eminently in discerning the capacities of those whose trust he had gained, and in enabling them to realise them to the full. He was able to channel into a creative and purposeful direction my diffused sense of compassion for the poor and oppressed. And so here he was now, while always mindful, in true African style, of the respect due to my age, taking hold of me, letting me a little more into his confidence, appreciative of the information I could, through my mobility and contacts with the white world, bring him, responding to my stated availability with suggestions of assignments that were always within both my capabilities and what was proper for me to perform. I am sure there was a lot going on of which I knew nothing – not because I was not trusted, but for my own protection. Should I be detained and interrogated – by now a real possibility – there were things it was better for me not to know.

There must have been other leaders of revolutionary struggles who have been similarly careful of the "troops" at their command. Gari-

baldi springs to mind, and Robert Sobukwe may well be a contemporary example. But I would have to go back to Jesus himself to find
a parallel to this extraordinary pastoral care which Steve had for his
own. I suppose this is why I was prepared to commit myself so whole-
heartedly to the care of his leadership. In this particular area I trusted
him with the same *kind* of trust I have in Jesus. I know this sounds
idolatrous to a Christian believer, but there was nothing idolatrous
in my attitude to him, as must be clear from our relationship as
sketched in this memoir. The main points here are the freedom Steve
allowed his followers, a freedom to be themselves; and the actual
rightness of his judgements and dispositions, a rightness which
flowed from his intelligence and from his essential revolutionary selflessness (see Section Twelve below). Whereas other leaders tend almost
insensibly to become Leaders with a capital L, I never saw any sign at
all of this happening with Steve. He remained to the end on all fours
with us, an example of what we all could be, above and beyond us
only in his vision, and in the depths of his commitment as his death in
detention showed.

And then, finally, there was the new quality that life in his company took on. It was like the Kingdom. The impossible became possible. Sometimes indeed it became actual, look at Zanempilo! And
this quality of life, while it might initially be 'caught' from him, could
become something inherent in oneself. This was pre-eminently true
of his black contemporaries but it could even happen to a non-black
like myself! Whatever his non-belief in the Christ of the historic
churches in his style of leadership Steve became an authentic (if un-
conscious) disciple of Jesus of Nazareth. This is why the movement
of which he is now the acknowledged "father" will never be destroyed. In fact the more it is crushed under the heel of the system the
more it will flower, the more it will proliferate. Herein, supremely,
lies the triumph of his death. And at the very heart of this man's life
was the quality of compassion – not the emasculated word of white
society with its paternalistic connotation of "feeling sorry for" someone in a worse situation than yourself, but the suffering-with that is
the word's true meaning, the compassion that was the driving force
in Christ's ministry to men. Steve extended this compassion not only
to his fellow blacks but also to whites whom he came to know. He
really understood, as from within, the agonising position of Beyers
Naude – an Afrikaner of Afrikaners, yet driven by his conscience to
oppose the policies and practice of the Nationalist Party.

On this occasion I expressed some concern at the strain of having to drive solo through the Transkei and Natal and so back to Johannesburg. He asked Mxolisi to accompany me. We left Zanempilo on the Tuesday morning, called on Pumzile Majeke, the former Zimele field worker who had been banned to his home village of Qumbu a few weeks earlier, and reached Pietermaritzburg that evening, where he left me with my Community Brethren while he took the car on to Durban. Next afternoon he returned, having picked up Diliza Mji, the current President of SASO, and another friend. We drove north, stopping for supper at the house of an old St Peter's student outside Ladysmith, and eventually arrived in Soweto at 3.45 on Thursday morning. After returning to the Priory and enabling Mxolisi to have half an hour's sleep, I drove him to the airport to catch a 'plane back to East London, and returned to the Priory to hear the bell ringing for Ascension Day Mass. I was cured!

NINE

Five days later I flew to England to visit my mother, and was there on 16 June when the killings of students in Soweto marked yet another irreversible step on the road to freedom. Returning to Johannesburg on 1 July one could only find words in W. B. Yeats to describe the revolution in the atmosphere:

> All, all is utterly changed . . .
> A terrible beauty is born.

That month scores of leading blacks were detained under the new Internal Security Act, which gave the Minister of Police power to imprison people for up to a year (which could be renewed) in preventive detention. They had the status of awaiting trial prisoners. I saw Steve briefly that month, to report on contacts I had made while overseas. For the first time in three and a half years he expressed frustration at being unable to move around at this crucial time, and be able to give direction to the heroic but uncoordinated protests of the young generation of students. It became clear to many that the Soweto uprising had altered the balance of black political forces and Steve, who would be 30 at the end of the year, was emerging as the new national leader, with good connections with the older generation who now moved up into the position of elder statesmen, and a natural role at the head of the new generation of idealistic but untutored schoolboys and girls.

It was an especial strength in the Black Consciousness movement that from the beginning in the late 1960s SASO had been open to Coloureds and Indians. I am not sure that the importance of this achievement, in the given social structures of South Africa, has been sufficiently emphasised. ANC, it is true, had been open to other than Africans; and because of a strong political tradition amongst elements of the Indian community many of the latter made a notable contribution. But the way in which SASO managed to overcome traditional barriers between Coloureds and Africans – barriers which had certainly caused tensions at our Alice Seminary – this was not only indicative of a new mood in the young Coloured community, but a significant achievement of non-ethnic black solidarity.

Now African and Coloured schoolchildren were converging on Cape Town in a joint protest march. Cape Town indeed emerged as one of the most militant centres of unrest in the country. The young Coloured, rejected and humiliated by years of discriminatory legislation in a city that was at many points traditionally integrated as far as whites and Coloured were concerned, had finally rejected the whites. Thus they brought a new injection of power into the movement. It has to be admitted that the detention of virtually all the leadership of the Black Consciousness movement during the second half of 1976 was effective in preventing the harnessing of the magnificent but in some respects undirected sacrificial spirit of the students. "In some respects" because initially they knew exactly what they wanted, and got it – the abolition of Afrikaans as a compulsory medium of instruction in schools. But the momentum imparted by the massacre on the 16th, together with the unrelenting harassing, rounding up, and beating to death of so many of the students – the internal security act detainees at Modder B could hear this going on – so that the leadership of the Soweto Students' Representative Council was constantly on the run – all this militated against an ordered plan of campaign such as the mature leadership of the Black Consciousness movement would have been able to offer. This is not to take away from the extraordinary achievement of the youngsters.

Zimele had begun to be too effective an organisation for the liking of the system. Earlier in the year the admirable field worker, Pumzile Majeke, was banned to his home in the Transkei. On 17 July Mapetla Mohapi, the administrator of the organisation, was detained under section 6 of the Terrorism Act. On 5 August at 11.30 p.m. Steve telephoned: "Mapetla has died in detention". This was a shattering blow. Already a number of men had died in detention, and their deaths had made an impact on their local communities proportionate to their reputations. Particularly horrifying to the Cape Town community had been the violent death in detention (allegedly by his "falling downstairs") in 1969 of Imam Abdullah Haroun, a respected leader of the Muslim community. An Anglican priest, the Reverend Bernard Wrankmore, went on a long hunger strike, much publicised, in an attempt to secure a judicial enquiry into the Imam's death. But Mapetla was the first member of the Black Consciousness Movement to die in detention. (Ongkopotso Tiro had been killed by a parcel-bomb in exile in Botswana; he with Nthuli Shezi (see last section of chapter 15 p 100 and pp 115ff) are the first two martyrs of the movement.

Steve and the community went into action at once. The family demanded that two doctors attend the autopsy on their behalf. Doctors Msauli and Ramphele were their choice. No-one believed the system's story that he had hanged himself with two pairs of jeans. The funeral took place ten days later at Mapetla's home, a remote kraal in hill country near the borders of Lesotho. Four thousand mourners came, from King, Durban, Port Elizabeth, Cape Town, Johannesburg. Dr (now Bishop) Manas Buthelezi preached the funeral oration. Cedric Mayson of the Christian Institute had a pilot's licence and flew down Beyers Naude, Manas and myself. The three of us, together with Francis Wilson and David Russell, were the only whites present. I will never forget the combination of anger and hope in that massive crowd. Steve of course could not attend because of his restriction order.

Two days later, on Tuesday 17 August, he and Thenjiwe Mtintso were detained under section 6 of the Terrorism Act. The previous week almost the entire leadership of BCP and BPC in King, as I have already mentioned, had been taken in under the Internal Security Act. But this detention of Steve and Thenjiwe was more serious. Knowing what had happened to Barney and others two years before, with Mapetla's death still raw in our minds, anxiety was deep. Surely they were aware of his international reputation? Donald Woods, editor of the East London *Daily Dispatch*, wrote an article syndicated in other leading South African papers, warning Kruger (Minister of Police) to treat Biko with kid gloves because one day one of his (Steve's) men might be occupying Kruger's position; and Africans have long memories! For whatever reason, Steve was, as he later told us, not seriously assaulted during his detention, though he lost a lot of weight because of the inedible food provided. The food his wife Ntsiki brought in helped: but the long intervals between visits meant it had to consist mainly of biscuits and tinned stuff, food he didn't particularly like.

If Steve was treated with relative mildness the same was not true of Thenjiwe, a brave and attractive young woman reporter on the *Daily Dispatch*. Comparing notes afterwards she and Steve discovered that whenever *he* had not been "co-operative" *she* had received 'the treatment'! Steve was kept in detention in East London for 101 days, and was then released without being charged. I flew down to see him about a week after his release, and found him much thinner. He could afford to lose some weight, and when he began to put it on again I threatened to get him re-detained. He said it had been an interesting experience. Apart from two members of the Branch who had tried to have a go at him for vindictive personal reasons (one of whom was so old Steve had just humoured him, the other was a distorted little man who had a posse of toughs outside in case Steve proved too much for him), and apart from the vile food, he had found it a useful time for reflection, and he was satisfied with the way he had coped with the questioning. He said he made it clear that he would only "co-operate" if they let him rest when he wanted to; and they complied with this. His principle was always to tell the truth if he possibly could because otherwise "things became complicated"; and he said that on the whole he had rarely found it necessary to depart from the truth! They asked him about me, but accepted his statement that I was his "spiritual father" and that our conversations were on deep personal matters. I could see that he was pleased with his "performance", and that it had not increased his respect for the system.

1976 came to its turbulent end with the release of all those detained under section 10 of the Internal Security Act, but Thenjiwe (who had been transferred more dead than alive from the Transkei, where she was held under section 6, back to King under section 10) was banned immediately, which meant the loss of her job on the *Daily Dispatch* (though the paper continued to pay her salary) and her removal to Orlando East, Soweto, where her mother lives. The scene was darkening and we all sensed we were living on borrowed time as the enemy became more desperate. Steve foresaw a period of up to five years of continued unrest, use by the police of their repressive powers, the situation "getting under control", some releases, fresh detentions, and so on. He was supremely confident of the outcome, but the immediate future was going to be tough. At no point did he ever give any hint of foreseeing his own death; and indeed the story of his treatment in detention, together with his growing prestige both outside and within the country, enhanced of course by his detention, made us confident that whatever other casualties we had to expect he at least was indestructible.

The release of the Black Consciousness leaders had two immediate results. First it meant that certain key people could have contact with the student leadership in Soweto and elsewhere and help them gain a sense of direction and strategy. Secondly, it enabled BPC to have a national meeting, in which far-reaching decisions and plans for the future were made, and Steve was elected Honorary President. It was the best way the political wing of the movement could openly acknowledge his leadership. Because of his banning order he could not accept the position; nor did he need to decline it. Honorary President he remains, despite his death, despite the banning of the organisation on 19 October.

Early in the new year the long-deferred inquest on Mapetla Mohapi took place in King. The two doctors asked by the family to represent them at the post-mortem, Dr Ramphele and Dr Msauli, had been detained almost immediately after the post-mortem, she before the funeral, he a week or two after it. Although the case now pales into insignificance in the light of Steve's own inquest, it was memorable at the time for the way Advocate Cooper made Captain Schoeman wriggle. A lawyer involved in the case said that Steve's contribution behind the scenes was "enormous". It was through his suggestions largely that the family lawyers were able to establish to any objective tribunal that Mapetla could not possibly have committed suicide: he must have been killed. The verdict after two weeks was that Mapetla "died by strangulation, and that no-one was to blame" – an odd conclusion! The court room was packed each day, and the humiliations suffered by Schoeman and the other members of the system were not calculated to make life easier for Steve once the inquest ended. During the next few months he was seldom free from harassment, including his indictment on a long and complicated charge of "defeating the ends of justice" – a case to do with some young boys detained in connection with the burning of the local secondary school. He was found not guilty, but it was exhausting – and expensive. All this time he was trying to continue his studies for a law degree by correspondence with UNISA. At first the authorities refused to grant him an aegrotat for having been so remiss as to be in detention during the examination period. Representations were made to the head of the Law Faculty. Furious with the Administration, he sent word that Steve should continue to prepare for the examination. After some delay permission to write was granted. Steve passed four out of the five subjects he attempted.

He was very keen that they should all be continuing their studies by correspondence, even while they were doing full-time work for BCP of Zimele, or in whatever sphere they were engaged. He gave the detainees no holiday on release from detention at the end of the year. He said they'd had quite enough holiday inside, and there was work to be done! Psychologically he knew it was much healthier to get straight down to work and have the machine running smoothly again; individuals could have holidays later, if needed. Besides, they had a responsibility both to the suffering people they served, and to their donors. The person who really needed a holiday was Nohle Mohapi, Mapetla's widow. She had turned up to work the day after her husband's death in detention. Then there was a period before the funeral when she observed the traditional customs. But from after the funeral she had been in sole charge at the BCP offices, with the help of two young women friends. She had kept the whole administration going in the Eastern Cape from mid-August to the end of the year.Then in January she had the ordeal of the inquest. She came through all this with serenity and beauty unimpaired. So there were no holidays, but there was a tremendous party at Zanempilo, with Donald Woods supplying champagne from the proceeds of an article on Steve.

I went down for the week-end in January, partly to attend the first day of the Mohapi inquest. I stayed at the Clinic; John Williams had left for England the previous month. There was a lot of system activity that week-end. Thenjiwe had come down to give evidence at the inquest and the system was determined to try to prevent communication between her and Steve. The Clinic and Steve's home were closely watched. He and I needed to talk undisturbed. In the end he managed to come over to the Clinic and I drove us out the "back" way to our usual rendezvous at the Dam.

When we were sitting on the grass by the water's edge he suddenly began to talk about his earlier life. There was no preamble, but I understood that he had reflected on all this while in solitary confinement. The narrative proved to be the justification (though told in no self-justifying tone) of the "confrontation" I had forced over two years before.

I understood why this was happening now. He knew that I now had such relationships of affection and mutual acceptance with the other two persons concerned as made it possible for him to speak to me of them with complete freedom.

If I say that it was a "confession" Christian readers must not take that in a technical sense. There was no formal confession of sin, still less any expression of purpose of amendment or prayer for forgiveness. Yet it was a "confession" in the sense that it was a simple telling of the truth of himself, and a particular area of his life, as he saw it. As I have said, there was no self-justification; but then from me there was no longer any accusation. There was simply the telling of the story; this is how it was, this is how it is, and only God knows how it will be.

When he had finished there was nothing that needed to be said, but I think that we both sensed that in this silence after the forth-telling the past was annulled and the future could be met with a deeper wholeness. For such matters we had, in fact, scant leisure. I noticed three blacks regarding us with interest. "BOSS", murmured Steve, and moved towards them. One proved to be the brother of the Chief Minister of the Ciskei, Mr Sebe, and another was the brother of an ordained minister I had taught at Alice. Steve was very civil to them, and introduced me; but when the senior of them asked me, "Were you born in this country, Father?" he retorted sharply: "What business is it of yours where Father Stubbs comes from?"

Soon afterwards another car with a large radio aerial and safari-suited driver swept up. Sergeant Viljoen of the Security Branch beamed at us in gratified relief. Apparently he had had orders to tail us, and had completely lost track of us. He could not go off duty until he had found us, and had come to Mamphela at the Clinic and begged her, almost in tears, to tell us where we were. She of course had answered that she had no idea where we had gone. At length BOSS had put him on the trail – hence the relieved smile. He asked us how long we would be here as Warrant Officer Hattingh (our old crony from Alice days) would now be taking over, but this curiosity Steve refused to gratify. He drove off. As it was time in any case to turn to other business we drove back into town, meeting Hattingh on the way. He of course immediately turned round and sat on our tail.

We stopped at a cafe as we had forgotten to take food and were hungry and thirsty. As I came out I went up to Hattingh and greeted him. He would not even look up, and merely grunted; the black system guy with him greeted me with a cheerful smile. So ended what proved to be our last visit to the Dam.

Early in the new year there was an interesting meeting. The "Urban Foundation" had been launched – an attempt by some top industrialists, led by Harry Oppenheimer and Anton Rupert, to improve the quality of urban life. They realised that if the country was ever to return to normal (itself a question-begging term!) the conditions of life for urban blacks must change. They hoped that by both working with the government and with the citizens of Soweto they could use their money to effect improvements which would be more than merely cosmetic. It was pointed out to those responsible within the Foundation that such a scheme could never succeed unless it had the support of the *young* blacks concerned. A meeting was accordingly arranged between three or four representatives of the Foundation and four members of BPC. The meeting was, by mutual agreement, secret and informal. Had it been known to the right wing of the Foundation, or to the left wing of BPC that it was taking place, explosions would have resulted! It seemed, at this early stage, as if some form of cooperation might be possible, e.g. for BCP to undertake some community development projects in Soweto and other black urban centres, the money to be put up by the Foundation.

But when the matter was brought before the BPC Executive, after a very long discussion, the decision was made that it would not be possible for the organisation to collaborate with such a body as the Urban Foundation. Although no reason was officially given it was clear that BPC could not afford to be even unofficially involved with an organisation which had openly stated its desire to work in concert with Bantu Administration Boards and other official government channels. Steve had been sympathetic to the informal meeting taking place, but he considered that the right decision had been made, and as the year wore on he found his opinion confirmed by the difficulties the Foundation ran into, and the image it began to have for the people of Soweto. I was bitterly disappointed at the time as by temperament and vocation I am a reconciler rather than confronter. Also I considered that the Foundation man through whom all projects would go for screening was admirably equipped to deal with people like BCP, to their and his profit and enjoyment. But I came myself to see that things had gone too far for such a gradualist proposal to have any chance of success. The people of Soweto might not all consciously know it, but their children certainly did. They did not primarily want electric light in all houses, good roads, fine community centres, and so forth. They wanted what they could only call "freedom", and nothing less. In other words they wanted an end to racial discrimination in every sphere of life: freedom of movement, freedom to sell their labour, equal educational opportunities with whites, i.e. free compulsory education for all, and of the same standard as whites; above all political representation which would recognise that South Africa is one society, not a conglomeration of arbitrarily determined ethnic groups radically unequal in economic wealth, and hence in political power. However well-intentioned the Foundation might be (and unfortunately it could not be denied that the proponents of the scheme obviously wanted to make South Africa safe for capitalism) their do-gooding in Soweto could have the most disastrous effect of all, that of making the people contented with their lot. The children could sense how easily their parents could be cajoled into accepting material benefits which made life temporarily easier without in any fundamental way changing the realities of their subjugation. If BPC had agreed to collaborate with the Foundation they would have betrayed those who had fallen to the police bullets in June the previous year. Not for the first time, after 18 years in South Africa, one realised with a sigh that things would have to get worse before they could get better. Just how much worse the unfolding year of 1977 would show.

TEN

My own position in South Africa had for some years been precarious. By coming out from England when the country was still in the Commonwealth, and then by registering when it became a Republic, I had been granted permanent residence; and a British citizen was exempted from visa requirements. This "privilege", however, could be withdrawn at any time at the discretion of the Minister of the Interior. After five years' residence one could apply for citizenship. This I did in 1964, but my application was refused because of the report put in on me by the Security Branch, in which it was said that I had been engaged in POQO activities – a unique honour for a white man! After my return from England in July 1976 I resolved not to leave the Republic until I had to visit my mother the following year

– no visits to Lesotho, Botswana, Swaziland or Zimbabwe.

At the beginning of April I flew down to Port Elizabeth to preach the Three Hours' Devotion at a Coloured parish of which an old student of ours was Rector. On our way from the airport to the Rectory our car was stopped by the system in a trap deliberately set for us, and we were ordered to accompany them to the local police station. There I was told to bring all my luggage into the station. Four men, led by Captain Siebert (the man who drove the dying Steve naked in the back of a Land Rover from Port Elizabeth to Pretoria, a distance of more than 700 miles, the night before he died), took me into a room. He ordered me to strip and conducted a body search, while the other three went through my luggage. After an hour and a half of this Siebert said I could go. They retained my intercession book, two address books, pocket diary, a folder of letters, six copies of a new Christian Institute publication *Torture in South Africa?* and a copy of a fine preaching of the Passion by the Reverend John Davies, *Crisis*. Both documents were subsequently banned. The Rector's wife, who was driving me, said she was politely treated but had to produce her handbag for a scrutiny and that they had made a minute search of the entire car.

When I drove across after Easter to recount the incident to Steve he was cross with me for meekly submitting to the order to strip! He said that when he was taken in under section 6 he had never let them search his clothes or his person, and in fact he had kept a piece of pencil in his overcoat pocket all the time he was in detention. All the same he was angry about the incident, and said I probably had a case against the police – a view which was confirmed by Counsel whom I consulted in Johannesburg. The Community had agreed for me to proceed against the Minister of Police and Captain Siebert when I had to fly to England early in June to see my mother, who was dying.

Something much more serious than this small incident happened while I was still down in the Eastern Cape. Mxolisi Mvovo was banned and put under house arrest in Dimbaza; and Mamphela Ramphele, the lady doctor who had been in charge of Zanempilo since it was built, and who had succeeded Steve as Branch Executive when he was prohibited from working for BCP, was banished to Tzaneen in the Northern Transvaal. The system entered the BCP office and compelled her to accompany them. Having manhandled her to the police van they then drove her straight to Tzaneen (800 miles away) without even allowing her to return to the Clinic and pack a bag. Arrived at a remote hospital in the Lebowa bantustan they said "Here is a room, and this is where you are going to work", and left. Steve told me all this when I arrived in King on my way back to Johannesburg, and asked me to use my influence with Mamphela not to do anything rash. Knowing her high-spiritedness we thought it unlikely she would take such a violent hi-jacking lying down; but Steve did not want her to land in gaol for an ill-considered act of defiance. He believed that even in her unpromising new situation she could use her peculiar skills to spread the gospel of Black Consciousness. Specifically he wanted a trusted white lawyer to visit her as soon as possible and scrutinise the restriction order so uncouthly served on her by Captain Schoeman.

Returning to Johannesburg after a sad week-end at Zanempilo without Mamphela I discovered that the lawyer would go and see her that Thursday 28 April. Later that afternoon she phoned me and said that he was with her and wanted directions for reaching the Priory from Pretoria. In the evening the lawyer himself phoned me and asked me to go across and see him at his home. He told me that Mamphela's restriction order had been incorrectly made out. Not only was her name wrongly spelt, but the order bore the wrong reference book number. The order clearly applied to someone other than Mamphela, and he had advised her accordingly.

At about half past midnight she arrived at the Priory with her bewildered young brother Tommy. He had just arrived to see her at Trichardtsdal, and all she had said was, "Good! I'm glad you've come. Now we're off!", bundled him into the car and driven the 200 miles odd to Johannesburg. At her request I had tried to contact Cedric Mason to fly her down to King, but he was away on holiday. So we put Tommy to bed and left a note under one of the Fathers' doors to look after him, and at 4 a.m. we slipped quietly out of the Priory and Johannesburg on our 600-mile drive to King. The drive was without incident, except that shortly after joining the national road I looked in the mirror and saw a police van on our tail with two white police in camouflage uniforms. I kept at the regulation 90km per hour, and it stayed on our tail for several miles. At length it swung out and passed us, and the man nearest us leaned out of the window and gave us a long, hard look. I didn't suppose they knew who Mamphela was, but I guessed they might charge us under the Immorality Act. Fortunately they were not waiting for us at the next town, and we arrived by the back way at the Zanempilo Clinic shortly before 4 p.m.

Mamphela knew that if she were seen by any of the local people they would make a noise which could be picked up by the system from their bugging device on the telephone, so she lay down on the floor of the car while I drove into the Clinic. She jumped out at the door of her house, and told me to tell any of the staff to come. I found Matron Nongause, Phumla Simanga (Secretary) and Mzoxolo Ndzengu (driver/clerk) in the telephone room.

Phumla: Fr Stubbs! . . . Are you alone?

A. Stubbs: I have a friend with me.

P. S.: Male or female?

A. S.: Female.

P. S. Oh, Fr Stubbs, you are a socialite!

A. S. Come and meet her!

By this time Mzoxolo had guessed the secret, but Phumla was still busy asking leading questions, and I had to lead her gently but firmly away from the telephone and take them to Mamphela's house, where the latter had chosen a room as far away from the 'phone as possible.

When they had all recovered from the shock I got one of them to phone Steve and ask him to come round. His first comment was "Fr Stubbs, I thought I told you to keep her where she was!" We phoned Donald and Wendy Woods, who came over from East London in time for breakfast next morning, Saturday. How should we arrange for the system to learn what had happened? It had been raining heavily before Mamphela left Trichardtsdal, so that the roads would have become impassable and they would not have discovered her flight. Her first plan was to enjoy an undisturbed week-end at Zanempilo, and let them discover her at work in the office in town on Monday morning. I asked her if it would not be still more satisfactory to have Donald run a lead story in the Monday *Dispatch*; and this is what happened. It was, of course, a short-lived triumph. An almost obsequiously polite Major Hansen arrived on Monday afternoon, deprecated the unseemly manner of her previous removal, and ended by asking for her correct reference book number. But it gave her ten days in which to come to terms with her banishment, with the help of Steve, and to set affairs at Zanempilo in order for her successor; and for the staff and surrounding community, by whom she was now so much beloved, to give her a proper farewell.

Steve and I had some talk on the Saturday morning about work I would do for them while overseas. He had, a short while before, refused an urgent invitation to visit the United States as a guest, under the auspices of the U.S.A./S.A. leadership exchange programme. He said that he would only accept such an invitation when America had given proof of a radically changed policy towards South Africa. For the same reason (and also because he felt a man in Young's position should first try to see Mandela and Sobukwe) he refused an invitation to meet Ambassador Andrew Young on the latter's visit to the Republic. The refusal to go to America (although of course it is only too probable the Vorster regime would have refused to relax his banning order or give him a passport) was costly, not only because a breath of outside air would have been refreshing and stimulating, but also because it might have given him an opportunity secretly to meet leaders of ANC and PAC and see if he could not effect a reconciliation between these two rivals with a view to presenting a common and united front for liberation. BPC was the only aboveground organisation working for radical change within the country. It was surely vital to the common goal for it now to be officially recognised as such by the two older bodies? He encouraged me, therefore, to investigate possible invitations to visit England or a European country, and in fact while I was overseas I was able to set in motion two such invitations. I flew back on the Saturday afternoon, having arranged for a quick return visit early in June before I left for England. Because of the news of my mother's serious condition this visit did not materialise, and I never saw Stephen again.

ELEVEN

The rest of the tale is quickly told. Mamphela duly returned to her place of banishment. The system at Tzaneen, having been made to look extremely silly, were correspondingly vicious, and enforced her order more rigorously than before. I visited her after she had been back a fortnight. Local Roman Catholic missionaries and African Sisters had been welcoming, and she had not even spent one night in the State-run hospital where – to give but one example of the prevailing ethos – an illiterate mother presenting her ailing infant for treatment was handed a death certificate in order that the doctor should not be disturbed in the night. She was in high spirits and already spreading the gospel of Black Consciousness.

But for Steve her going left a big gap; and Ntsiki had had to leave St Matthews Mission Hospital which had been taken over by the government, and was seeking a new post at All Saints, Engcobo, Transkei. We spoke regularly on the 'phone during these weeks –

never satisfactory because both our 'phones were tapped. One good recruit he had collected for King at the beginning of the year was Peter Jones, a strong BPC man from Cape Town. Peter was a trained accountant, and when Mamphela was banished he in due course succeeded her as the Eastern Cape Branch Executive, and lived among the small and very demoralised Coloured community on the edge of King. Nothing was more impressive than this continuing succession of totally committed young men and women. Thoko Mpumlwana, who got married to Malusi as soon as both were released from detention in December 1976, was banned at the height of the arrangements for the production of *Black Review*, which she was editing. Immediately Steve was able to call on Asha Rambally, a young Indian woman in Durban, to "come over and help us".

After visiting Bennie Khoapa in Durban for last-minute instructions on BCP contacts in Europe and Britain I flew to London on 6 June. My mother died on 2 July. Exactly a fortnight after the funeral I was at Mirfield, the headquarters of my Community, when a dapper young man from South Africa House arrived and presented me with the document I most feared to receive; notice from the Minister of the Interior that in my case he had decided to withdraw the visa exemption facilities which are accorded to certain citizens of the United Kingdom.

Steve and I had more than once discussed what I should do – subject to obedience to my Community of course – if this were to happen. We both felt strongly that I should if possible not leave South Africa. I had in fact for more than two years been drawn to a more contemplative way of life, and I had discussed with him my idea for living a life of prayer on an old mission station between King and East London. He was against this primarily because he considered that my gifts were best exercised in direct contact with people. The incident with the system in Port Elizabeth had any way made clear to me the impossibility of carrying through my plan in its original form.

But now that I could not return to South Africa the possibility arose of living this life of prayer in a country adjacent to the Republic. There was Masite in Lesotho where a community of enclosed nuns has lived the life for twenty years. My Superior and Chapter agreed, the Bishop of Lesotho and Prioress of the Society of the Precious Blood were welcoming, and I flew from London to Maseru on Saturday 20 August, spending the night of Sunday 21 in the international transit lounge of Jan Smuts airport, Johannesburg. From there I telephoned Steve. His mother answered the 'phone and said he had been detained two days earlier, together with Peter Jones. She thought they were being held in Grahamstown (in fact they had already been moved to Port Elizabeth though the family was not informed). The rest is history. He died in detention exactly three weeks after my arrival in Lesotho.

Five weeks after his death, on 19 October, all the Black Consciousness organisations were banned. Zanempilo, the apple of his eye, was handed over to the Provincial Health Department. The medical superintendent and secretary were dismissed; the rest of the staff could stay on but must accept the drastically lower salary scales fixed by the government for "bantu". The Njwaxa leather-working cottage industry was closed down; police came and removed the machinery, thus depriving a whole community of its means of livelihood. By the stroke of a ministerial pen work all over the country that had given life and hope to thousands of men and women and children was smashed.

Of his closest friends and colleagues only his immediate family, Mamphela, and Ben Khoapa are not in detention. Ben is in Europe; Mamphela is in her place of banishment in Lebowa. Barney was detained under section 6 three days before Steve and Peter, and is still held in Port Elizabeth. Thami Zani, who two years ago endured over 400 days in detention, the greater part in solitary, is in again under section 6. Stanley Ntwasa has now been in for a year under section 6. No-one has seen him during that whole year. On 19 October, when the organisations were banned, too many friends to mention by name were taken in under the Internal Security Act; let those of Kenny Rachidi, President of BPC, Drake Tshenkeng, Vice-President, Mxolisi (Steve's brother-in-law), Malusi, Dimza (Barney's wife) and Thenjiwe suffice. The night has come.

TWELVE

What did Steve die for? In what sense, if any, can he be called a Christian martyr? I want to end this short and highly subjective memoir by trying to answer these questions. I do so from an inner necessity, rather than for any "propaganda" purposes. In this section I am grateful to be allowed to quote from a memorandum Steve sent to Fr David Russell in 1974, which sets forth his basic ideas about God, the Church and Christ. It would not be fair to print the memorandum in full as it was a response to a document which David had sent Steve.

Nevertheless, a good deal of it seems to reflect fairly his mature views on these subjects.

Does God exist?
I have never had problems with this question. I am sufficiently convinced of the inadequacy of man and the rest of creation to believe that a greater force than mortals is responsible for the creation, maintenance and continuation of life. I am also sufficiently religious to believe that man's internal insecurity can only be alleviated by an almost enigmatic and supernatural force to which we ascribe all power, all wisdom and love. This is ultimately what makes us tick. As Napoleon put it, if God was not there it would be necessary to create him. Of course my conviction is much stronger than merely to conceive of a God as of convenience for man. I go further therefore to believe that God has laid for man certain basic laws that must govern interaction between man and man, man and nature at large. These laws I see as inscribed in the ultimate conscience of each living mortal. I speak of ultimate conscience here because I believe man has enough power to dull his sensitivity to his own conscience and hence become hard, cruel, evil, bad, etc. But intrinsically somewhere in him there is always something that tells him he is wrong. This is then his awareness of the unexpressed and unwritten laws that God has laid down to regulate human behaviour.

What is God's nature?
This is where problems begin. In my mind I find it completely unnecessary for me to even contemplate the nature of the God I believe in; whether he is spiritual, human or plant-like, I find completely irrelevant to the issue. I rather like to know God not in terms of what exactly he is made of but more in terms of his characteristics. This is not completely foreign to human experience in our times. We speak in certain terms of subatomic particles, of types of light rays, of different forms of energy, all of which we have neither actually located nor seen. However invisible bodies can be studied and a fair understanding reached of what they are all about. Equally then we need not know the absolute quintessence of God's nature. Suffice it to trace back to him all that happens around us and out of this to begin to understand somewhat his powers.

But the real stumbling block for Steve was the South African phenomenon of the historic churches as they presented themselves to him.

Most of the time one is born into or within a particular religion and denomination and very little individual thinking is done to consider the fundamental relationship between man and God. I was likewise born into the Anglican Church. At a certain stage in my life I considered strongly the question of why I was not a Catholic, or a Methodist, etc. Besides rationalising the established fact of my being an Anglican I found very little reason for my being Anglican other than the fact that my parents worshipped in that context. I have since become extremely critical of denominationalism. Beyond this I've also grown to question in fact that very need for worship in an organised way. In other words do organised churches necessarily have a divine origin or should one view them as mancreated institutions probably in the same category as soccer clubs?

The existence of a multiplicity of denominations convinces me of the uselessness of organised worship in investigating man's duty to God. Churches have tended to complicate religion and theology and to make it a matter to be understood only by specialists. Churches have tended to drive away the common man by immersing themselves in bureaucracy and institutionalisation. Where does the truth lie – with the Methodists or Anglicans, with the Catholics or Jews, with Jehova's Witnesses or the Seventh Day Adventists? In my view the truth lies in my ability to incorporate my vertical relationship with God into the horizontal relationships with my fellow men; in my ability to pursue my ultimate purpose on earth which is to do good.

My attitude to the Church – i.e. organised denominational worship – is therefore completely down to earth. I see them more as social man-made institutions without any divine authority. Though probably useful and potentially much more useful, organised worship, I feel, is not a prerequisite to proximity to God. I can reject all Churches and still be Godly. I do not need to go to Church on Sunday in order to manifest my godliness. Yet I do appreciate that all too often people's moral convictions are reinforced by constant revival meetings. If then I go to Church it is more for this type of limited service than because I regard them as

having a monopoly on truth and moral judgement. If then my
motives for going to Church are bound to be limited expectations I
feel free to withdraw without any compunctions if and when my
expectations are not met. For this purpose also, the ultimate
denomination which serves me is only of relative importance. It
could be Anglican or Catholic or Methodist depending on whether
either the minister in charge or part of the congregation are likely
to help me in a concrete way in shaping up for my calling.

But what about Christ?
From the above it becomes obvious that I am underplaying the
role of Christ. My problem is that the most unbelievable aspects of
organised religion are to do with the advent and subsequent role of
Christ on earth. As a historical fact I find it easily acceptable that
Christ did come to earth. What I find difficult to accept, however,
are the many dogmatic pronouncements that accompany
explanations about Christ's advent and subsequent role on earth.
The Catholic Church demands that I believe that Christ was true
Man and true God at the same time. How can I? All true men have
mortal fathers and mothers. But the Church does not accept that
Joseph was Christ's father. I remember saying to my tutors at a
Catholic School – the choice is simple; it is either we are
worshipping an illegitimate child as our God or we are elevating a
normal human being into the status of God's son. Nuns used to
blush and be hysterical at such statements and call upon us to have
faith and accept these things as divine "mysteries". That is easier
said than done, especially to those of us who are extremely
sceptical anyway of the historical context in which we view
Christianity. Any religion which comes to replace another must be
able to acquit itself reasonably well before insisting on acceptance
on the basis of faith.

In addition then one finds transmitted into the Theology of
many of the orthodox Churches a characteristic conservatism that
makes me shudder a lot. Probably a lot of this is due to the role
played by St Paul. His Roman citizenship tended to colour a lot of
his interpretations.

He saw Rome not as the enemy people were hoping to be rid of
by the advent of the Messiah but as an institution to which God
had given sanction and somewhat urged people to accept her
authority. Calvinism as represented in the strongly conservative

Dutch Churches fetches its origin from his philosophy. My dilemma then regarding Christ starts here. My God – if I have to view Christ as such – is so conservatively interpreted at times that I find him foreign to me. On the other hand if I accept him and ascribe to him the characteristics that flow logically from my contemplation about him and his work, then I must reject the Church almost completely; and this includes my own Anglican Church whose structure is foreign to me and whose theology is so amorphous as to have sometimes no substance.

This is where the prospects of Black Theology seem to be so attractive to me.

He concludes:

I have felt better protected from becoming completely agnostic by rejecting therefore, as I have said, all denominationalism as divinely instituted protagonists of God's law and basing my whole understanding of God on my own contemplations about him. As I have said also I have accepted Churches only in the limited role of being man-made institutions attempting to organise into units those who worship God.

Two facts concerning his belief about Christ seem to emerge. First, that it was not Christ he rejected, only the "unbelievable" Church dogmas about him. Second, that "Black Theology" seemed to give him hope. What is "Black Theology"? In a recent article in *The Month* ('God and the Christian Theologian', October 1977) Fr Robert Butterworth, S.J., has suggested that "phrases like 'the theology of revolution', 'the theology of hope', etc. and therefore (though he does not mention it) by implication 'black theology', do not in the end amount to any thing more than "a way of providing what in more traditional . . . parlance would be better called a Spirituality for would-be Christian revolutionaries" etc. – or, in our case, for would-be Christian blacks. Certainly the insights of "Black Theology" only make sense as black Christians try to express them in their lives. At the heart of "Black Theology" is the perception that Jesus belonged historically in a situation ⊍f oppression, that he was a member of an oppressed people in an oppressive society, and that he came to set his people free. The classic text around which the whole of "Black Theology" clusters is Isaiah 61, 1f., quoted by Christ as the text of his first sermon (Luke 4. 18f.)

The spirit of the Lord is upon me because he has anointed me;
he has sent me to announce good news to the poor,
to proclaim release for prisoners and recovery of sight for
the blind;
to let the broken victims go free,
to proclaim the year of the Lord's favour.

This provides the basis for a meaningful spirituality for the man in a situation of oppression, but it does not have anything to say about God (except for the one vital fact that he is against oppression and with the oppressed, working in Christ with them for their liberation), nor about Christ as God. I suggest that Steve found "Black Theology" attractive as offering this paradigm of spiritual praxis in the contemplation and imitation of the black Christ. (Such a paradigm is not confined to blacks, as the white South African Albert Nolan, O.P., has shown in his *Jesus before Christianity*).

The last page and a half of the memorandum is devoted to a criticism of David's thoughts on obedience:

Obedience to God in the sense that I have accepted it (i.e. in the belief that God reveals himself in his laws inscribed in our conscience) is in fact at the heart of the conviction of most selfless revolutionaries. It is a call to men of conscience to offer themselves and sometimes their lives for the eradication of an evil. To a revolutionary, State evil is a major evil for out of it flow countless other subsidiary evils that engulf the lives of both the oppressors and the oppressed. The revolutionary sees his task all too often as liberation not only of the oppressed but also of the oppressor. Happiness can never truly exist in a state of tension, even if the tension is only of conscience. Hence in a stratified society like ours, those who have placed themselves upon a pedestal spend far too much time on the lookout for disturbances and hence can never have peace of mind. The South African society abounds with fear and is constantly in a state of frenzy. The revolutionary seeks to restore faith in life amongst all citizens of his country, to remove imaginary fears and to heighten concern for the plight of the people. To the revolutionary the Church is anti-progress and therefore anti-God's wishes because long ago it decided not to obey God but to obey man; long ago the Church itself decided to accept the motto "white is value"; etc.

If therefore one speaks of "obedience", one opens himself up to tremendous challenges. Obedience to God implies deliberate "maladjustments" to so many evils in the Church and State. Where do we draw the line? Do we allow ourselves to be obedient to God and at the same time obedient to a white-controlled, power-mongering institution like the Church of the Province?

The phrase "selfless revolutionary" seems to me the clue to what Steve himself meant to die for, and to be crucial to the answer we give to the second of my questions, namely "In what sense can he be called a Christian martyr?". From a very early age (I am not yet in a position to say just when) Stephen was possessed with a passion for the liberation of his people, and he gave himself to this passion with a single-minded integrity which consistently proved stronger than his fear of imprisonment, torture or death. In this vision he saw himself, the "selfless revolutionary", fighting for the "liberation not only of the oppressed but also of the oppressor". There is an almost irresistible temptation here for the Christian moralist to examine the term "selfless", always with the pre-suppositions of the doctrine of original sin. I suggest that it would be more in accordance with the mind of Christ to look at Steve's actual achievement. He in fact, as we now know through the inquest, endured dreadful degradations and torture without breaking and without losing his "ubuntu" (humanness). On 9 September, when the brain damage suffered two days earlier was irreversible and he was thus already a dying man, he told Mr Fitchett (a prison warder in Port Elizabeth) he wanted to kiss him because Mr Fitchett had given him "mageu" and water (*Rand Daily Mail* Saturday, 19 November 1977). However unreliable some of the witness's evidence may have been, there seems no cause to doubt the veracity of this detail. Nothing in the whole narrative of the inquest moved me more than this little incident, because it was so true to Steve's nature.

He was, moreover, consistently free from any spirit of hatred, bitterness or resentment. When questioned once about this he laughed and said these would take too much time and energy and must be eschewed. It may be said that at the very heart of an authentic Christian witness is the spirit of forgiveness. To suggest that words of forgiveness were at any time during his passion on Steve's lips would be, in my view, unjustifiable; but that does not make him an unforgiving person. He was fighting for his life against men whose dehumanised condition made them far more dangerous and unpredictably malignant than wild animals. There is no reason to suppose that Steve did not meet expressions of repentance with demonstrations of forgiveness. The whole aim of the "selfless revolutionary" as defined by Steve above, "the liberation not only of the oppressed but also of the oppressor", presupposes not only that the oppressor can be brought to a state of repentance for what he has done, but also that at that moment he is embraced, and so liberated by the forgiveness extended to him by the oppressed. I personally cannot pray for the *forgiveness* of those responsible for his death. I can and do pray for their *repentance*, which will then make possible and efficacious their forgiveness. The real miracle of the Gospel, as Coleridge saw, is not forgiveness but repentance.

Steve died to give an unbreakable substance to the hope he had already implanted in our breasts, the hope of freedom in South Africa. That is what he lived for; in fact one can truly say that is what he *lived*. He was himself a living embodiment of the hope he proclaimed by word and deed. That is why I call this little personal memoir "Martyr of Hope". Martyr means witness. He was in his person a witness to the hope that all men, women and children in South Africa, the oppressed and oppressor alike, could be free. His writings attest it; the works of BCP and Zimele and above all the community at King proclaim it; his passion and death seal it. The Church of the province of South Africa, in which he was baptised and which (largely because of respect for his mother's faith) he never repudiated, this Anglican church does not have the right at present to claim him as its martyr. "He was too big for the Church", Lawrence Zulu, Bishop of Zululand, remarked to me after Steve's death. And that about sums it up!

But in the purified Church that will be reborn out of the destruction of this racist society, a Church whose lineaments can be traced even now in one or two communities, in certain Christians here and there, in that Church he will be venerated everywhere, as he is by some of us now, as a true martyr of Christ – the Christ whom he maybe could not consciously be often in communion with because of the disfiguring disguises with which the Church had distorted him – the Christ nevertheless of the poor and the oppressed, whose compassion he displayed, and whose passion for righteousness it was that drove him to his death.

I shall end by quoting, without his permission, from a letter received from Malusi Mpumlwana, one of the Christians who give hope for the future of the Church in Southern Africa, a devoted friend of Steve, prominent in BCP and BPC, and currently in detention in King under the Internal Security Act. Let him who reads understand! (N.B. Steve's other name was Bantu which means "people".)

Your Christmas message was warm and strengthening, Father, just like you'd have been in person. I was very much pleased to hear from you on the occasion of the birth of the Son of Man. Your card was stamped at the Post Office on December 19. Allow me to assume that it was written on the previous day – December 18. Is that relevant at all? If it brings the Bible any closer to some of us, perhaps it is, because once upon a time there was a son of man. He had been born on December 18 and had his Good Friday in Spring instead of Autumn as is normally the case in the southern hemisphere. Your Christmas prayer for me written on December 18 says, "May Christ be born in your heart anew this Christmas . . ." It is indeed a significant prayer, and with your permission I will amend it to read "may the son of man be born anew this day" When the Son of Man called himself that, during his lifetime on earth, his followers never knew the meaning of the term. But the full meaning of his person was outlined by Cleopas, after the memorable events of the Passover, in the Gospel according to St Luke 24, verses 18–21. The words of Cleopas are this day echoed by all those who are followers of the son of man ("a prophet powerful in speech and action before God and the whole people; how our chief priests and rulers handed him over to be sentenced to death, and crucified him. But we had been hoping that he was the man to liberate Israel"). If Christ had not died, there would be no question of him being "born anew" (as you put it) in any body's heart; and therefore because the son of man is no more, we talk of him being born anew. If all good days lasted for years there would be nothing good about them. But then because they last only till the dusk, they are always remembered with longing when bad days come. They serve the purpose of brightening the spirit of mortals on bitter wintry days.